The BRICS in the New International Legal Order on Investment

Silk Road Studies in International Economic Law

Edited by

Wenhua Shan (*Xi'an Jiaotong University School of Law*)

Associate Editor

Jinyuan Su

VOLUME 4

Silk Road Studies in International Economic Law offers incisive analysis of the latest developments in international and comparative law, with particular attention to interactions with China.

The titles published in this series are listed at *brill.com/srsl*

The BRICS in the New International Legal Order on Investment

Reformers or Disruptors

Edited by

Congyan Cai
Huiping Chen

Assistant Editor

Yifei Wang

BRILL
NIJHOFF

LEIDEN | BOSTON

Library of Congress Cataloging-in-Publication Data

Names: Cai, Congyan, editor. | Chen, Huiping, 1968– editor. | Wang, Yifei, 1994– editor.
Title: The BRICS in the new international legal order on investment : reformers or disruptors / edited by Congyan Cai, Huiping Chen ; assistant editor Yifei Wang.
Description: Leiden ; Boston : Brill Nijhoff, 2020. | Series: Silk Road studies in international economic law, 2352–5681 ; volume 4 | "This book derives from the Conference of Brazil, Russia, India, China, South Africa (the BRICS) and International Legal Order on Investment, which Professor Congyan Cai convened in Xiamen in November 2017 ... Based on the 2018 Symposium, we further develop this book ... This book is one of outcomes of two research projects that Professor Congyan Cai hosts." —ECIP acknowledgements.
Identifiers: LCCN 2020003241 (print) | LCCN 2020003242 (ebook) | ISBN 9789004376984 (hardback) | ISBN 9789004376991 (ebook)
Subjects: LCSH: Investments, Foreign—Law and legislation—BRIC countries—Congresses.
Classification: LCC K3829.8 . B75 2020 (print) | LCC K3829.8 (ebook) | DDC 346/.092—dc23
LC record available at https://lccn.loc.gov/2020003241
LC ebook record available at https://lccn.loc.gov/2020003242

Typeface for the Latin, Greek, and Cyrillic scripts: "Brill". See and download: brill.com/brill-typeface.

ISSN 2352-5681
ISBN 978-90-04-37698-4 (hardback)
ISBN 978-90-04-37699-1 (e-book)

This book is printed on acid-free paper and produced in a sustainable manner.

Contents

Acknowledgements

This book derives from the Conference of Brazil, Russia, India, China, South Africa (the BRICS) and International Legal Order on Investment, which Professor Congyan Cai convened in Xiamen in November 2017. More than ten international investment law scholars and policy makers from the BRICS, Western states and international organizations were invited to explore whether, and to what extent the BRICS, a new power hub in international society, have a common approach to investment treaties and the potential to bring new inputs to international legal order on investment. The conference produced the *Symposium on the BRICS Approach to the Investment Treaty System* at the AJIL Unbound (Vol. 112, 2018), which included seven short essays.

We developed this book based on the 2018 Symposium. Five parts (Chapters 2, 3 and 5, 6 and the Conclusion) of this book are substantially rewritten based on essays published at the AJIL Unbound while others are contributed by other participants of that Conference. We believe that this book is unique for academia, professionals and legal officials in international investment law. This is not only because it is the first one to extensively and currently explore the BRICS's approach to and, influence on, investment treaty regime, but also, presumably more importantly, because it is produced by international investment specialists with BRICS background, which expects accurate knowledge of legal policies and practice on international investment of the BRICS.

This book is financially supported by research projects that Professor Congyan Cai hosts. They include "Improve Chinese Discourse in International Economic Legal Rules-Making" and "The Rise of China and International Legal Order", which are funded by China's National Social Science Planning Office (NSSPO) and Xiamen University respectively.

We are truly grateful to Yifei Wang, a PhD student in international law at Xiamen University School of Law, for her tremendous assistance in the production of this book.

Congyan Cai and Huiping Chen

Abbreviations

AIIB	Asian Infrastructure Investment Bank
BIT	Bilateral Investment Treaty
BRI	Belt and Road Initiative
BRICS	Brazil, Russia, India, China, and South Africa
CFIA	The Cooperation and Facilitation Investment Agreement
CIETAC	China International Economic Trade Arbitration Commission
CSR	Corporate Social Responsibility
ECT	Energy Charter Treaty
EU	The European Union
FDI	Foreign Direct Investment
FET	Fair and Equitable Treatment
FIFD	Friends of Investment Facilitation for Development
G20	Group of 20 Countries
GATS	The General Agreement on Trade in Services
ICC	International Chamber of Commerce
ICSID	The International Centre for Settlement of Investment Disputes
IFA	Investment Facilitation Agreement
IIA	International Investment Agreements
IMF	The International Monetary Fund
ISDS	Investor-State Dispute Settlement
LDCs	Least Developed Countries
MERCOSUR	Mercado Común del Sur
MFN	Most-favoured Nation
MIGA	Multilateral Investment Guarantee Agreement
NAFTA	North Africa Free Trade Agreement
NDRC	National Development and Reform Commission of China
NIEO	New International Economic Order
RSFSR	Russian Soviet Federative Socialist Republic
SADC	South African Development Community
SCC	Stockholm Chamber of Commerce
SCIA	Shenzhen Court of International Arbitration
SPC	Supreme People's Court
TFA	Trade Facilitation Agreement
TFS	Trade Facilitation in Services Agreement
TPP	Trans-Pacific Partnership
TTIP	Transatlantic Trade and Investment Partnership
UN	The United Nations

UNCITRAL	The United Nations Commission on International Trade Law
UNCTAD	The United Nations Conference on Trade and Development
USSR	Union of Soviet Socialist Republics
WB	The World Bank
WTO	World Trade Organization

Notes on Contributors

Andreas Buser

is a research associate at the chair for international law and German public law, Prof. Dr. Heike Krieger at Freie Universität Berlin. At Freie Universität he teaches international law and German administrative law and has recently handed in his PhD thesis on "Emerging Powers, Global Justice and International Economic Law". Currently he also works as a trainee lawyer for the German Federal Ministry for Economic Affairs and Energy. Mr. Buser has published several articles on international law and European Union law in renowned journals and law blogs such as EJIL Talk. His research interests more broadly include international economic law, theories of global justice and international law, human rights, law & development and Third World Approach to International Law.

Congyan Cai

is a Professor of International Law at Fudan University and an Honorary Professor of East China University of Political Science and Law (ECUPL), China. Before he joined Fudan Law School in 2020, he was a professor at Xiamen University School of Law since 2008. Professor Cai focuses on international legal theory, foreign relations law, international investment law, and Chinese legal policies and practice in the international arena. Professor Cai has published many Chinese and English articles in journals like *American Journal of International Law*, *European Journal of International Law*, and *Journal of International Economic Law*. Recently, Professor Cai published *The Rise of China and International Law* (Oxford University Press, 2019). Professor Cai was a former director of Xiamen University International Economic Law Institute (IELI), a Fulbright Scholar and Global Research Fellow at the New York University School of Law (2011–2012), a visiting professor at Columbia Law School (2014), a senior fellow at Humboldt University School of Law (2016), and visiting professor at Kobe University School of Law (2016, 2017, 2018). Professor Cai is a member of Editorial Boards of several journals including *Chinese Yearbook of International Law* and *Journal of East Asia and International Law*.

Huiping Chen

is Professor of international law at Xiamen University. Professor Chen received her PhD degree in international law from Xiamen University in 1999. Professor Chen teaches international investment law, public international law and international human rights law. Professor Chen was visiting research fellow at the East Asian Institute of National University of Singapore during June to September 2005, visiting scholar at Faculty of Law of Leiden University (the Netherlands) during 2000–2001, Fulbright Researcher at Georgetown University Law Center (USA) during 2006–2007, and Freeman Fellow at the University of Illinois during 2012–2013. Currently, Professor Chen is Secretary-General of the Administrative Council of Xiamen Academy of International Law (Xiamen Academy), deputy Secretary-General of the Chinese Society of International Economic Law (CSIEL), a Vice President of China International Investment Arbitration Forum (CIIAF), and the director of International Economic Law Institute (IELI) at Xiamen University. Professor Chen has varieties of publications in both Chinese and English focusing on international investment law and transboundary water, including *OECD's Multilateral Agreement on Investment: A Chinese Perspective* (Kluwer Law International, 2002).

Xiuyan Fei
is the lecturer at the Institute of BRICS Legal Studies of the East China University of Political Science and Law (ECUPL). Dr. Fei's research interests include international economic law, arbitration and dispute settlement, and Indian law. Dr. Fei obtained her PhD in law from the University College Dublin with full scholarship under the State Scholarship Fund of China. Dr. Fei was sitting doctoral researcher at New York University School of Law (2011–2012). Dr. Fei has papers published in journals such as *The Chinese Economy* and the *Journal of the Indian Law Institute*. Her chapter is supported by Renmin University Research Program "On the Treaty Interpretation by the WTO Dispute Settlement Body" (15XNB001).

Felipe Hees
is a Brazilian diplomat with a strong background in trade negotiations. He holds a PhD in Brazilian History from the University of Brasília, Brazil, and a Master's degree in Economics from the University of Campinas (UNICAMP), Brazil. As trade negotiator, Mr. Hees has significant professional experience, ranging from services, investment, e-commerce, agriculture, antidumping, safeguards, subsidies, countervailing measures, SPS, and other issues in the multilateral, regional and bilateral context (Mercosur, Free Trade Area of the Americas, Mercosur/European Union, WTO). Mr. Hees has also served as panelist in WTO dispute settlement cases and has authored several publications in his field. He was the Director of the Brazilian Trade Remedies Authority between 2011 and 2014 and headed the unit responsible for trade negotiations with Egypt, Jordan and Morocco.

Currently Mr. Hees serves at Minister-Counselor for economic and commercial issues at the Embassy of Brazil to China, in Beijing.

Dmitry K. Labin
is a Professor of International Law at the International Law Department, Moscow State Institute of International Relations attached to the Ministry of Foreign Affairs (MGIMO-University, Russia), Arbiter of the Moscow Chamber of Commerce and Industry Arbitration, and a member of editorial board of the Moscow Journal of International Law. Professor Labin is the author of many articles published inter alia in the *American Journal of International Law* and the *European Journal of International Law* and several books including *The International Law on Encouraging and Protecting Foreign Investments* (Wolters Kluwer, 2008, second edition published in 2019).

Xiaoxia Lin
is a litigation analyst, Debevoise & Plimpton LLP (New York). Ms. Lin's academic interests include international investment law, international disputes resolution, and the interconnection of international investment law with human rights and environmental protection. Ms. Lin received her LLM degree from New York University School of Law in International Legal Studies. Ms. Lin also holds a LLM degree from Xiamen University School of Law in International Law in China. She is the recipient of the prestigious International Finance & Development Fellowship with the International Institute for Sustainable Development (IISD) in Geneva. During the fellowship she provided legal commentaries and advisory opinions in international investment law and sustainable development for developing countries. Ms. Lin was a visiting scholar at Columbia Law School (2016–2017).

Henrique Choer Moraes
is a diplomat working in the Ministry of Foreign Affairs of Brazil. Throughout his career, he has been involved in a number of areas of economic diplomacy, with postings in Brasilia, Brussels (Mission of Brazil to the EU, where, for the second time, he is now posted) and Montevideo (Mission of Brazil to the Mercosur). He is also the author of academic work in the field of global economic governance, including articles and chapters covering topics such as transgovernmental networks, global financial governance and intellectual property rights.

Engela C. Schlemmer
is a professor of law and assistant dean Academic Planning in the Faculty of Commerce, Law and Management at the University of the Witwatersrand, Johannesburg. She teaches and publishes in international economic law, international investment law, international business transactions law and real and personal security law. Her research interests also include aspects of banking law, insurance law, and law of property. She is a member of the editorial board of the *Journal of Contemporary Roman Dutch Law* and assistant editor of the *South African Yearbook of International Law*. She was a fellow of the International University in Germany and has been a visiting professor/scholar at the Universities of Antwerp, Leuven, Namibia, Münster, Saarbrücken and Tokyo. She is a member of the International Law Association's (ILA) committee on the Rule of Law in International Investment Law and ILA's committee on International Monetary Law. Professor Schlemmer has published numerous articles in accredited law journals and chapters in international books.

Alena V. Soloveva
is an Associate at an international law firm, Kennedys, where she is heavily involved in complex commercial litigation cases. Ms. Soloveva is also a PhD Candidate in International Law at the Moscow State Institute of International Relations (MGIMO- University, Russia). Before that, she studied international law of foreign investment and obtained a Master's degree from University College London. In addition, she worked at London's only public international law boutique focusing on high-value investment treaty arbitrations. Ms. Soloveva has been advising private entities and States on a variety of international law issues, including foreign investment and M&A contentious and non-contentious legal matters.

Yifei Wang
is a PhD student in international law at Xiamen University, LLM in maritime law at Erasmus University Rotterdam (EUR), and LLB & Juris Master at China University of Political Science and Law (CUPL). Her researches focus on international legal theory, international law of the treaty and maritime law.

CHAPTER 1

Introduction

Congyan Cai and Yifei Wang

The twenty-first century has been witnessing an overall transformation of international investment law, which was unprecedented either in the nineteenth century or in the twentieth century. Indeed, States long quarreled with each other as to how to regulate foreign investment, but the context, actors and content of debates have substantially changed today. In the nineteenth and twentieth century, developed states and developing states held totally opposite positions concerning how to treat foreign investment which almost exclusively flowed the former to the latter. The South-North divide characterized the history of international investment law in the nineteenth century and in the twentieth century.[1] In any case, most developing states finally yielded to the many demanding commitments required by developed states, for instance, the "prompt, adequate, effective" compensation for expropriation or nationalization of foreign investment first advocated by the US in the 1920s. Actually, it was widely acknowledged that developed states were the "rule-makers" of the investment treaty regime while all developing states could do was to either accept or reject it. In short, developing states did not play perceivable roles in the development of the investment treaty regime. By contrast, since the late 1990s common interests have begun to emerge between developed states and developing states so as to make investment treaty regime more balanced, efficient and predictable. The main reasons include that, economically, some developing states have begun to emerge as new major investment sources in addition to being investment destinations, which induces them to embrace a more investment-friendly legal policy, and that, legally, investment treaties are frequently used or abused by foreign investors to challenge the public authority of host states which include not only developing states but also developed states. The public-private debate, namely, how the regulatory power of host states is duly exercised toward private business, has thus emerged a new major concern for all countries.[2] The shift from the South-North divide

1 Wenhua Shan, From North-South Divide to Private-Public Debate: Revival of the Calvo Doctrine and the Changing Landscape in International Investment Law, 27 *Northwestern Journal of International Law & Business* 610 (2007).

2 Id.

 | DOI:10.1163/9789004376991_002

to the public-private debate implies that, if technically workable, any reform proposal of a State, either a developed state or a developing state, is likely to win support from other States, thereby playing a substantial role in reforming the investment treaty regime. This encourages many states, individually or collectively and in different forums, to propose varieties of proposals reforming the investment treaty regime. These proposals have commonalities on some aspects while differing on other aspects. Generally speaking, different States have taken a number of similar measures to improve some investment legal rules, for instance, the definition of indirect expropriation, the content of fair and equitable treatment (FET),[3] but they remain divided on others, especially on how to reconstruct the investor-state investment dispute (ISDS) mechanism. Different approaches, incremental, systemic and paradigmatic, have been adopted and attained more or less universal support.[4] The reason is simple: because the ISDS mechanism, which empowers foreign investors to bring international claims against host states, is a major instrument to put substantive commitments States have made into place.

In 2001, O'Neill, an economist from GoldmanSachs, coined the acronym "BRIC" basing on the initial letters of the names of Brazil, Russia, India and China. He predicted that the BRIC nations would emerge as an economic group comparable to the Group of 7 states (G-7) 7.[5] Another two economists assumed that by 2025 the economies of BRIC could account for half the size of the G-6 (except Canada) and that China's economy could overtake Japan by 2015 and the US by 2039 respectively.[6] In June 2009, the first BRIC Summit was convened in Ekaterinburg, Russia.[7] From then on, a summit would be convened annually. During the third Summit in Sanya, China, South Africa was admitted to the BRIC, bringing about the "BRICS".[8] The BRICS is not a proper international organization like the United Nations (UN) or World Trade Organization (WTO). Be that as it may, the BRICS leaders often announce principled policies

3 See for instance 2012 U.S. Model BIT, arts. 5, 6 and Annex B; China-Canada BIT (2012), art. 4 and Annex B.10. See also Federico Ortino, Defining Indirect Expropriation: The Transatlantic Trade and Investment Partnership and the (Elusive) Search for Greater Certainty, 43 *Legal Issues of Economic Integration* 351 (2016); Kendra Leite, The Fair and Equitable Treatment Standard: A Search for a Better Balance in International Investment Agreements, 32 *American University International Law Review* 363 (2016).

4 See for instance Anthea Roberts, Incremental, Systemic, and Paradigmatic Reform of Investor-State Arbitration, 112 *American Journal of International Law* 410 (2018).

5 Jim O'Neill, *Building Better Global Economic BRICs*, November 30, 2001, GoldmanSachs.

6 Dominic Wilson, Roopa Purushothaman, *Dreaming with BRICs: The Path to 2050*, 1 October 2003, GoldmanSachs.

7 Joint Statement of the BRIC Leaders Ekaterinburg, Russia, 16 June 2009.

8 Sanya Declaration, Sanya, Hainan, China, 14 April 2011, para. 2.

toward a wide range of international affairs at annual Summits, which are followed by more operative coordination among the relevant authorities among BRICS countries. For instance, in 2010, the BRICS proposed proposals to reform the International Monetary Fund (IMF) and the World Bank (WB). At the Brasilia Summit in April of that year, the BRICS announced:

> The IMF and the World Bank urgently need to address their legitimacy deficits. Reforming these institutions' governance structures requires first and foremost a substantial shift in voting power in favor of emerging market economies and developing countries to bring their participation in decision making in line with their relative weight in the world economy ... We do also agree on the need for an open and merit based selection method, irrespective of nationality, for the heading positions of the IMF and the World Bank. Moreover, staff of these institutions needs to better reflect the diversity of their membership. There is a special need to increase participation of developing countries. The international community must deliver a result worthy of the expectations we all share for these institutions within the agreed timeframe or run the risk of seeing them fade into obsolescence.[9]

Arguably, the strong voice from the BRICS countries has made a difference. In December 2010, the Board of Governors of the IMF approved a package of reforms which were scheduled to finish by October 2012.[10] Unfortunately, any perceivable progress was not achieved. As a response, at the Sixth BRICS Summit in 2014 the BRICS countries warned that that situation would damage "the IMF's legitimacy, credibility and effectiveness" and that the reform "must lead to the modernization of its governance structure."[11] In particular, they called for developed countries to "meet their commitment to cede two chairs on the Executive Board of the IMF."[12]

However, the BRICS countries disagree with each other on some issues. For instance, China and India insist that the Kyoto Protocol approach, which creates mandatory limits on greenhouse gas (GHG) emission from developed states and several transitional economies including Russia while not imposing

9 BRIC – Brazil, Russia, India and China Grouping II Summit of Heads of State/Government, Brasilia, April 15, 2010, Joint Statement, para. 11.

10 "Press Release: IMF Board of Governors Approves Major Quota and Governance Reforms," available at https://www.imf.org/en/News/Articles/2015/09/14/01/49/pr10477. (last visited October 10, 2018).

11 VI BRICS Summit Fortaleza Declaration, July 15, 2014, para. 18.

12 8th BRICS Summit – Goa Declaration, Goa, India, October 16, 2016, para. 32.

such obligation on developing states including China and India,[13] be maintained, but Russia tends to abandon this approach.[14] This may prevent the BRICS countries from acting with "one voice" on some issues. Furthermore, in recent years the BRICS countries appear to have lost economic clout, which may reduce their potential to exert influence on international law. An important thing, however, is that there has continually existed a permanent mechanism which can facilitate cooperation and coordination among BRICS countries.

Arguably, the investment treaty regime is a major field on which the BRICS countries can exert substantial influence in light of their growing roles in the flow of international capital, that is, they not only have been major investment destinations but also have emerged as new major investment sources.[15] As will be seen in the following chapters, each BRICS country, in different ways, has reformed their investment treaty policy and practice respectively. Some observers may be frustrated to find that discrepancies among BRICS countries in terms of investment treaties appear to have enlarged, and may be larger than those between a BRICS country (say, China) and a non-BRICS country (say, the U.S.). It should be noted, however, that they have begun to harmonize their approaches to investment treaties.

This book is unique for readers because it is the first one exploring the BRICS approach to investment treaties and, equally importantly, because it is produced by specialists with BRICS backgrounds, which ensures an accurate description of the legal policies and practice of BRICS on international investment. It mainly purports to investigate why and how the BRICS countries modernize their approach to investment treaty regime, whether they can develop some common approach to investment treaties, and, most importantly, what BRICS countries will bring to the investment treaty regime in the future, or they are reformers or disruptors of international legal order on investment.

Brazil has long been a major investment destination. Interestingly, it was not until 2015 that Brazil ratified its first BIT with Angola, even though it had signed over ten bilateral and regional investment treaties.[16] With the adoption

---

13 United Nations Framework Convention on Climate Change, Annex I; Kyoto Protocol, Annex B.

14 See "COMMENT: Russia stands firm on abandoning Kyoto, kills hopes for legally binding climate deal", at http://www.bellona.org/articles/articles_2011/kyotono_russia (visited December 10, 2011).

15 See Karl P. Sauvant, New Sources of FDI: The BRICs – Outward FDI from Brazil, Russia, India and China, 6 *Journal of World Investment & Trade* 639 (2005).

16 A list of Brazil's investment agreements including BITs and treaties with investment provisions, see "Investment Policy Hub: Brazil", available at https://investmentpolicy.unctad.org/international-investment-agreements/countries/27/brazil (last visited August 10, 2019).

of the Brazilian Model BIT in 2015, that is, Cooperation and Facilitation Investment Agreements (CFIA),[17] based on which the Brazil-Angola BIT (2015) was signed, Brazil started its new investment treaty practice. In Chapter 2, Felipe Hees and Henrique Choer Moraes, two legal officials from Brazil, do not simply explain the history of Brazil's reluctant to ratify BIT.[18] Rather, they focus on the unique approach of investment facilitation embedded in the CFIA, which is considered by them "at the centre" of the lawmaking of Brazil on international investment. They explain why Brazil recently has preferred an investment facilitation-oriented approach to investment treaty regime and introduce the efforts that Brazil has made at the bilateral, regional and multilateral levels. According to Hees and Choer Moraes, Brazil is developing a pragmatic methodology to reform investment treaty regime currently under fierce backlashes, that is, to find common denominators among States while leaving those controversial issues of investment protection aside. Hees and Choer Moraes suggest that investment facilitation "injects fresh air in a regime long in need of new, non-contentious, approaches." Importantly, the investment facilitation approach, in the view of Hees and Choer Moraes, can also function to enhance investment protection.

Although Russia, as one of five permanent members of the United Nations Security Council, plays a prominent role in international relations, the investment treaties of Russia have not yet been received much attention. Dmitry K. Labin and Alena V. Soloveva, in Chapter 3, provide a very informative description of the development of Russian investment treaty policy and practice and the underlying dynamic. They examine the evolution of four generations of Russia's investment treaties, explaining the political, economic and legal contexts, respectively. They further explain the Russian approach to the core provisions of investment treaties, for instance, national treatment. In particular, Labin and Soloveva explain Russia's "private law" or commercial arbitration-oriented approach to investment arbitration, which is extraordinary in the current trend where most countries, given that the investment arbitration is an instrument used to resolve the "public-private" disputes between host states and foreign investors, support the idea that investment arbitration should be reframed with the inclusion of some "public law" elements, for instance, transparency.

As a leading state in the movement of New International Economic Order (NIEO) in the 1960s and 1970s which was characterized by hostility toward

17 "Cooperation and Facilitation Investment Agreement Between the Federative Republic of Brazil and ___", available at http://investmentpolicyhub.unctad.org/Download/TreatyFile/4786 (visited on October 14, 2018).

18 *See generally* Nancy A. Welsh, Andrea Kupfer Schneider, and Kathryn Rimpfel, Using the Theories of Exit, Voice, Loyalty, and Procedural Justice to Reconceptualize Brazil's Rejection of Bilateral Investment Treaties, 45 *Journal of Law & Policy* 105 (2014).

foreign investment and liberal investment treaties and full support for the economic sovereignty of host states, the twists and turns of India's investment treaty policy and practice does merit special attention. In Chapter 4, Xiaoxia Lin first reviews the evolution of Indian legal policies on foreign investment. Then, Lin investigates the evolution of India's investment treaty policy and practice in the 1990s and the early 2000s, which culminated in the adoption of the Model BIT in 2003 representing India's turn to embrace the Western liberal approach to investment treaties. Based upon the Model BIT newly adopted in 2015, Lin further examines how India recalibrates its investment treaty policy and practice, which was mainly triggered by the *White Industries–India* case from 2011 in which India was, for the first time, found in breach of its BIT obligations by an international tribunal. While Lin supports the inclusion of several innovative elements, for instance, corporate social responsibility (CSR), she argues that, generally speaking, the Model BIT (2015) might go too far and thus it is doubtful to what extent it could be accepted by negotiating partners. Finally, Lin analyzes the China-India BIT which was signed in 2006 but which, as a result of the Model BIT (2015), did not continue to apply after its first ten-year application expired in 2016.

The "Belt & Road" Initiative (BRI or Initiative) was proposed by China's President Xi Jinping in 2013. For China the BRI aims to further integrate China into the global economy and to fuel the global economy through close cooperation with BRI countries in trade, investment, infrastructure construction, connectivity, and other development projects. However, it is also considered a part of the grand strategy of China, a rising great power, to expand its geopolitical and geo-economic power in the twenty first century.[19] The BRI is believed to have substantial implications for Chinese international investment law both at the national level and at the international level. In Chapter 5, Huiping Chen examines what China has done to enhance the BRI, how the BRI influences China's approach to investment treaty regime, and, in particular, how China seeks to reframe the framework of the settlement of investor-state disputes which, given that most BRI countries are developing states, is a big concern for Chinese investors. Chen informs us how China seeks to build itself as a major international centre for the settlement of investor-state disputes by innovating its domestic dispute settlement infrastructures and increasing international cooperation.

South Africa started its investment treaty program in the early 1990s, which was believed to be a part of the State's re-engaging international society after

19 See generally Zheng Yongnian; Zhang Chi, The Belt and Road Initiative and China's Grand Diplomacy, 56 *China International Studies* 52 (2016).

decades of international exclusion and sanctions as the result of apartheid policy. It thus comes as no surprise that South Africa initially embraced liberal investment treaties. As *White Industries–India* did to India's investment treaty policy, the *Foresti* case[20] largely contributed to South Africa's new investment treaty policy. In 2012 South Africa decided to terminate the investment treaties that it had signed. As of September 2019, ten out of a total of twenty-two South African BITs no longer applied. Furthermore, South Africa approved the Protection of Investment Act in 2015, which "localized" foreign investment affairs by incorporating some investment treatment and protection prevailing in investment treaties and, in particular, excluding international dispute settlement mechanisms.[21] In contrast to India, however, there are more complicated domestic public policy considerations underlying South Africa's new investment treaty policy. They are, in particular, the policy of "promoting a more equitable distribution of wealth by supporting and favouring the economic empowerment of persons from historically disadvantaged communities".[22] The experience of South Africa in investment treaties informs people the dynamic underlying its international legal policy and practice, and, in particular, how international legal policy of a State has to be compromised to accommodate domestic public policy. In Chapter 6, Engela C. Schlemmer reviews the evolution of South Africa's investment treaty policy and practice. She examines the content of the Protection of Investment Act of 2015 which constitutes limitations on South Africa's future negotiations of investment treaties. In particular, she discusses how South Africa reconciles the Protection of Investment Act of 2015 and investment treaties to which South Africa has entered into.

In the 1960s and the 1970s, given their shared history of being colonized by Western powers and their similar disadvantaged role in the international economic order, nearly all developing states, if not all, adopted the similar or same policies on the regulation of foreign investment and other economic activities, which were totally different from those of developed states. Those regulation policies were characterized by overwhelmingly stressing the economic sovereignty of host states while attaching far less importance on the protection of foreign investment. This situation has significantly changed since the 1980s. Some developing states have begun to ideologically embrace the Western neoliberalism which supports de-regulating and privatizing economic sectors

---

20 *Foresti v. South Africa*, ICSID Case No. ARB(AF)/07/1 (Aug. 4, 2011).

21 Protection of Investment Act of 2015, sections 6, 7, 8, 9, 11 and 13.

22 Lance Fleiser, What is Black Economic Empowerment Enterprise, 9 *Juta's Business Law* 22 (2001) 22. See also Engela C. Schlemmer, An Overview of South Africa's Bilateral Investment Treaties and Investment Policy 31 *ICSID Review* 167 (2016)172.

and activities. More importantly, some developing states have significantly increased their economic power, which arguably does make feasible or necessary the substantial adjustment of the traditional economic regulation, even though they may not actually do so. Thus, whether and how these developing states adjust their regulation of foreign investment is highly relevant to whether developing states can unite as a whole as they had done in the 1960s and the 1970s. In Chapter 7, Andreas Buser, by conducting a comparative examination of the investment treaty policies of BRICS members, demonstrates that developing states have divided and developing states have no common approach to the regulation of foreign investment, even though they rhetorically embrace the recalibration of investment treaties in order to maintain more regulatory policy space for host states. It should be noted that Buser only compares investment treaty polices of Brazil, India, China and South Africa (especially the first three) because he argues Russia is not a "former" developing state like the other four BRIC countries. Buser heavily relies on the typology of Anthea Roberts who, in analyzing diverse approaches to the ongoing investment treaty reform, identifies countries as loyalists/traditionalist, and reformers or revolutionaries respectively.[23] According to his survey, Brazil and India belong to "reformers" because they support incorporating several very innovative BIT elements (say, investment facilitation for Brazil) while also substantially rewriting several fundamental provisions prevailing in traditional investment treaties (say, the ISDS provisions for India) or excluding them (say, the FET for India). Compared with Brazil and India, South Africa goes further by terminating many of investment treaties. Thus, it is considered to be a "revolutionary". According to Buser, the sole loyalist to investment treaties is China, but he notes that China's BIT practice is not always consistent and often ambiguous. Buser appears to have high expectations for China because he argues that "Now, much depends on the future course of China's investment treaties. If China resists the temptation to strengthen investment protection and instead further recalibrates its BITS not only a common BRICS approach is possible, but China may also calm host States wary of increased Chinese influence and competition."

Xiuyan Fei, in Chapter 8, uses a specific and unique perspective of investment barriers to explain why BRICS countries are reluctant to fully subject themselves to investment treaties and why BRICS countries highlight the approach of investment facilitation both in the reform of their investment

23 *See* Anthea Roberts, The Shifting Landscape of Investor-State Arbitration: Loyalists, Reformists, Revolutionaries and Undecideds, June 15, 2017, available at https://www.ejiltalk.org/the-shifting-landscape-of-investor-state-arbitration-loyalists-reformists-revolutionaries-and-undecideds/ (visited 8 August 2017).

treaty regimes and in the efforts to negotiating multilateral rules on investment. The existence of a wide range of investment barriers, according to Fei, is a major reason explaining why BRICS countries reject investment treaties, are reluctant to negotiate liberal investment treaties or terminate those liberal investment treaties. Fei, however, finds that BRICS do make efforts to reduce investment barriers. These efforts are made not only at the domestic level but also at the international level. Therefore, BRICS countries, especially Brazil and China, attach great importance to investment facilitation. In one word, investment facilitation is considered by BRICS countries to be an important instrument which can help reduce investment barriers while not imposing substantial obligations on host states.

CHAPTER 2

Investment Facilitation and the Contribution of the Brazilian Approach to the Reform of the Investment Treaty Regime

Felipe Hees and Henrique Choer Moraes

1 Introduction

International investment law is experiencing a period of unprecedented experimentalism.[1] Recently, this was a field that seemed unscathed by many of the challenges that were confronted by international law. Accordingly, while portraying international law as an area marked by "stagnation",[2] as of August 2019 international investment law can boast about 3,000 investment agreements[3] and an impressive record of more than 900 known investor-State disputes.[4]

Nevertheless, several developments concerning real impacts of investment rules in both developed and developing countries have led many to consider the system to have been tilted too much towards the protection of investors and investments, to the detriment of public interests. Lawmaking in the investment area thus began to display a degree of innovation not witnessed until then, with most new provisions in investment treaties aimed at safeguarding the space enjoyed by States to implement public policies.[5] On some cases, States decided to leave the system altogether.[6] Irrespective of the different

---

1 Wolfgang Alschner, The Global Laboratory of Investment Law Reform Alternatives, 112 *AJIL Unbound* 237 (2018).

2 Joost Pauwelyn, Ramses Wessel and Jan Wouters, When Structures Become Shackles: Stagnation and Dynamics in International Lawmaking, 25 *European Journal of International Law* 733 (2014).

3 The exact number as of August 2018 is 3,299 investment agreements, comprising 2,911 Bilateral Investment Agreements (BITS) and 388 other treaties with investment provisions. *See* UNCTAD Investment Policy Hub, available at http://investmentpolicyhub.unctad.org/IIA (visited on August 10, 2019).

4 *See* http://investmentpolicyhub.unctad.org/ISDS (visited on August 14, 2019).

5 See generally Andreas Kulick (ed.), *Reassertion of control over the investment regime* (Cambridge: Cambridge University Press, 2017).

6 Such as when Bolivia, Ecuador and Venezuela decided to withdraw from the ICSID Convention ("Convention on the Settlement of Investment Disputes between States and Nationals of Other States").

 | DOI:10.1163/9789004376991_003

views States might have concerning the need to modify the investment system,[7] there is no doubt this field finds itself on a reformed mode for the past years.

A remarkable aspect of the discussions on the reform of the international investment regime is that it is by and large a *multilateral agenda*. A panoply of international organizations – such as the Organization for Economic Co-operation and Development (OECD), the United Nations Commission on International Trade Law (UNCITRAL), the United Nations Conference on Trade and Development (UNCTAD), World Bank/the International Centre for Settlement of Investment Disputes (ICSID) and the World Trade Organization (WTO) – is now contributing in one way or another to the discussions on the need to modify investment rules and governance. The tendency is a welcome development, as it allows for open, multilevel and multi-stakeholder discussions on what seems to amount to one of the most pressing challenges of global economic governance today. Debates benefit from a diverse pool of inputs emerged over the past few years in the full range of international fora that now contribute to these discussions.

Despite that, it is equally interesting to note that solutions adopted within the context of the current period of reform are primarily national or, occasionally, regional. There are very few multilateral solutions addressing the contentious issues at stake in the debates on the investment regime.

It could be arguable that this is because the main subject of the discussions – often inscribed in provisions of bilateral investment agreements (BITs) or other investment agreements – is not multilateral rules. While this would be a correct assessment, it does not preclude the importance of potential multilateral solutions to the reform debate. However, would it be feasible to conceive of multilateral solutions aimed at addressing at least some aspects of the reform of the international investment regime? Alternatively, does the shadow of past failed attempts still inhibit looking in the direction of multilateral understandings in this area?

Brazil developed its approach to investment agreements precisely in the present period of reform. Still, unlike the other states – which were engaged in reforming their pre-existing policies on investment agreements –, Brazil was joining the system of investment agreements altogether. Although Brazil signed fourteen BITs in the 1990s,[8] it was not a party committed to any investment

7 Anthea Roberts, Incremental, Systemic, and Paradigmatic Reform of Investor-State Arbitration, 112 *American Journal of International Law* 410 (2018).

8 "Investment Policy Hub: Brazil", available at https://investmentpolicy.unctad.org/international-investment-agreements/countries/27/brazil (visited August 10, 2019). As to the history of Brazil's BITs, see Nancy A. Welsh, Andrea Kupfer Schneider and Kathryn Rimpfel, Using the Theories of Exit, Voice, Loyalty, and Procedural Justice to Reconceptualize Brazil's Rejection of Bilateral Investment Treaties, 45 *Journal of Law & Policy* 105 (2014); Fabio

agreement until July 2017 when Brazil-Angola BIT was signed in January 2015 and entered into force. This unique position enables Brazil to craft its investment agreements closer to its actual needs, and a vital feature of the Brazilian approach is the role of *investment facilitation*, instead of the traditional concern with *investment protection* enshrined in the BITs.

In this chapter, the authors argue that investment facilitation is a topic that ranks as a candidate for multilateral treatment. This argument is formulated drawing on the Brazilian experience with investment lawmaking, as well as on several recent examples emerging from debates taking place in different international settings. Investment facilitation comprises a set of measures, mechanisms and actions aimed at putting in place favourable national investment environments. Because investment facilitation measures have an active procedural or practical component, a multilateral approach to investment facilitation can direct discussions on the reform of the regime towards a constructive and productive path, while simultaneously avoiding the controversies surrounding proposals for multilateral rules on topics that have proven very contentious, namely investment protection and dispute resolution.

Following the introduction, the first section presents the experience of Brazil with its investment agreements, the experience on many counts but especially so for being structured around the concept of investment facilitation. A look at the Brazilian approach will reveal it has a degree of "interoperability": although it represents a significant departure from the traditional design of the BITs, Brazil has signed bilateral agreements with countries sometimes holding extensive BIT portfolios, as well as a regional protocol with the other Mercado Común del Sur (MERCOSUR countries), namely, Argentina, Paraguay and Uruguay.[9] These developments suggest that multilateral initiatives on investment facilitation are not incompatible with alternative preferences of investment policies. The subsequent part turns to the state of the art of multilateral discussions on investment facilitation, with an emphasis on the work of the World Trade Organization (WTO), a forum which might be relevant to advance this agenda, among other reasons for having hosted the successful case of the Trade Facilitation Agreement (TFA). The last part concludes with reflections on why investment facilitation might be a suitable candidate for a multilateral approach.

Morosini; Ely Caetano Junior Xavier, Foreign Direct Investment Regulation in Brazil: From Resistance to Investment Bilateral Treaties to the Emergence of a New Regulatory Model, 12 *Brazilian Journal of International Law* 421 (2015).

9 A list of Brazil's investment agreements including BITs and treaties with investment provisions, see "Investment Policy Hub: Brazil", available at https://investmentpolicy.unctad.org/international-investment-agreements/countries/27/brazil (visited August 10, 2019).

2 Investment Facilitation at the Centre of Investment Lawmaking: the Experience of the Brazilian Investment Agreements

Brazil is in a virtually unique position in the universe of international investment agreements. As noted above, although Brazil signed more than ten BITs, the first investment treaty it ratified is that with Angola signed in April 2015 and entered into force in October 2017. Brazil-Angola BIT is based on the Model BIT, Cooperation and Facilitation Investment Agreements (CFIA) approved in 2015.[10] As of 2019 ten Brazil's BITs or CFIAs based on the CFIA, including Brazil-Angola BIT, have been signed.[11]

The investment agreements ratified by Brazil are not only recent; they are also inspired by a *rationale* that departs from that of the BITs in many ways.[12]

Firstly, and what is perhaps more salient, they deliberately avoid traditional features of BITs such as the standards of "fair and equitable treatment" to investors, as well as provisions prescribing compensation for measures that could deem acts of "indirect expropriation". Most notably, Brazilian investment agreements do not foresee the possibility of investor-State dispute settlement mechanisms (ISDS).[13] The Brazilian approach focuses instead on dispute prevention mechanisms. If a dispute leads to arbitration proceedings, the procedure will take place in the State-State format, much like the dispute settlement system of the WTO.

However, that does not mean the Brazilian investment agreements do not provide for guarantees to investments. They contain provisions guaranteeing non-discrimination (national treatment and most-favoured-nation treatment), transparency, specific conditions for direct expropriation, compensation in case of conflicts and guarantees for international transfers.[14]

Nevertheless, Brazil's CFIAs stand out because they are premised on an innovative and constructive approach that seeks to foster institutional cooperation,

---

10 "Cooperation and Facilitation Investment Agreement Between the Federative Republic of Brazil and ___", available at http://investmentpolicyhub.unctad.org/Download/TreatyFile/4786 (visited on October 14, 2018).

11 A list of Brazil's new BITs, see "Investment Policy Hub: Brazil", available at https://investmentpolicy.unctad.org/international-investment-agreements/countries/27/brazil (visited August 10, 2019).

12 Henrique Choer Moraes and Felipe Hees, 'Breaking the BIT Mold: Brazil's Pioneering Approach to Investment Agreements', 112 *AJIL Unbound* 197 (2018).

13 Volterra, R.G.; Mandelli, G., India and Brazil: Recent Steps towards Host State Control in the Investment Treaty Dispute Resolution Paradigm, 6 *Indian Journal of Arbitration Law* 90 (2017).

14 See the CFIA, arts. 5, 6, 7, 8, 9.

and the facilitation of mutual investment flows between the Parties, while, at the same time, providing for legal protection to investments.

The CFIA seeks particularly to facilitate investments by meeting investors' needs in a concrete, pragmatic and proactive manner, while at the same time, respecting the development strategy and the regulatory space of host countries.

This latter concern is essential for Brazil: although it signed several BITs in the traditional model in the 1990s, these treaties triggered such degree of resistance during debates in the Congress that the government eventually opted for withdrawing them from parliamentary approval. They have never ever been applicable. The criticisms levelled against the BITs by the Brazilian lawmakers at the time (the early 2000s) resemble a large extent the debates taking place today: ISDS provisions were considered discriminatory against national investors, rules on indirect expropriation were possible hindrance in the adoption of public policies and little or no causal link was seen between signing BITs and attracting FDI.[15]

For this reason, the CFIA seeks to strike a balance between public and private interests at a different point of the spectrum where the BITs do. Accordingly, the Brazilian investment agreements contain substantial provisions regarding corporate social responsibility encouraging investments to benefit society, local communities and workers.[16] The more recent agreements also prescribe obligations to investors,[17] as well as some carve-out provisions that safeguard the space to put in place public policies.[18]

In order to give expression to the goal of investment facilitation and cooperation, the Brazilian agreements establish a two-level institutional framework comprising:

(i) a joint committee of the States Parties,[19] which provides a setting for discussing investment matters of interest to the Parties (and their investors), coordinating the implementation of programs of investment facilitation

15 Martino Maggetti and Henrique Choer Moraes, The Policy-Making of Investment Treaties in Brazil: Policy Learning in the Context of Late Adoption, in Claire Dunlop et al., *Learning In Public Policy: Analysis, Modes And Outcomes* (New York: Palgrave, 2018) 295; Daniela Campello and Leany Barreiro Lemos, The Non-Ratification of Bilateral Investment Treaties in Brazil: A Story of Conflict in a Land of Cooperation, 22 *Review of International Political Economy* 1055 (2015).

16 See the CFIA, art. 14.

17 Article 14 of the CFIA, among others, explicitly requires that foreign investors "refrain from any undue interference in local political activities". See also the Mercosur Protocol on Cooperation and Facilitation of Investments, art. 13.

18 See, for example, the CFIA, arts. 12 and 13.

19 The CFIA, art. 17.

as well as preventing and managing possible disputes arising out of investments in one of the Parties;[20] and

(ii) The establishment of national *focal points* (or Ombudspersons) mandated to support investors from the other States Parties, including by liaising with the authorities of the host State to channel demands from investors of the other State Parties.[21] In Brazil, the office of the national focal point has been set up within the Chamber of Foreign Trade (CAMEX), an inter-ministerial body comprising government agencies involved in trade policy, which gives the work of the focal point a whole-of-government reach.

The CFIA also provides for the establishment of investment facilitation and cooperation *agendas* in areas where further work may improve the investment environment.[22] Such agendas may vary depending on the possibilities and challenges of each bilateral investment relationship. The agendas make the CFIA a dynamic tool that facilitates the gradual evolution of specific commitments between the Parties.

The new template was developed based upon inputs from international organizations and in close consultations with the Brazilian private sector.[23] The outreach to the Brazilian investors revealed a strong demand for support in setting up shop in third countries more than anything – in other words, a demand for investment facilitation.

This demand has oriented the Brazilian strategy in investment treaty-making. Accordingly, since 2015, a total of nine bilateral investment agreements have been signed with countries where investments play an essential part in the bilateral economic relations. The first three agreements were signed with African partners (Angola, Mozambique and Malawi), followed by agreements with Latin American countries (Chile, Colombia, Mexico and Peru) and most recently, in 2018, with Ethiopia and Suriname. In addition to these bilateral agreements, in April 2017, MERCOSUR countries (Argentina, Brazil, Paraguay and Uruguay) signed the MERCOSUR Protocol on Cooperation and Facilitation of Investments, which also draws enormously on the Brazilian

---

20 The CFIA, art. 17(4) (e). See further Vivian Gabriel, The New Brazilian Cooperation and Facilitation Investment Agreement: An Analysis of the Conflict Resolution Mechanism in Light of the Theory of the Shadow of the Law, 34 *Conflict Resolution Quarterly* 141 (2017).

21 The CFIA, art. 18.

22 The CFIA, art. 17(4).

23 Michelle Ratton Sanchez Badin and Fabio Morosini, Navigating Between Resistance and Conformity with the International Investment Regime: The Brazilian Agreements on Cooperation and Facilitation of Investments (ACFIs), in Michelle Ratton Sanchez Badin and Fabio Morosini (eds.), *Reconceptualizing international investment law from the Global South* (Cambridge: Cambridge University Press, 2017) 248.

model agreement.[24] What is interesting to note in this case is that the Protocol regionalizes the Brazilian approach to investment lawmaking since the other three MERCOSUR countries agreed to discipline the relations amongst themselves – and not only their bilateral relations with Brazil – based on the Brazilian approach. All reflect the *rationale* of the Brazilian model agreement, although there is an evolution in their wording over time.

Although the design of the CFIA owes a great deal to the Brazilian experience with the investment regime, the template has shown a high degree of "interoperability" with a wide range of investment policy options, which is particularly true regarding the provisions on investment facilitation. Not only has it been possible for Brazil to enter bilateral agreements with countries sometimes possessing considerable portfolios of BIT, but furthermore the Brazilian model became the regional blueprint for the investment disciplines across the MERCOSUR States Parties.

This points to a feature of investment facilitation disciplines that sets them apart from the other topics debated in the context of the investment regime reform: they are compatible with differences in investment policy preferences. Investment facilitation measures do not affect the options made by States for investment dispute settlement mechanisms, standards of protection, or the scope recognized for the right to regulate, among other items that put States in different camps in the context of the reform of the investment regime.[25] This is a crucial element to enable multilateral discussions on this area.

3 Investment Facilitation: Is This a Friendlier Approach to Multilateral Lawmaking?

In 2016, the G20 leaders endorsed the non-binding Guiding Principles for Global Investment Policymaking.[26] Given the divergence of views among

24 For a comment on the Protocol, see Facundo Perez Aznar and Henrique Choer Moraes, The MERCOSUR Protocol on Investment Cooperation and Facilitation: regionalizing an innovative approach to investment agreements, *EJIL Talk!*, September 12, 2017, available at https://www.ejiltalk.org/the-mercosur-protocol-on-investment-cooperation-and-facilitation-regionalizing-an-innovative-approach-to-investment-agreements/ (visited on October 14, 2018).

25 Anthea Roberts, The Shifting Landscape of Investor-State Arbitration: Loyalists, Reformists, Revolutionaries and Undecideds, *EJIL Talk!*, June 15, 2017, available at https://www.ejiltalk.org/the-shifting-landscape-of-investor-state-arbitration-loyalists-reformists-revolutionaries-and-undecideds/ (visited on October 14, 2018).

26 G20 Guiding Principles for Global Investment Policymaking (adopted by the G20 trade ministers in Shanghai, July 10, 2016), available at http://www.g20.utoronto.ca/2016/160710

countries concerning the future shape of this regime, it is no mean feat that the diverse membership of the group has reached a minimally substantive understanding.[27]

The Guiding Principles recognize, among other things, that (a) "investment policies should establish open, non-discriminatory, transparent and predictable conditions for investment" (principle II); (b) "regulation relating to investment should be developed in a transparent manner with opportunity for all stakeholders to participate (…)" (principle IV); (c) "Governments reaffirm the right to regulate investment for legitimate public policy purposes" (principle VI); and (d) "investment policies should promote and facilitate the observance by investors of international best practice and applicable instruments of responsible business conduct and corporate governance" (principle VIII).

Still, it is telling that the Guiding Principles do not touch upon thorny issues in the debates on investment treaty reform such as investor-State disputes settlement. This particular topic, for instance, was couched with comprehensive language recognizing that investment policies should provide for "access to effective mechanisms for the prevention and settlement of disputes, as well as to enforcement procedures" and that "[d]ispute settlement procedures should be fair, open and transparent, with appropriate safeguards to prevent abuse" (principle III). Regarding standards of protection – another controversial issue –, the convergence within the G20 could not go beyond the recognition that "[i]nvestment policies should provide legal certainty and strong protection to investors and investments, tangible and intangible (…)" (principle III).

The Guiding Principles – both in scope and depth – should be seen as the most recent testimony of the difficulties to deliver at the multilateral level on topics that stand at the core of the reform of the regime. One possible exception would be the European Union (EU) proposal to establish a multilateral investment court, designed among others as a possible remedy to address the criticisms against ISDS mechanisms. However, even this example seems to be a partial exception as the initiative does not challenge the prerogative

-trade-annex3.html (visited on October 14, 2018). The G20 Leaders later endorsed the Guiding Principles at the Hangzhou summit, see G20 Leaders' Communiqué: Hangzhou Summit (Hangzhou, September 5, 2016), paragraph 29, available at http://www.g20.utoronto.ca/2016/160905-communique.html (visited on October 14, 2018).

27 James Zhan, G20 Guiding Principles for Global Investment Policymaking: a facilitator's perspective, The E15 Initiative (ICTSD-WEF), E15 investment theme think piece, December 2016; Karl Sauvant, China moves the G20 toward an international investment framework and investment facilitation, 2017, available at https://ssrn.com/abstract=2901156 (visited on October 14, 2018).

of investors to bring States before international tribunals, one of the primary sources of those criticisms.

However, there seems to be at least one area in which some further multilateral development seems possible: investment facilitation.[28] Actually, some countries have attached much importance to investment facilitation.[29]

In the same meeting where the Group of 20 countries (G20) Guiding Principles were adopted, the G20 trade ministers stated that they value "(...) discussions on investment promotion and facilitation, and encourage UNCTAD, the World Bank, the OECD and the WTO to advance this work within their respective mandates and work programmes, which could be useful for future consideration by the G20."[30]

In several ways, the guidance provided by G20 trade ministers draws on a body of work on investment facilitation that has already been underway at the multilateral level. Prominent among these is UNCTAD, which devised its Global Action Menu for Investment Facilitation as a mean to highlight the importance of investment facilitation measures to spur growth and development.[31] Nevertheless, according to UNCTAD, "[t]o date, in the overwhelming majority of the existing 3,300 plus IIAs, concrete investment facilitation provisions are either absent or weak".[32] Relevant work on investment facilitation has also been undertaken by the OECD[33] and the World Bank.[34] Together, the contributions of those three international organizations – and the World Association of Investment Promotion Agencies (WAIPA) as well – constitute a valuable source of soft law and best practices in terms of investment facilitation.

---

28 See Ahmad Ghouri, What Next for International Investment Law and Policy: A Review of the UNCAD Global Action Menu for Investment Facilitation, 15 *Manchester Journal of International Economic Law* 190 (2018).

29 Ruki Baruti, Investment Facilitation in Regional Economic Integration in Africa: The Cases of COMESA, EAC and SADC, 18 *Journal of World Investment & Trade* 493 (2017).

30 G20 Trade Ministerial Meeting Statement – Final Draft (Shanghai, July 10, 2016), paragraph 18, available at http://www.g20.utoronto.ca/2016/160710-trade.html (visited on October 14, 2018).

31 available at http://investmentpolicyhub.unctad.org/Publications/Details/148 (visited on October 14, 2018).

32 UNCTAD, Investment facilitation: a review of policy practices, Feb. 2017, p. 6.

33 OECD Policy Framework for Investment, available at http://www.oecd.org/investment/pfi.htm (visited on October 14, 2018).

34 World Bank Investment Policy and Promotion, available at https://www.worldbank.org/en/topic/investment-climate/brief/investment-policy-and-promotion (visited on October 14, 2018).

Compared to the international organizations mentioned in the previous paragraph, the WTO is a late-comer regarding investment facilitation,[35] although the issue "investment" is not new to the Organization.[36]

Investment facilitation was first brought to the consideration of WTO members in October 2016, with the submission by India of a concept note on a Trade Facilitation in Services Agreement (TFS). In its contribution, India recognized that the Trade Facilitation Agreement was a significant milestone concerning trade in goods and suggested that there is the need for a counterpart agreement that can foster the reduction of transaction costs associated with unnecessary regulatory and administrative burdens on trade in services. The concept note was followed in November 2016 by a contribution focusing on possible elements of the TFS. Finally, on the same day, the TFA entered into force – February 22, 2017 –, India submitted a draft legal text of the TFS.

By putting forward legal language encompassing "commercial presence" ("Mode 3" as defined in the General Agreement on Trade in Services (GATS)), the Indian initiative on TFS represents, *de facto*, a proposal on investment facilitation, even though confined to the services sector.

The Indian proposal raised the issue of whether, from a public policy perspective, it would make sense to improve domestic institutional arrangements or to adopt regulatory measures to facilitate exclusively investment in services, rather than investment in general. It seemed instead that serious consideration should be given to the establishment of one common framework encompassing investment facilitation in general, i.e. for both services and goods. A comprehensive approach would be even more important in a scenario, such as the current stage of the global economy, in which the distinction between the provision of services and the production of goods is progressively blurring – the so-called "servicification" of the production of goods.

Against the background provided by the discussions in the G20 and the submission by India, a series of contributions on investment facilitation have been tabled since then within the WTO.

35 Felipe Hees and Pedro Mendonça Cavalcante. 'Focusing on investment facilitation: Is it that difficult?' Columbia FDI Perspectives, n. 202, June 19, 2017, available at http://ccsi.columbia.edu/files/2016/10/No-202-Hees-and-Cavalcante-FINAL.pdf (visited on October 14, 2018).

36 "Investment" was one of the four issues referred to in paragraph 20 of the WTO Singapore Ministerial Declaration, in 1996, and discussions regarding the relationship between trade and investment have been carried out under the Working Group on Trade and Investment (WGTI) between 1997 and 2003.

Russia was the first one to circulate, in March 2017, a proposal specifically focused on investment facilitation,[37] suggesting that "discussion on coherent multilateral investment facilitation rules in the WTO is necessary for further improvement of the investment climate in WTO Members and to increase their efficiency for both investors and recipient economies". The MIKTA countries (Mexico, Indonesia, Korea, Turkey and Australia) submitted a communication[38] making the point that "investment facilitation could be a good starting point for discussions to complement the recently concluded Trade Facilitation Agreement and current discussions on trade facilitation for services". The group of "Friends of Investment Facilitation for Development – FIFD"[39] followed suit with the suggestion to establish a WTO informal dialogue on investment facilitation for development.[40] According to the FIFD, "[t]he informal dialogue will seek to explore – without limiting or prejudging possible outcomes – the role that the WTO could play as a forum to discuss measures that Members could take to facilitate investment."

Already within the framework of the informal dialogue, China submitted a contribution on possible elements of investment facilitation which could be further discussed:[41] enhancing the transparency of the investment policy framework; options for improving the efficiency of administrative procedures relating to investment; and options for responding do develop and least-developed members' needs. Finally, Brazil and Argentina tabled a communication with "possible elements of a WTO instrument (an agreement or a ministerial decision) on investment facilitation".[42]

The success of the "High-Level Trade and Investment Facilitation Forum for Development"[43] – held in Nigeria (November 2017) and attended by senior business leaders and trade and investment officials from over 30 African countries – was a clear indication that an investment facilitation agenda was

37 Communication from the Russian Federation – Investment Policy Discussion Group, JOB/GC/120 (30 March 2017).

38 MIKTA investment workshop reflections, JOB/GC/121 (6 April 2017).

39 Argentina; Brazil; Chile; China; Colombia; Gambia; Guatemala; Hong Kong, China; Kazakhstan; Liberia; Mauritania; Mexico; Nigeria; Pakistan; Qatar; Republic of Korea; and Uruguay.

40 Proposal for a WTO informal dialogue on investment facilitation for development – Joint communication from the Friends of Investment Facilitation for Development, JOB/GC/122 (21 April 2017).

41 Possible elements of investment facilitation – Communication from China, JOB/GC/123 (21 April 2017).

42 Possible elements of a WTO instrument on investment facilitation – Communication from Argentina and Brazil, JOB/GC/124 (24 April 2017).

43 WT/MIN(17)/4.

of interest to developing countries. The Buenos Aires Presidential Declaration, adopted during the WTO's Ministerial Conference in December 2017, can corroborate the same conclusion.[44]

However, the most crucial development in this area so far was the 2017 Buenos Aires Joint Ministerial Statement on Investment Facilitation for Development,[45] co-sponsored by 70 WTO Members, representing virtually all the informal groupings within the WTO – Least-Developed Countries (LDCs); African Group; developed countries; developing countries; BRICS;[46] African, Caribbean and Pacific countries (ACPs); Small, Vulnerable Economies (SVEs); Bolivarian Alliance for the Americas (ALBA). This Joint Statement can be considered an authentic birth certificate of investment facilitation at the WTO.

Regarding the discussions on investment facilitation in the WTO during 2017, two issues are worth highlighting:

(i) The focus on the issue "investment" has moved from *protection* to *facilitation*. This change made clear with the adoption of a *negative approach* of investment facilitation, whereby. Members agreed to exclude from its scope investment protection (including expropriation), market access and investor-state dispute settlement. This new approach is what renders "investment facilitation" a different issue from the traditional WTO understanding of the topic "investment", which dates back to the 1996 WTO Singapore Ministerial Conference. Some additional work remains to be undertaken to clarify the distinction between *investment facilitation* and *investment promotion*;[47] and

(ii) Interest in investment issues seems no longer an exclusively OECD-driven agenda, as developing countries are becoming the home country of foreign direct investment (FDI) increasingly.

Following the call made in Buenos Aires for the beginning of "structured discussions with the aim of developing a multilateral framework on investment

44 WT/MIN(17)/53. On behalf of Argentina; Brazil; Chile; Colombia; Guyana; Mexico; Paraguay; Peru; Suriname; and Uruguay.

45 WT/MIN/(17)/59.

46 The BRICS agenda displays already some results on investment facilitation. In August 2017, their trade ministers endorsed the "Outlines for BRICS Investment Facilitation", a non-binding, voluntary instrument that captures "good practices of various BRICS countries concerning enhancing transparency, improving efficiency and promoting cooperation", available at http://www.brics.utoronto.ca/docs/170802-trade.html (visited on October 14, 2018).

47 Felipe Hees and Pedro Barreto da Rocha Paranhos, Investment facilitation: moving beyond investment promotion, Columbia FDI Perspectives, n. 228, June 18, 2018, available at http://ccsi.columbia.edu/files/2016/10/No-228-Hees-and-Paranhos-FINAL.pdf (visited on October 14, 2018).

facilitation", Brazil submitted, on January 31, 2018, a draft of an Investment Facilitation Agreement (IFA)[48] containing a concrete illustration of a possible WTO multilateral framework for investment facilitation. The submission was meant to be a platform to promote more focused and text-based discussions as well as recognition of the "importance of continuous outreach to WTO Members, especially developing and least-developed Members". In so doing, Brazil drew on its recent experience with investment facilitation in the CFIAs.

The discussion so far has allowed WTO Members to explore – under a positive approach – a wide array of disciplines with an active procedural or practical component that, if implemented, could contribute to a favourable national investment environment.

Although the Brazilian draft remains for the moment the only contribution containing concrete suggestions for disciplines, many commonalities can be spotted across the positions already put forward. For example, the concept of a *single-window* appears explicitly in the communications by Brazil and Argentina, China and Russia, and it was fully incorporated into the Brazilian draft agreement. *Transparency* is a pervasive element across all proposals as well as *technical assistance* and *attention to individual needs of LDCs*. The Russian paper and the proposal by Brazil and Argentina articulate the notion of dispute prevention and resolution of disputes. The communications submitted by Brazil and Argentina as well as the one by China encourage the voluntary adoption of corporate social responsibility standards by investors.

Besides convergence on several issues, discussions have also shown that investment facilitation could be understood differently by different WTO Members. China, for instance, has suggested that Members should "use clearly-defined lists or catalogues to indicate which sectors are allowed, restricted or prohibited for foreign investment, as well as to create clear criteria for the approval process". China has also suggested discussions to simplify administrative processes, "which means to reduce or remove approval requirements as much as possible. If the approval is still necessary, Members are encouraged to shorten the timeframe for administrative decisions; to simplify document and procedural requirement and to keep the fees at a minimum". Regarding the Chinese suggestion to include the topic of entry and sojourn of investment personnel, concerns are that the highly controversial nature of the topic, combined with the sensitive nature of screening disciplines and market access issues, could render the structured discussion more complicated rather than helping move the issue forward.[49]

48 Communication from Brazil, dated 31 January 2018, JOB/GC/169.

49 China's statement during the third meeting of the structured discussion on investment facilitation, held in Geneva July 23.

Debates on investment facilitation are recent on the WTO agenda, and discussions are still evolving. Nevertheless, the degree of engagement so far witnessed suggests that WTO can deliver a promising contribution to the reform of the international investment regime.

4 The Gap: Policy Debates on Investment Facilitation and the Current Academic Narrative on the Reform of the International Investment Regime

Multilateral work on investment facilitation could benefit from inputs coming from academic debates, which have been adding much-needed sophistication and legitimacy to the discussion on the other topics covered under the reform of the international investment regime. There seems to be a disconnection between the state of play of the debates on investment facilitation at the policy level and the current academic agenda.

One example is the analyses of the Brazilian investment agreements. They are often singled out by, for example, the fact that they are one of the few instruments in force to prescribe State-to-State dispute settlement. These analyses remain within the realm of what is familiar to the community of investment lawyers and policy-makers. This is a partial assessment of this model agreement. Although it is controversial that Brazil stands as a "revolutionary"[50] State for exercising the option not to follow the ISDS approach, the Brazilian model investment agreement is not defined exclusively by this option.

The whole segment of investment facilitation – particularly what its introduction to the repertoire of rules implies to the investment regime – seems to be left unaddressed.

What could explain this situation? One reason that could be in response is that discussions on investment facilitation are relatively recent in the context of the reform of the regime. This should explain the time lag between policy debates and academic discourse.

However, if one takes, as a reference for comparison, the initiative promoted by the EU for a multilateral investment court, this type of argument is not borne out. Despite also being a rather recent proposal, the EU initiative seems to have received much more academic attention – both in the literature and academic events – than the debates on investment facilitation.

50 Anthea Roberts, The Shifting Landscape of Investor-State Arbitration: Loyalists, Reformists, Revolutionaries and Undecideds, *EJIL Talk!*, June 15, 2017, available at https://www.ejiltalk.org/the-shifting-landscape-of-investor-state-arbitration-loyalists-reformists-revolutionaries-and-undecideds/#more-15339 (visited on October 14, 2018).

This comparison should lead to a second possible explanation for the apparent academic disregard for investment facilitation. Moreover, this is that the topic does not seem to fall easily under the conceptual categories that have so far framed the vocabulary of investment policies and rules. The EU initiative, in contrast, is undeniably drafted in this vocabulary.

Indeed, rules on investment facilitation – and, by extension, treaties enshrining them – are designed for a different purpose than standards of investment protection. The reform debates are often depicted as an interplay of forces occurring on a sliding scale between the private interest of investors and the public power of the state to regulate. Two actors seem to play the leading roles in this legal narrative of the reform – the States and the adjudicators – as the academic conversation predominantly revolves around the dispute settlement stage.[51]

By contrast, it is more difficult to see where investment facilitation measures – a set of procedures to streamline the establishment and operation of investors in a third country – fit under these categories or narratives. They are hardly the result of a tug of war between investors' and States' interests. Similarly, the role disputes are expected to play on the enforcement of such rules is likely to be minimal. Instead, it seems to be precise because investment facilitation rules are compatible with the different policy preferences in questions such as dispute settlement that this topic has been gaining traction at the multilateral level.

51 Two recent works that try to make sense of the reform suggest that the debates are confined to the traditional categories emerging from the experience of the BITs. In *Shifting Paradigms in International Investment Law* (Stephan Hindelang and Markus Krajewski (eds.), Oxford: Oxford University Press, 2016), the dynamics underlying the reform is presented as one where "[t]*he balance of the international investment law regime may shift away from a strong emphasis on interests of private property protection*" in the direction of "*more firmly securing a State's right to regulate in the public interest*" (at 5). In its turn, in *Reassertion of Control over the Investment Treaty Regime* (Andreas Kulick (ed.), Cambridge: Cambridge University Press, 2017) the interest lies in examining the many instruments States have been employing in order to exert more control over the investment treaties, particularly investment treaty arbitration. It is not clear how these conceptual framings would apply – nor if they do – to investment treaties where the emphasis is not on dispute settlement nor the calibration between public and private prerogatives. The same reasoning seems to apply to the *clash of paradigms* outlined by Anthea Roberts, which is equally a portrayal of the struggle between public and private interests with a strong emphasis on the dispute stage (107 *American Journal of International Law* 45 (2013)). Still, one of her insights on the evolution of the investment regime could be seen as able to also accommodate the emergence of agreements centered on investment facilitation, as the latter could be viewed as "*treaty provisions that they* [States] *are happy to live with on either side of the equation*", i.e., capital exporters or importers (at 92).

To be sure, investment facilitation rules are different from investment protection ones. Still, they might be complementary. Both are part of the menu of options in the context of the reform of the international investment regime.

It is for this reason that academic debates should factor in the contribution of investment facilitation to the reform of the international investment regime. For example, to what extent can investment facilitation rules address the concerns that drive the debates on the reform? Inputs from academic discussions would be a welcome element to enrich the policy-making options.

5 Concluding Remarks

Some 60 years ago, BITS began their global dissemination having among their purposes the alleged need to compensate for perceived shortcomings in domestic governance of host States. Measures dedicated to investment facilitation seek to do just that.

This chapter has argued that, for the first time in a long time, the political will might be there to advance multilateral discussions on investment facilitation – a non-trivial event in this area. The experience of Brazil, aside from a growing body of intelligence gathered by international organizations, suggests that this might be an opportunity to engage in discussions that might better correspond to what we can expect from an investment regime resembles very little to the one that witnessed the emergence of the BITS. As argued in this chapter, one of the critical aspects of the Brazilian investment agreements – and hence of its investment facilitation provisions – is its *interoperability*. They can coexist with previous commitments States might have made under BITS with other states. This element seems to be crucial in a scenario where the 'new normal' is pluralism, instead of the predominance of the BIT model.

When compared to the other items on the menu of the reform of the international investment regime, investment facilitation does not bring forward the legacy associated with the issues that stand at the core of the reform debates, and which currently divide countries. Quite the opposite, investment facilitation injects fresh air in a regime long in need of new, non-contentious, approaches.

CHAPTER 3

Russia's Foreign Investment Policy: Recent Developments and Future Trends in Terra (In)Cognita

Dmitry K. Labin and Alena V. Soloveva

1 Introduction

The past 15 years have seen dramatic changes in Russia's investment treaties and arbitration practice. As a major player in international investment activities and a prominent constituent of the group of Brazil, Russia, India, China and South Africa (BRICS) which is considered to be a new power hub in international relations in the twenty first century, Russia's divergent approaches to investment treaties and arbitration practice have attracted wide attention and debates. What adds to that curiosity is that Russia is a significant participant in the United Nations Commission on International Trade Law (UNCITRAL) discussions to reform the investor-state dispute settlement (ISDS) mechanism, and the world has been watching any slight shifts in its approach closely. Hence, it is necessary to gain insight into the underlying consideration of Russia's legal practice.

Up until 2016, all of Russia's bilateral investment treaty (BIT) negotiations were primarily based on Russian Model BIT (2001),[1] which replaced the 1992 Russia Model BIT.[2] However, the ever-changing political and economic landscape revealed the technical inadequacy of the existing legal tools, which had fallen behind new mechanisms of investment promotion and protection. Any treaty structure should be designed in light of the circumstances and needs of the state concerned.[3] In this regard, Russian Model BIT (2001) was not very

1 Decree of the Government of the Russian Federation dd. June 09, 2001 No. 456 "On Entering into International Treaties on the Encouragement and Mutual Protection of Investments between the Government of the Russian Federation and the Governments of Foreign States" (Collection of Russian Federation Legislation, June 18, 2001, No. 25. P. 2578).

2 Decree of the Government of the Russian Federation dd. June 11, 1992 No. 395.

3 Wenhua Shan and Hongrui Chen, Chine-US BIT negotiation and the emerging Chinese BIT 4.0, in C.L. Lim (ed.), *Alternative Visions of the International Law on Foreign Investment: Essays in Honour of Muthucumaraswamy Sornarajah* (Cambridge: Cambridge University Press, 2016) 248.

 | DOI:10.1163/9789004376991_004

helpful in addressing the market needs of Russian investors and host states. As a result, in September 2016 the Government of the Russian Federation adopted the new Regulation on Entering into International Treaties on the Encouragement and Mutual Protection of Investments (Regulation (2016)).[4] Regulation (2016) contains non-binding guidelines for drafting and negotiating future investment protection treaties (Guidelines (2016)). As a result, a new, fourth, generation of Russian BITs seems to be taking shape.

This chapter attempts to dissect the evolution of four generations of Russian BITs by exploring the background against which these generations of treaties have developed. It will then discuss specific issues presented by the complex web of legal protection standards which become prescribed in investment treaties over time. Furthermore, the chapter examines Russia's approach to the ratification of the relevant arbitration conventions, and in particular, the Convention on the Settlement of Investment Disputes between States and Nationals of Other States of 1965 (Washington Convention or the ICSID Convention).[5]

Before proceeding with the above-mentioned topics, one preliminary matter needs to be addressed. Russia delved into foreign investment relations initially as part of the Union of Soviet Socialist Republics (the USSR, or the Soviet Union).[6] Of 15 constituents, the Russian Soviet Federative Socialist Republic (RSFSR) was the largest republic.[7] Following the dissolution of the USSR in 1991, Russia became a state successor to the USSR.[8] Under the Agreement on the Creation of the Commonwealth of Independent States (CIS)[9] signed in

4 The Regulation of the Government of the Russian Federation dd. September 30, 2016 No. 992 "On Entering into International Treaties on the Encouragement and Mutual Protection of Investments".

5 Available at https://icsid.worldbank.org/en/Documents/icsiddocs/ICSID%20Convention%20English.pdf (visited July 10, 2019).

6 The USSR was a socialist state in Eurasia that existed from 1922 to 1991.

7 In total, the USSR was composed of 15 Soviet Socialist Republics (SSR): Armenian SSR, Azerbaijan SSR, Byelorussian SSR (Belarus), Estonian SSR, Georgian SSR, Kazakh SSR, Kirghiz SSR (Kyrgyzstan), Latvian SSR, Lithuanian SSR, Moldavian SSR (Moldova), RSFSR, Tadzhik SSR (Tajikistan), Turkmen SSR, Ukrainian SSR, and Uzbek SSR.

8 On 8 December 1991, the presidents of Russia, Ukraine and Belarus signed the Belavezha Accords which declared the dissolution of the Soviet Union, and the creation of the Commonwealth of Independent States.

9 Commonwealth of Independent States is a regional intergovernmental organization formed following the dissolution of the Soviet Union and which consists of post-Soviet republics in Eurasia including Azerbaijan, Armenia, Belarus, Kazakhstan, Kyrgyzstan, Moldova, Russia, Tajikistan, Turkmenistan, Ukraine and Uzbekistan. Georgia was a member of the CIS in 1993–2009. In 2014 Ukraine announced its ambitions to leave the organisation. However, no formal withdrawal process has been initiated so far.

December 1991 in Belarus, Russia assumed the rights and obligations under international agreements entered into by the USSR. What is particularly interesting is that the Ministry of Foreign Affairs signed a note in December 1990 which essentially confirmed its succession under the investment treaties. Therefore, we refer to Russia's investment practice as also covering the USSR legacy.

2 Four Generations of Russia's BITS

As of August 2019, in addition to several treaties with investment provisions, Russia has signed over 84 BITS, 63 of which have been ratified.[10] Like many other developing countries, Russia started its BIT programme in 1989 in the hope it would attract foreign investments amidst the new political and economic landscape which was taking shape after the fall of the Berlin Wall.[11] This is when the actual "BIT era" began, as exhibited through the growth in BITS numbers over time: since the 1989 marker, over the next ten years their number grew from 385 to 1,857, a four-fold increase.[12]

The important numbers to consider are those for the growth in the number of Russian BITS over time. As can be seen in Figure 3.1 below, the highest number of BITS was signed in 1989 when the Soviet Union debuted in the foreign investment arena. The number of BITS gradually decreased, settling at the moderate pace of two BITS per year.

It seems reasonable to observe that Figure 3.1 indicates a definite downward trend. Perhaps more surprising than this steep downward trend in BITS

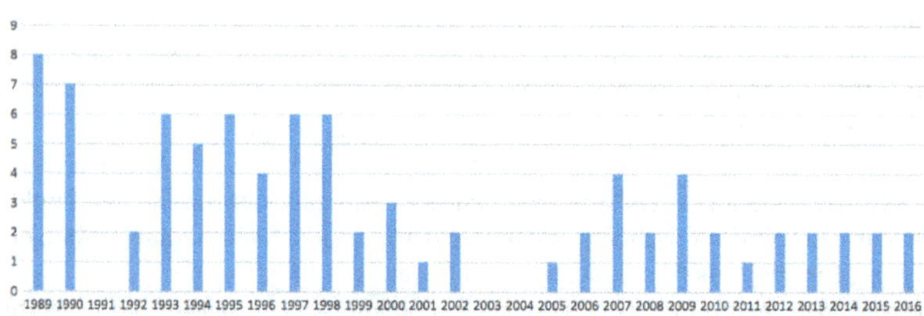

FIGURE 3.1 Annual growth of Russia's BITS, 1989–2016

---

10 "Investment Policy Hub: Russia-BITs", available at https://investmentpolicy.unctad.org/international-investment-agreements/countries/175/russian-federation (visited October 10, 2019).

11 O. Thomas Johnson and Jr., Jonathan Gimblett, From Gunboats to BITs: The Evolution of Modern International Investment Law, in Karl P. Sauvant (ed.), *Yearbook on International Investment. Law & Policy 2010–2011* (2012) 685.

12 Id.

numbers is the rapid drop in numbers after the adoption of the pilot 1992 Russia Model BIT.

Historically, there are four easily identifiable generations of Russian BITs:

(1) 1989–1991: the launch of BIT programme and the first generation of BITs reinforced by the geopolitically sensible attitudinal shift toward foreign investment by the end of the Cold War;

(2) 1992–2000: the adoption of Russia's first Model BIT in 1992 and the second-generation BITs, arguably, in response to a rapid increase in foreign investment flows into developing countries in 1991–1992, "increasing from a total annual inbound investment of less than US$40 billion in 1989 to US$200 billion in 1999;"[13]

(3) 2001–2015: the adoption of Russia's second Model BIT in 2001 and the third generation of BITs which explicitly allowed foreign investors to have access to international arbitration mechanism administered by the *International Centre for Settlement of Investment Disputes* (ICSID), which was established in 1966 in accordance with the ICSID Convention, via the ICSID Additional Facility Rules;[14]

(4) 2016–present: the emergence of the fourth generation of BITs spurred by the adoption of the Guidelines (2016) with some briefly canvassed changes to the established investment treaty practice.

The proposed categorization – like any other BITs categorization – is not perfect and will likely be a subject of future debate. There is, however, a rationale for the identification of these periods in Russia's BITs practice. Our categorization derives from the idea that rule-making follows law-making, and each new series of BITs mirrors the development in Model BIT approaches by the Russian Government. That is, however, in sharp contrast to other observations made in different contributions to the subject by Russian scholars.[15] We proceed with further scrutiny of each generation through the lens of standards of investment treatment and protection, including national treatment and most-favoured nation treatment (MFN), as well as full protection and security and dispute settlement mechanisms.

BITs are of significance in the context of national laws on investment promotion and protection which are well-recognized often incoherent. Of particular interest on this issue is that BITs can, by operation of Russian constitutional principle,[16] fill the gaps in national laws, thereby having a bearing on

13 Id.

14 Created on September 27, 1978.

15 For example, Vasily Gushchin and Alexey Ovchinnikov, *Investment Law* (Moscow: EKSMO, 2009).

16 Art. 15(4) Constitution of the Russian Federation reads: "The universally recognised principles and norms of international law and the international treaties of the Russian

regulatory power to be exercised toward foreign investment. Russian BITs with other states conveniently echo the standards recognized in international practice and cover an array of essential aspects. However, each Russian BIT is unique as it is negotiated to reflect the contracting parties' investment policies and laws.

2.1 *First Generation of Russia's BITs*

Profoundly influenced by worldwide BITs practice, the USSR first became interested in investment treaties in the late 1980s when the sheer basics of the market economy were receiving an enhanced definition. In 1987, the USSR adopted a Model BIT,[17] based on which the first-generation of Russian BITs were negotiated until the collapse of the USSR.

In 1989 Russia signed the first set of BITs with eight developed countries of Netherlands, France, Germany, the UK, Luxembourg, Belgium, and Finland. Next year, in 1990, Russia secured five more lucrative additions such as Austria, Denmark,[18] Spain, Switzerland, and the Republic of Korea.[19] The socio-political context cannot be separated the content and form of investment treaties. Therefore, Russia's mindset when signing such BITs was cautious, if not conservative, aiming to preserve the sovereignty of Russia as a host state as much as possible.

Incidentally, almost all first-generation BITs vividly demonstrate an unstable approach toward a national treatment standard, bordering on complete rejection. In this regard, the USSR-UK BIT (1989) became the first BIT which included a "best effort" provision regarding national treatment, that is, each Contracting Party shall "to the extent possible", accord the same treatment to the investments of investors of the other contracting State as to the investments of "its own investors."[20] Some four months later, Russia signed another

Federation are a component part of its legal system. If an international treaty of the Russian Federation stipulates other rules than those stipulated by law, the rules of the international treaty apply."

17 Resolution of the Council of Ministers of the USSR of 27 November 1987, No 1353: On Conclusion between the Government of the USSR and Governments of Foreign States of Agreements on Reciprocal Protection of Investments.

18 The USSR-Denmark BIT (1990) was later replaced by a new Russia-Denmark BIT (1993). For this reason, most Russian and international scholars claim that during 1989–1990 Russia signed 14 BITs (not 15, as with Denmark). We reached an informed decision to include the BIT (1990) in the statistics to ensure fair and inclusive analysis of Russia's investment treaty practice.

19 That year, Russia also signed BITs with two developing economies of China and Turkey.

20 The USSR-UK BIT (1989), art. 3(3).

BIT with France which included a similar provision on national treatment whereby a contracting State shall accord to the investors of the other contracting State treatment no less favourable than that to its investors "in accordance with its laws and regulations."[21] By the end of 1989 the scales had tilted again to the soft reading which resulted in the USSR-Canada BIT containing a national treatment which mirrored the UK "best effort" standard ("to the extent possible").[22] Such rule-making reached its culmination in the USSR-Korea BIT (1990), which included a "grandfathered" national treatment clause,[23] which allowed only "limited exceptions to national treatment."[24] Other highlights include the USSR-Luxembourg BIT (1989) with a full protection and security clause qualified only by a public order exception,[25] and the USSR-Canada BIT (1989), which has no termination date ("this Agreement shall remain in force unless either Contracting Party notifies in writing the other Contracting Party of its intention to terminate it").[26] On a separate note, Russia-Germany BIT (1989) explicitly stated that it would apply "irrespective of whether there are diplomatic or consular relations between the states."[27] Surprisingly, while the USSR-Netherlands BIT, the first Russian BIT, contained a MFN clause, but excluded a national treatment. Importantly, early BITs of this period offered full access to the ISDS mechanism, traditionally under the UNCITRAL Arbitration Rules or the Arbitration Rules of the Arbitration Institute of the Stockholm Chamber of Commerce (SCC Rules).

Therefore, we suggest that 1989–1990 represented a starting point for Russian BIT practice. Arguably, this practice was inspired by Russia's own strong expectation that it would integrate itself into the Western-countries led international economic order after Russia, as a part of the USSR, was largely isolated from the international economic order. This background can help inform the interplay of practice and the development of the legal rules that formed the basis of Russia's foreign investment policy. Since Russia had no previous experience in BIT-drafting and had not developed a relevant national legal framework to assist in rule-making, there were many variations in the content, structure and form of the first-generation Russian BITs.

---

21 The USSR-France BIT (1989), art. 3(4).
22 The USSR-Canada (1989), art. 3(4).
23 The USSR-Korea BIT (1990), art. 3(2).
24 The USSR-Korea BIT (1990), art. 3(3).
25 The USSR-Luxembourg BIT (1989), art. 4(2).
26 The USSR-Canada BIT (1989), art. 14.
27 The USSR-Germany BIT (1989), art. 12.

2.2 *Second Generation of Russia's BITs*

The disappearance of the USSR on December 25, 1991 made Russia a separate sovereign state. The turn to the Western world was initially established by Russia as its fundamental national strategy. Western-style political, economic, social regimes and ideology were introduced and boomed in Russia. This process of state construction included the updating of the BIT program. In 1992, Russia published its first Model BIT. In 1995, Russia adopted a Resolution,[28] which "did not modify the actual Model BIT, but related solely to the intra-governmental procedures for the conclusion of investment treaties."[29] Furthermore, the Russian Ministry of Economic Development, "in lieu of the Ministry of Finance, acquired extended powers to negotiate investment treaties with foreign states and sign them (prior to that, treaties had to be presented to the Russian Government in order to be signed)",[30] which presumably aimed to facilitate the conclusion of BITs. However, some of 1992–1993 Russian BITs did not include provisions that were provided in 1992 Model BIT because they had already been approved before the Model BIT (1992) was adopted.

The BITs concluded by Russia after the breakup of the USSR contain a provision on national treatment. However, all of these BITs were subject to a general exception clause.[31] The exception clauses to the national treatment in Russian BITs with Greece, Sweden, Denmark and Italy BIT are clear-cut. However, Contracting Parties had great discretion in some other BITs (for example with Bulgaria, Czech Republic, Hungary, Lithuania, Romania, and Slovakia) as to how to apply those exception clauses. For instance, Russia-Bulgaria BIT (1993) reads that "each Contracting Party reserves the right to determine sectors and areas of activities where activities of foreign investors shall be excluded or restricted",[32] This made Russian BITs nearly incapable of providing a stable and predictable investment climate for foreign investors.

---

28 Government Resolution of 26 June 1995, No. 625: On the Insertion of Changes and Additions to the Resolution of the Government of the Russian Federation of 11 June 1992, No. 395.

29 Tilman Dralle, A Glance into the Future: The Prospective Investment Law Regime between the European Union and the Russian Federation, *Dresden Research Papers on International Economic Law, Research Paper No. 2* (2013), at 37–38.

30 Id.

31 Russia-Bulgaria BIT (1993), art. 3(3); Russia-Czech Republic BIT (1994), art. 3(2); Russia-Denmark BIT (1993), art. 3(3); Russia-Greece BIT (1993), art. 3(3); Russia-Hungary BIT (1995), art. 3(3); Russia-Italy BIT (1996), art. 3(2); Russia-Lithuania BIT (1999), art. 3(3); Russia-Romania BIT (1993), art. 3(2); Russia-Slovakia BIT (1993), art. 3(2); Russia-Sweden BIT (1995), art. 3(3).

32 Russia-Bulgaria (1993), art. 3(3).

A similar thing happened to the ISDS mechanism which is generally considered a fundamental component of a BIT effectively providing protection for foreign investment. The Russia Model BIT (1992), together with Russian BITs based upon that Model,[33] provided a list of suggested ISDS mechanisms including an ad hoc arbitration provision under the UNCITRAL Arbitration Rules or the Arbitration Institute of the Stockholm Chamber of Commerce (SCC), a leading commercial arbitration institution. However, it should be stressed that, while most of the BITs provided for the ISDS mechanism, they did not include a provision requiring the awards be final and binding upon the Contracting Parties.[34] This was an absolutely abnormal phenomenon in BITs. It seriously damaged the reliability of the ISDS mechanism because a request to enforce an award unfavorable to Russia could be easily denied.

Two possible reasons may be presented to explain Russian BIT policy in this period. First, as a transitional economy, Russia hoped that it could maintain its own regulatory power as much as possible, even though it had become more friendly to foreign investment. Second, Russia was a successor of the socialist USSR, which was particularly reluctant to subject itself to international adjudication.[35]

Nevertheless, the Russia-US BIT, which was signed on June 17, 1992, represented a landmark. This was the first BIT between the U.S. and a CIS Member State that was submitted to the US Senate for advice and approval. The US Senate quickly ratified that BIT in 1993; however, until 2019 that BIT has not been ratified by Russia. Some commentators suggested that the US should pursue a new treaty with Russia because the Russia-US BIT (1992) has become old and outdated.[36] Actually, in 2008 the state leaders of Russia and the United States agreed to enhance efforts to negotiate a new BIT that would "promote a state and predictable framework for investment, to the benefit of the business communities in both countries".[37] However, no progress has been achieved yet. It is suggested that the absence of a new BIT with high standards of investment

33 *See, e.g.*, Russia-Denmark BIT (1993), art. 8.

34 *See, e.g.*, Russia-Denmark BIT (1993), art. 8.

35 As to the USSR policy to international adjudication, see G. Shinkaretskaya, A Changing Attitude Towards International Adjudication in the Soviet Union, 3 *Leiden Journal of International Law* 59 (1990).

36 Samuel Charap and Andrew C. Kuchins, Economic Whiplash in Russia: An Opportunity to Bolster U.S.-Russia Commercial Ties?, *A Report of the CSIS Russia and Eurasia Program* (2009), at 9–10.

37 "Fact Sheet: U.S.-Russia Strategic Framework Declaration", available at https://georgewbush-whitehouse.archives.gov/news/releases/2008/04/20080406-5.html (visited July 5, 2019).

treatment and protection between the two states is a major factor discouraging substantial US investment flow to Russia.[38]

Be that as it may, the Russia-US BIT (1992) is important because that BIT is distinct in terms of its structure and content. That BIT, in Article 2, provides the standard of investment treatment which includes "relative treatment" and "absolute treatment". Under the "relative treatment" standard Russia must treat US investments "on a non-discriminatory basis".[39] Under the "absolute treatment" standard, Russia has the obligation to accord the US investments with "fair and equitable treatment".[40] It should be noted that the United States successfully persuaded Russia to embrace a "pre-establishment commitments" with a negative-list approach. This was the first and last time these terms entered into Russia's political and economic life. Under the BIT, Russia committed itself to the pre-establishment national treatment subject to exceptions which had existed or were to be claimed in coming years.[41] These exceptions "generally relate to matters such as land, power production, state loans, banking, and mass media."[42] For instance, Russia reserved the right to make exceptions on the "ownership of land and use of subsoil and natural resources."[43] There must be a "strong political will to follow such a challenging path of reform"[44] to change the national interest in having such exceptions. The gauntlet thrown down by the United States was subsequently picked up by Russia. Attached to the BIT is a letter between the United States and Russia "containing an understanding of the BIT shared by both countries,"[45] which constitutes an integral part of the BIT. Therefore, even though Russia reserved the right to make exceptions to national treatment, in that letter Russia appeared to suggest – without making a binding commitment – that it would not deny national treatment to the US investments in natural resources in Russia.[46]

From 1994 to 2000 there was a spree of Model BIT-based agreements with 18 states including Czech Republic, India, Portugal, Hungary, Albania, Norway,

---

38 Samuel Charap and Andrew C. Kuchins, Economic Whiplash in Russia: An Opportunity to Bolster U.S.-Russia Commercial Ties?, *A Report of the CSIS Russia and Eurasia Program* (2009), at 9–10.

39 Russia-U.S. BIT (1992), art. 2.1.

40 Russia-U.S. BIT (1992), art. 2.2. *See also* N. Stephan Kinsella and Paul E. Comeaux, The United States Bilateral Investment Treaties with Russia and Other CIS Republics, 2(3) *Russian Oil & Gas Guide* 23 (1993) 24.

41 Russia-U.S. (1992), art. 2(1).

42 N. Stephan Kinsella and Paul E. Comeaux, supra note 40, at 24.

43 Id.

44 Wenhua Shan and Hongrui Chen, *supra* note 3, at 231.

45 N. Stephan Kinsella and Paul E. Comeaux, *supra* note 40, at 24.

46 *Id.*

Sweden, Egypt, Lebanon, Turkey, Argentina, Kazakhstan, South Africa, Ukraine, Tajikistan, Italy, Ethiopia. Russia's mentality as a capital-importing state did not materially change during the late 1990s. At the end of this period, Russia secured a new lucrative BIT with economically powerful Japan.

2.3 *Third Generation of Russia's BITs*

The third generation of Russian BITs was practiced in a substantially different context. Politically, Vladimir Putin took office as President in May 2000. The ambitious new President pledged to regain the status of a great power by reconstructing its national governance, and increasing its participation in the international system, in particular, the accelerating WTO accession negotiations, etc. It should be noted that, largely benefiting from the sharp grow of oil price in the early 2000s, the Russian economy, which had been at the edge of a collapse largely attributable to the "shock therapy" that Russia adopted in the 1990s, significantly restored and grew. As a result, Russia began to emerge a new investment source.[47]

In 2001, Russia adopted a new Model BIT. Surprisingly, "for unknown reasons, this Model BIT initially lacked any provisions on national treatment, most-favoured nation regime and fair and equitable treatment."[48] What went unnoticed by some authors[49] was that this lacuna was swiftly closed by an amendment of 2002, which reintroduced those rules into the Russian Model BIT (2001).[50] Nevertheless, Russia's investment treaty practice became "much more conservative with the beginning of Putin's administration",[51] which was still reflected in the Russian Model BIT (2001). The new amendment of 2010 stipulated that "the investment treaty negotiations should be conducted according to a plan to be administered by the Ministry of Economic Development of the Russian Federation."[52]

The WTO accession negotiations were another major factor that had a significant impact on Russia's BIT practice in the first ten years of the twenty

47 *See* Karl P. Sauvant, New Sources of FDI: The BRICs Outward FDI from Brazil, Russia, India and China, 6 *The Journal of World Investment & Trade* 639 (2005).

48 Tilman Dralle, *supra* note 29, at 9.

49 David Collins, *The BRIC States and Outward Foreign Direct Investment* (Oxford: Oxford University Press, 2013) 61.

50 Government Resolution of 11 April 2002, No. 229: On the Insertion of Additions and Changes to the Model Agreement adopted by Resolution of the Government of the Russian Federation of 9 June 2001, No. 456.

51 Noah Rubins and Azizjon Nazarov, Investment Treaties and the Russian Federation: Baiting the Bear?, in Jacques Werner and Arif Hyder Ali (eds.), *A Liber Amicorum: Thomas Wälde – Law Beyond Conventional Thought* (London: CMP Publishing, 2009) 242.

52 Government Resolution of 17 December 2010, No. 1037: On the Insertion of Changes to the Resolution of the Government of the Russian Federation of 9 June 2001, No. 456.

first century. The Russian Model BIT (2001) sought to accommodate WTO requirements by containing a reference to Russia's commitments under the WTO regime, primarily the General Agreement on Trade in Services (GATS) which actually constituted the upper limit of what Russia would undertake under a BIT. In the WTO accession negotiations, Russia admitted that its BITs guaranteed national treatment but "with exemptions."[53] Thus, the Russian Model BIT (2001) stated that "[each] Contracting Party reserves the right to apply and introduce exemptions from national treatment of foreign investors and their investments."[54] As a result, Russia's BITs during this period showed no departure from its general reluctant attitude towards the national treatment standard.[55] To clarify the exact meaning of national treatment under a particular Russian BIT, it is helpful to first examine Russia's Schedule of Specific Commitments under the GATS.[56] In light of these existing commitments, many countries insisted on the introduction of exemptions of MFN and national treatment into the BIT drafts, which in turn created more challenges in the negotiation process.

In a further development on this issue, Russia has recently adopted a more cautious stance concerning the MFN. First, Russia limited the effect of the MFN clause by introducing a "saving clause specifying that the most-favoured nation clause cannot create any obligations for Russia over and above the existing WTO commitments."[57] Second, Russia linked the MFN to the fair and equitable treatment (FET) standard. Thus, the scope of the MFN embodied in the Russian Model BIT (2001) is "significantly restricted vis-à-vis a most-favoured nation clause that follows the standard wording,"[58] because its application is confined exclusively to the FET.[59] However, Russia has successfully

53 General Agreement on Trade in Services (GATS) is a treaty of the World Trade Organization (WTO) that entered into force in January 1995.

54 Russian Model BIT (2001), art. 3(3), available at http://docs.cntd.ru/document/9012573 (visited May 3, 2019).

55 *See* Russia-Singapore BIT (2010), art. 4(3) and Russia-China BIT (2006), art. 3(2); Russia-Algeria BIT (2006), art. 4(2); Russia-Indonesia BIT (2007), art. 3(3); Russia-Jordan BIT (2007), art. 3(3); Russia-Angola BIT (2009), art. 5(5); Russia-Qatar BIT (2007), art. 4(3); Russia-Libya BIT (2008), art. 3(3); Russia-Syria BIT (2005), art. 3(3); Russia-Thailand BIT (2002), art. 3(3); Russia-Yemen BIT (2002), art. 3(3); Russia-Venezuela BIT (2008), art. 4(3); Russia-Turkmenistan BIT (2009), art. 4(3); Russia-Zimbabwe BIT (2012), art. 5(3).

56 *See* WTO, Trade in Services, Russian Federation – Schedule of Specific Commitments, GATS/SC/149.

57 Tilman Dralle, *supra* note 29, at 27.

58 Id.

59 See *Renta 4 S.V.S.A. et al. v. Russian Federation*, SCC Case No. 24/2007, Award on Preliminary Objection, 20 March 2009, para. 105.

pushed for such an unconventional version of the MFN obligation in many of its recent BITs.[60]

The Russian Model BIT (2001) introduced a ground-breaking provision which recommended the ICSID as an arbitral institution. Foreign investors may have access to ICSID arbitration in accordance with the ICSID Additional Facility Rules[61] in investment treaties with countries that have not ratified the ICSID Convention as long as it is explicitly provided for in the investment treaty. Russia is precisely such a country. Although Russia is not a Contracting Party to the ICSID Convention, it accepted the ICSID mechanism by agreeing the ICSID Additional Facility Rules in many BITs that it has concluded. However, awards made in accordance with ICSID Additional Facility Rules are not as enforceable, credible and predictable as those made in accordance with the ICSID Convention.[62] Unlike the ICSID Additional Facility Rules, "awards rendered under the ICSID Additional Facility Rules are subject to the supervision of a national court, and their enforcement is covered by the New York Convention."[63]

Russian third-generation BITs, including those with China,[64] Singapore,[65] UAE,[66] Equatorial Guinea,[67] Zimbabwe,[68] Guatemala,[69] Uzbekistan,[70] Azerbaijan,[71] Bahrain,[72] Iran,[73] and Cambodia[74] explicitly provide that investors

60 *See, e.g.*, Russia-Libya BIT (2008), art. 3(2); Russia-Indonesia BIT (2007), art. 3(2); Russia-Jordan BIT (2007), art. 3(2); Russia-Venezuela BIT (2008), art. 4(2); Russia-Syria BIT (2005), art. 3(2); Russia-Turkmenistan BIT (2009), art. 4(2); Russia-Singapore BIT (2010), art. 4(2); Russia-Qatar BIT (2007), art. 4(2). One exception is the Russia-China BIT (2006), art. 3(3).

61 Created on September 27, 1978.

62 Tian Wenjing, Investing in Russia? – Lessons learnt from the Yukos and Sanum Cases, *China Law Insight* (2017), available at https://www.lexology.com/library/detail.aspx?g=bfbafe0f-1486-429f-99a9-cedf908adaaa (visited May 3, 2019).

63 Yarik Kryvoi, Ratification of Arbitration-Related Conventions by CIS States: Global and Regional Framework, *CIS Arbitration Forum* (2018), available at http://www.cisarbitration.com/2018/05/18/ratification-of-arbitration-related-conventions-by-cis-states-global-and-regional-framework/ (visited April 21, 2019).

64 Russia-China BIT (2006), art. 9(2)(b).

65 Russia-Singapore BIT (2010), art. 9(2)(b).

66 Russia-UAE BIT (2010), art. 9(3).

67 Russia-Equatorial Guinea BIT (2011), art. 8(2).

68 Russia-Zimbabwe BIT (2012), art. 13(2)(iii).

69 Russia-Guatemala BIT (2013), art. 8(2)(c).

70 Russia-Uzbekistan BIT (2013), art. 8(2).

71 Russia-Azerbaijan BIT (2014), art. 8(2)(b).

72 Russia-Bahrain BIT 2014, art. 8(2)(c).

73 Russia-Iran BIT (2015), art. 9(2)(b).

74 Russia-Cambodia BIT (2015), art. 8(2)(c).

may submit disputes for ICSID arbitration. Thus foreign investors from these countries can submit disputes with Russia to ICSID through the mechanism of the ICSID Additional Facility Rules.[75] Unlike the ICSID awards, "awards rendered under the ICSID Additional Facility Rules are subject to the supervision of a national court, and their enforcement is covered by the New York Convention."[76]

Apart from ICSID arbitration, Russian Model BIT (2001) maintains two traditional ISDS options, i.e. an ad hoc arbitration court in accordance with the UNCTIRAL Arbitration Rules and a competent court within the territory of the host state. In a further twist, the Russian Model BIT (2001) allows an investor to choose ICSID-bound arbitration instrument, as investors now have a real opportunity to submit disputes to ICSID which is regarded as the epitome of investment treaty arbitration. This freedom of choice is doubly important when the host State has not ratified the ICSID Convention. In this sense the Model BIT can also be seen as illustrating the hypothetical intellectual transcendent premises for ICSID case law with Russia's involvement even though it has never transformed into empirical arbitration practice.[77]

2.4 *Fourth Generation of Russia's BITs*

While foreign direct investment (FDI) to Russia in 2014 dropped by 70%, to an estimated US$19 billion, since regional conflict, sanctions, and negative growth prospects demotivated foreign investors from the region,[78] foreign investors have gradually adapted to the new market realities, and currently continue to invest in the primary sector.[79] For example, Gaetano LLC, a UK-based private equity firm, acquired Komi Oil Ltd. in Russia.[80] In 2016, there was a 62% uptick in inflows of direct investment to Russia,[81] which owed to the privatization of state-owned assets.[82]

---

75 For example, Russia-China BIT (2006), art. 9(1)(b).

76 Yarik Kryvoi, Ratification of Arbitration-Related Conventions by CIS States: Global and Regional Framework, *CIS Arbitration Forum* (2018), available at http://www.cisarbitration.com/2018/05/18/ratification-of-arbitration-related-conventions-by-cis-states-global-and-regional-framework/ (visited April 21, 2019).

77 There is no known investment arbitration case against Russia which was resolved under the ICSID Additional Facility Rules, despite a treaty provision allowing such an option.

78 UNCTAD, Global Investment Trends Monitor No. 18, 2015, at 5.

79 UNCTAD, Global Investment Trends Monitor No. 22, 2016, at 6.

80 Komi Oil Ltd operates an oil refinery. The company is based in Russia. As of December 3, 2015, Komi Oil Ltd operates as a subsidiary of Gaetano LLC.

81 UNCTAD, Global Investment Trends Monitor No. 25, 2017, at 5.

82 The Russian Government sold a 19.5% stake in the state-owned oil company Rosneft in a deal worth around US$11 billion to a consortium led by Glencore (Switzerland) and the Qatari sovereign wealth fund.

Russia's recent move towards the fourth generation BIT is a result of a combination of economic, political, and international factors. Economically, Russia's shift from being mainly a capital-importing state to being both a capital-importing and a capital-exporting state now requires the country take a more open approach to investment treaties. Politically, domestic reform has also reached a new stage under the Guidelines (2016),[83] which in turn requires Russia's investment regime to be looked at afresh. Finally, from an international perspective, the new generation of Russian BITs also demonstrates Russia's response to the new international landscape of investment treaty and arbitration practice.

An important innovation in Russian investment treaty architecture is that treaty negotiations must now follow the customised recommendations.[84] Under the recommendations contained in the Guidelines (2016), Russia's government can now adapt treaty text for each new BIT partner. This tailor-made approach is presumably designed to resolve certain problems occasionally experienced by Russian investors in a particular marketplace, and to assess investment capabilities of prospective partners who wish to invest in Russia.[85] This approach allows Russia proposes to include additional elements that it deems necessary in a particular treaty negotiation for a particular partner's situation.

As discussed above, Russian Model BIT (2001) included a provision that allowed each Contracting Party to introduce exemptions from the national

83 Recent years have cemented Russia's approach toward investment treaty regime through national interests perspective. The newly adopted regulatory measures (including the Guidelines) demonstrate an attempt to safeguard national sovereignty and restrict market liberalization for foreign investors. For instance, investment treaty protection will cover only companies which have a so called "substantial business activity" in the host state. And there are no fixed criteria what "substantial" means. The Guidelines do not even contain a nonexclusive list of indicators such as location of registered office or headquarters, number of employees, turnover, and the nature of activities. That probably means that the "substantial business activity" will be assessed and established in each specific case on its own merits.

84 Published as enclosures to the Guidelines 2016 as its integral part including Criteria for the Assessment of the Reasoning to Negotiate and Conclude International Treaties of the Russian Federation concerning the Encouragement and Reciprocal Protection of Investment (Enclosure 1 to the Guidelines 2016) and General Approaches to the Conclusion of International Treaties of the Russian Federation concerning the Encouragement and Reciprocal Protection of Investment (Enclosure 2 to the Guidelines 2016).

85 The Ministry of Economic Development of the Russian Federation changes approaches to the entering into treaties concerning the encouragement and reciprocal protection of investment [Minekonomrazvitiya menyaet podkhody k zaklyucheniyu soglashenii po voprosam pooshchreniya i zashchity kapitalovlozhenii] in Russ, available at http://economy.gov.ru/minec/about/structure/deptorg/2016050802# (visited May 3, 2019).

treatment of foreign investors and their investments. It is, however, silent as to the nature of exemptions applied against a current or prospective investors and their investments. The Guidelines (2016) allows Contracting Parties to agree upon the list of particular exemptions from national treatment during the negotiations, thereby ensuring transparency and predictability for all investors.

One particular highlight concerns a list of persons who can enjoy the BIT benefits. Historically, BITs are designed to govern investors only from the Contracting Parties of a BIT. However, international arbitration practice shows that there have been several attempts to circumvent the requirement of the investor's nationality. To clarify this issue, the Guidelines (2016) expressly excludes those investors and investments of the host state which are: companies owned or controlled by nationals of the host state or of a third state and investments made by individuals who were nationals of the host state at the time when the investment was made.[86] Therefore, any new investment treaty should not apply to investments made by companies which do not have significant business activity in the country of their incorporation or companies which are controlled by the beneficiaries from the host state or a third country. It was suggested that new Russian investment treaties "would likely make it difficult for investors to structure investments solely for the purposes of gaining protection under a Russian BIT."[87]

The Guidelines (2016) introduces a more rigorous approach to some of the key provisions in Russian Model BIT (2001). The Guidelines (2016) do not specify which international arbitration rules are to be included in new investment treaties. Therefore, Russia and its BIT negotiating partners can designate any arbitration centre during the negotiation. However, the Guidelines (2016) do encourage the parties to choose the UNCITRAL Arbitration Rules where a dispute is submitted to an ad hoc arbitration.[88] Importantly, the Guidelines (2016) specify that any new investment treaty should expressly exclude the

---

86 Russian BITs normally limit the notion of "investor" to citizens or nationals of a contracting party. That is the approach adopted in the Model BITs 1992 and 2001, as well as the Guidelines (2016). However, three BITs (with Canada, Germany and Kazakhstan) also extend protection to permanent residents of a contracting party. The Argentina BIT disqualifies Russian citizens who, at the time when the investment was made, had been living in Argentina for more than two years, unless the source of the investment was foreign.

87 Norton Rose Fulbright, Russia's new guidelines on future bilateral investment treaties in International Arbitration Report, June 2017, at 30–31.

88 Art. 53 Enclosure 2 to the Guidelines (2016).

UNCITRAL Rules on Transparency in Treaty-based Investor-State Arbitration approved in December 2013.[89] Instead, the Guidelines (2016) establishes a duty of confidentiality concerning any information about the dispute. Arguably, this conception of privacy and confidentiality "originates primarily from the foundational underpinnings of international commercial arbitration, but it has also to a considerable extent been translated into the investment context."[90] This can explain the rationale for Russia's clear reluctance to support enhanced transparency in the ISDS system. This disinclination to incorporate arbitration considerations into the Guidelines (2016) is presumably a response to recent developments in investment treaty and arbitration practice in the rest of the world.

The Guidelines (2016) also includes a series of procedural elements[91] related to the ISDS which previously were deliberately left for the disputing parties to agree upon once the actual dispute arose. Protections under any new investment treaty should not be granted to investments made by citizens of the host state. Furthermore, any new investment treaty should not apply to investments made by companies which are controlled by the beneficiaries from the host state or a third country. Accordingly, new investment treaties will likely make it difficult for investors to structure investments solely for the purposes of gaining protection under a Russian BIT, thereby excluding any possibility of a foreign company shopping for treaty protection. This new legal innovation can arguably be seen as adding its own transparency element into corporate nationality shopping and protecting the public interests of the host state by substantially closing loophole that allowing treaty shopping provides.

Furthermore, the Guidelines (2016) instructs that any new treaty should provide for a limitation period of two years after the events giving rise to the dispute for the claimant to send the notice of dispute to the host state, and arbitration must be commenced with three years from the date of that notice.

---

89 The UNCITRAL Rules on Transparency in Treaty-based Investor-State Arbitration includes several innovative obligations with limitations and exceptions. These obligations include the publication of information at the commencement of arbitral proceedings (art. 2), publication of documents (art. 3), submission by a third person (art. 4) and n by a non-disputing Party to the treaty (art. 5), hearing open to the public (art. 6).

90 *See generally* Cindy Buys, The Tensions between Confidentiality and Transparency in International Arbitration, 14 *American Review of International Arbitration* 121 (2003).

91 The new Regulation contains some mapped ISDS reform elements such as a mandatory 180-days "cooling-off period" and detailed requirements on notification of disputes; a limitation period of two years after the events giving rise to the dispute for the claimant to send the notice of dispute to the host state, and arbitration must be commenced within three years from the date of such notice.

Investors therefore should be aware of prescription periods for the filing of a claim. Hence, the pursuit of improved transparency and inclusion of procedural aspects in the Guidelines (2016) will likely have a chilling effect on the ability of disputing parties to arbitrate.

Despite these aggressive moves, it is too early to draw a definitive conclusion about the future trajectory of Russia's BIT policy. The Guidelines (2016) cannot be used to interpret existing investment treaties, but they usefully demonstrate what future Russian BITs could look like. The Guidelines (2016) represent a lesson learned from recent investment treaty disputes involving Russia, including the arbitration brought by former shareholders of *Yukos* against the Russian Federation. The introduction of the Guidelines (2016) implies that Russia might be willing to negotiate BITs which are restricted only to protections readily available to foreign investors in Russia. Consequently, investors could benefit from more certain protections than they currently have.

3 Overview of Substantive Protections and Procedural Rights

3.1 *Fair and Equitable Treatment*

Almost all Russian BITs in force[92] include a FET clause, and most Russian BITs provide the FET in a general manner. For instance, the Russia-Thailand BIT (2002), while providing that each Contracting Party shall "in its territory in any case accord such-investments by investors of the other Contracting Party fair and equitable treatment and full protection",[93] does not further define the meaning of the FET. Only a few BITs[94] refer to the FET as being "in accordance with principles of international law." Interestingly, in a departure from earlier Russian BIT practice, the Guidelines (2016) do not envision that future BITs should contain a FET clause. However, it does provide for a prohibition on arbitrary treatment in future BITs, stating all relevant laws and other regulations "shall be applied reasonably, objectively and impartially."

3.2 *National Treatment and Most-Favoured Nation Treatment*

While the majority of Russian BITs feature both national treatment and most-favoured nation clauses, some provide neither.[95] In the Soviet-era BITs, national treatment was either referred to not at all,[96] or it was watered down

92 With the exception of Russia-Ukraine BIT (1998) and Russia-Armenia BIT (2001).

93 Russia-Thailand BIT (2002), art. 2(2).

94 *See, e.g.*, USSR-Canada BIT (1989) and Russia-France BIT (1989).

95 *See, e.g.*, Russia-Armenia BIT (2001).

96 *See, e.g.*, the BITs with Austria (1990), Belgium (1989), Finland (1989), Germany (1989) and the Netherlands (1989).

to a "best effort" commitment or subjected to the domestic legal framework of the respective host State, like for instance, the BITs with France,[97] Spain[98] and the UK.[99] Russian BITs from the Soviet-era generally contained a provision on the MFN, which made it only subject to a set of standard exceptions such as customs unions, free trade areas and regional economic integration agreements. The second wave of BITs concluded between 1992 and 2000 basically followed this approach, with the only exception being that economic cooperation agreements between Russia and the former Soviet republics were not covered by the MFN obligation.[100] This carve-out, which is also reflected in Russian Model BIT (2001),[101] allows Russia to conclude "more favourable investment protection agreements with former USSR countries without having to extend these benefits to other BIT partners."[102] The Russian Model BIT (2001) also provides that the Contracting Parties will accord to each other a regime "no more favourable" than that imposed by the WTO.[103] Most Russian BITs also contain exceptions along these lines. The Guidelines (2016) specifies that a MFN clause cannot be used to import dispute resolution mechanisms from other treaties.

3.3 *Full Protection and Security*

Most Russian BITs contain a full protection and security guarantee. However, the precise formulation varies from treaty to treaty. The 1992 Russia Model BIT refers to a somewhat robust formulation such as "full and unconditional protection in accordance with legislation [of the host state]", while Russian Model BIT (2001) offers a slightly narrowed protection, and stipulates that the host state "guarantees full protection, in accordance with its legislation, of investments in its territory by investors of the other Contracting Party." Incidentally, the Guidelines (2016) does not envisage including the full protection and security guarantee in future BITs. The doctrinal interpretation suggests that the exclusion of a full protection and security clause crowns the paradigmatic move towards the protection of public interests as opposed to foreign investor's interests. Incidentally, while most of the Russian BITs contain a full

97 The USSR-France BIT (1989), art. 3(4) – "en conformité avec sa législation nationale."

98 The USSR-Spain BIT (1990), art. 5(4) – "con arreglo a su legislación nacional."

99 The USSR-UK BIT (1989), art. 3(3) – "to the extent possible' and 'in accordance with its laws and regulations."

100 *See, e.g.*, Russia-Czech Republic BIT (1994), art. 3(3); Russia-Denmark BIT (1993), art. 3(4); Russia-Hungary BIT (1995), art. 3(4); Russia-Italy BIT (1996), art. 3(3); Russia-Slovakia BIT (1993), art. 3(3); Russia-Sweden BIT (1995), art. 3(4). This additional exception is not based on the then valid Russian Model BIT of 1992.

101 Russian Model BIT (2001), art. 3(4).

102 Tilman Dralle, *supra* note 29, at 27.

103 *See, e.g.*, BITs with Venezuela (2008), Jordan (2007), Singapore (2010) and Syria (2005).

protection and security guarantee (except for the BIT with Singapore), not all BITs allow disputes relating to full protection and security to be submitted to investment arbitration by the investor and thus can only be decided via inter-State arbitration.[104]

3.4 *Umbrella Clause*

The Russian Model BITs of 1992 and 2001, like the majority of Russian BITs, do not include umbrella clauses. Likewise, the Guidelines (2016) do not envisage the inclusion of such clauses in Russia's future BITs. Nevertheless, 12 Russian BITs currently in force contain umbrella clauses.[105]

3.5 *Dispute Settlement*

Each BIT is a result of a negotiation process, which may involve particular political considerations, trade concerns, and the distinct elements of the parties' national legal systems. Such rule-making may thus be "haphazard, messy, and uneven, depending on what is needed and what is feasible in a given constellation of interests and forces."[106] These rationales for divergence play out in different procedural combinations and to differing degrees concerning states' regional ambitions. Recent examples include a mandatory exhaustion of local remedies clause (India), the use of an investment court with an appellate mechanism (EU), a recourse to national court in the event of a dispute relating to investments (South Africa), the use of specialised investment courts (Iraq and Kazakhstan), institutional mediation based on a national court system (Morocco and Republic of Korea), state-to-state arbitration (Australia), and the use of joint committees or ombudspersons (Brazil).

A major weakness of Russia's investment treaty system is that many of the Soviet-era BITs between Russia and EU Member States suffer from a lack of reliable access to ISDS mechanism. The Russia 1992 Model BIT gave the investor a choice between arbitration under the SCC Rules or ad hoc arbitration under the UNCITRAL Rules. Russian BITs concluded in the 1990s generally provide

104 *See, e.g.*, USSR-Germany BIT (1989), art. 10(2); USSR-France BIT (1989), art. 9(1); USSR-Netherlands BIT (1989), art. 9(2); USSR-Austria BIT (1990). art. 7(1); USSR-Spain BIT (1990), art. 10(1); USSR-Turkey BIT (1990), art. 6(1).

105 USSR-France BIT (1989), Russia-China BIT (2006), USSR-Germany (1989), Russia-Greece (1993), Russia-Denmark (1993), Russia-Japan (1998), USSR-Korea (1990), Russia-Kuwait (1996), USSR-Netherlands (1989), USSR-Switzerland (1990), Russia-Turkey (1997) and USSR-UK (1989).

106 Karl P. Sauvant, Lessons from the negotiations of the United Nations Code of Conduct on Transnational Corporations and related instruments, in C.L. Lim (ed.), *Alternative Visions of the International Law on Foreign Investment: Essays in Honour of Muthucumaraswamy Sornarajah* (Cambridge: Cambridge University Press, 2016) 192.

for SCC arbitration and UNCITRAL ad hoc arbitration,[107] while some subsequent BITs provide a choice between the ICSID (and the ICSID Additional Facility arbitration) and UNCITRAL ad hoc arbitration.[108] Several BITs only provide for ad hoc arbitration, with no rules stipulated at all[109] or arbitration under the UNCITRAL Rules for ad hoc arbitration.[110] Russian Model BIT (2001) replaced SCC arbitration with arbitration under the ICSID Convention or the ICSID Additional Facility Rules. The Guidelines (2016) provides for the possibility of both institutional and ad hoc arbitration, as agreed in future BITs, but it does not prescribe any specific institutional rules.

4 Russia and Multilateral Investment Treaties

Russia's approach to multilateral treaties related to investment demonstrates an unstable relationship with international trade regimes. For instance, Russia is a state successor to the USSR which signed and ratified the United Nations Convention on the Recognition and Enforcement of Foreign Arbitral Awards (New York Convention) in 1960 and is a signatory to the Kyev Convention on Settling Disputes Related to Commercial Activities (Kyiv Convention) of 1992. Russia signed the ICSID Convention in 1992, but never ratified it. Russia signed the Energy Charter Treaty (ECT) in 1994 but then withdrew from the Treaty in 2009. Illustrating this see-saw relationship, from 1994 to 2009, Russia applied the Treaty provisionally, but the application was relatively limited. First, Russia never considered itself bound by the ECT in its broad sense, largely due to this provisional application. Russia's authorities consistently claimed that there were no legal obligations per se for Russia under the Treaty. Thus, Arkady Dvorkovich, in his role as an Assistant to the President of Russia, once said that "Russia signed the ECT, but never ratified it which means that we do not interpret ourselves as obligated to abide by its provisions." Second, the ECT proved to be an imperfect legal instrument when it failed to resolve the dispute between Russia and Ukraine in 2009 in which Ukraine breached the ECT provisions. Russia highlighted the lack of adequate assessment of this breach by the EU and its Member States, and the remarkable inactivity of the ECT Secretariat to help settle the conflict. Third, while the ECT was a regarded as a mutually beneficial deal, it remains unclear what benefits would have been

107 *See, e.g.*, Russian BITs with Belgium/Luxembourg (1989), the UK (1989) and Spain (1990).
108 *See, e.g.*, Russian BITs treaties with Yemen (2002), Syria (2005) and Singapore (2010).
109 *See, e.g.*, the treaties with the Netherlands (1989), Switzerland () and Germany (1989).
110 BITs with Canada, France and Egypt.

gained by Russia after its ratification. Back in 2006 President Putin shed some light on internally conflicting provisions in the ECT which purported to establish mutual access to energy production and transport infrastructure. Whilst Russia could give an access to its infrastructure for other Contracting States, which Contracting State could potentially provide a similarly exquisite access to its energy production infrastructure, or or trunk pipelines?[111] Overall Russia saw the ECT as a treaty which protected the interests of those countries which were net importers of energy, and did not protect the interests of net exporters of energy. Hence Russia abandoned the Treaty. This step confirms again Russia's move away from the philosophy and interest of a pure capital-importing state.

Most recently, a brand-new transparency-dedicated legal instrument, the United Nations Convention on Transparency in Treaty-based Investor-State Arbitration ("Mauritius Convention") signed by twenty-two States and entered into force on 18 October 2017, has been ratified by three States.[112] However, Russia is not even a signatory to the Mauritius Convention. Thus, notwithstanding its significant economic and political influence in the world, "Russia has not developed as a major international arbitration jurisdiction."[113]

At present, there is no official position of Russia's authorities as to the ratification of the ICSID Convention. While the ICSID Convention is not a panacea for Russia's international issues, it arguably can help improve the image of Russia as open to international jurisdiction. The ICSID Convention has consistently attracted attention from major developed, capital-exporting countries and developing capital-importing countries, with the most recent valuable addition to the ICSID system being Mexico.[114] Therefore, it seems that the ratification of the ICSID Convention is a desirable step to increase confidence of foreign investors to make investment in Russia.[115]

---

111 A Brief on Energy Charter Treaty, available at https://ria.ru/20090130/160544072.html (visited June 10, 2019).

112 So far five States have ratified the Convention including Cameroon, Canada, Gambia, Mauritius, and Switzerland.

113 Steven Finizio, Kenneth Beale, Russian Arbitration Reforms. Repatriating Russian disputes, 5 *Commercial Dispute Resolution* (2014) 21.

114 Mexico signed the International Centre for Settlement of Investment Disputes (ICSID) Convention last January 11, 2018. Upon the Senate's approval of the Convention, Mexico's president published the instrument in Mexico's Public Gazette ("Diario Oficial de la Federación") and submitted the ratification instrument to the ICSID on July 27, 2018. As a result, based on art. 68(2) of the ICSID Convention, this instrument formally came into force for Mexico on August 26, 2018. With Mexico, there are now 162 signatory states of the ICSID Convention and 154 members.

115 Tian Wenjing, Investing in Russia? – Lessons learnt from the Yukos and Sanum Cases, *China Law Insight* (2017), available at https://www.lexology.com/library/detail.aspx?g=bfbafeof-1486-429f-99a9-cedf908adaaa (visited May 3, 2019).

As discussed above, Russia began to offer a treaty-based recourse to arbitration under the ICSID Additional Facility Rules in the third-generation BITs, and this practice continues in the newly signed treaties with Morocco[116] and Palestine.[117] Although investors have not yet pursued claims under the ICSID Additional Facility Rules, this ICSID-bound mechanism is still a promising shift in Russia's arbitration legacy.

5 Russia and International Arbitration

On the whole, Russia has traditionally adopted European-style dispute resolution clauses with particular Russian characteristics. In many Russian BITs, the provisions for the settlement of both state-to-state and investor-state disputes are rather short and lack detail. Notably, the USSR-Finland BIT (1989) contains a decidedly short provision on state-to-state dispute settlement, stating that "[d]isputes between the Contracting Parties regarding the interpretation or application of this Agreement shall be settled through the diplomatic channel."[118] Arbitration clauses in more recent Russian BITs are visibly broader.

Several Russian BITs concluded in the late 1980s and the 1990s include an arbitration clause of limited jurisdiction, providing consent to resolve disputes only related to the "amount or mode of payment of compensation for expropriation"; these include for instance, the BITs signed in 1991 with Belgium/Luxembourg, Finland and Spain. The scope of the arbitration clause of several other BITs is limited to matters regarding the breach of the free transfer provision, as well as the amount of compensation for expropriation, for instance the BITs with Austria, Germany, Switzerland, Korea, the Netherlands and the UK. In some cases in which Russia is a Respondent, claimants argued that such narrow arbitration clauses should be interpreted to authorise the tribunal to determine whether expropriation has taken place. While the tribunal rejected this argument in *Berschader and Berschader v. Russian Federation*,[119] it later accepted as rendering the clause to be interpreted sufficiently broad to determine the fact of expropriation as well as appropriate compensation in *Renta 4 SVSA and ors v. Russian Federation*.[120] Claimants also tried to invoke the MFN

116 Russia-Morocco BIT (2016), art. 9(2)(b).

117 Russia-Palestine BIT (2016), art. 8(2)(c).

118 The USSR-Finland BIT (1989), art. 9.

119 *Berschader and Berschader v Russian Federation*, SCC Case No. 080/2004, Award, 21 April 2006, paras. 151–158.

120 *Renta 4 SVSA and ors v. Russian Federation*, SCC Case No. 24/2007, Award on Preliminary Objections, 20 March 2009, paras. 19–67.

clauses in Russian treaties to access less restrictive arbitration clauses in other Russian BITs, with varied success.[121]

Russia ranks itself one of top ten respondent States during the period of 1987–2017 with the total number of known cases reaching 24. Of these, 18 cases were dealt with under the UNCITRAL Arbitration Rules.[122] On the other hand, Russian investors submitted only 22 known cases, more than 50% of which were arbitrations under the UNCITRAL Arbitration Rules.[123] Currently 11 of these cases are pending with the oldest case dating 2007.[124] Out of the other 11 cases, three were discontinued and one was settled. Thus, there are only seven cases in which decisions have been rendered, and in three of these cases the awards have not been published. Surprisingly, some cases do not disclose even information about tribunal composition.[125]

Since 2016 Russian investors have become more active,[126] initiating most disputes under the UNCITRAL Arbitration Rules with the only ICSID[127] claim filed by subsidiaries of a Russian corporation.[128] Most of those claims were initiated under the UNCITRAL Arbitration Rules with only one claim in accordance with the ICSID Additional Facility.[129]

---

121 The tribunal in a case brought under the UK – Russia BIT used the MFN clause in that treaty to import a more favourable arbitration clause from the Denmark – Russia BIT. *RosInvestCo UK Ltd v. Russian Federation,* SCC Case No. Abr. V 079/2005, Award on Jurisdiction, 5 October 2007, paras. 73–74. In other cases, however, tribunals rejected the use of the most-favoured nation clause to expand the scope of limited arbitration clauses in this way. See for instance, *Berschader and Berschader v Russian Federation, SCC* Case No. 080/2004, Award, 21 April 2006, paras. 159–208; *Renta 4 SVSA and ors v Russian Federation,* SCC Case No. 24/2007, Award on Preliminary Objections, 20 March 2009, paras. 68–120.

122 “Russian Federation: Cases as Respondent State”, available at https://investmentpolicy.unctad.org/investment-dispute-settlement/country/175/russian-federation (visited August 15, 2019).

123 “Russian Federation: Cases as Home State of Claimant”, available at https://investmentpolicy.unctad.org/investment-dispute-settlement/country/175/russian-federation (visited August 15, 2019).

124 Sergei Paushok, *CJSC Golden East Company and CJSC Vostokneftegaz Company v. The Government of Mongolia* (2007).

125 *Oleg Deripaska v. Montenegro,* PCA Case No. 2017–07.

126 For example, *Ministry of Land and Property of the Republic of Tatarstan v. Ukraine (2016); Roscosmos State Corporation for Space Activities, RKTs Progress, KBOM and TsENKI v French Republic (Case No. 16/01314); Ms Olga Ovchinnikova v the Kingdom of Sweden (2016).*

127 International Centre for Settlement of Investment Disputes.

128 *Emergofin B.V. and Velbay Holdings Ltd. v. Ukraine (ICSID Case No. ARB/16/35)* where two subsidiaries of the Russian aluminium producer Rusal, Emergofin BV and Velbay Holdings, incorporated in the Netherlands and Cyprus respectively, filed a request for ICSID arbitration against Ukraine under Article 9 of the Netherlands-Ukraine BIT.

129 *Emergofin B.V. and Velbay Holdings Ltd. v. Ukraine* (ICSID Case No. ARB/16/35) where two subsidiaries of the Russian aluminium producer Rusal, Emergofin BV and Velbay

Importantly, Russia declines to enforce any awards which it deems against its public interest. It sought to challenge awards in local courts at the seat of arbitration (e.g., in Swedish courts in the case of *RosInvestCo v. Russian Federation*),[130] and has strongly resisted the seizure of its assets by foreign courts pursuant to arbitral awards against it (e.g., in German and Swedish courts in the case of *Sedelmayer v. Russian Federation*).[131] On 18 July 2014, the Tribunal in the three parallel *Yukos* arbitrations against Russia brought under the ECT rendered the largest-ever awards in the history of international arbitration totalling US$50.2 billion in damages.[132] The Russian Government challenged these awards in Dutch courts and on 20 April 2016, the District Court in the Hague set them aside, holding that the Tribunal could not have established jurisdiction based on the provisional application of the ECT. Arguably then, Russia's withdrawal from the ECT in 2009 via an effective termination of the provisional application could be construed as a smart strategic move since the PCA award in *Yukos* was revoked essentially because the ECT had not been ratified by the signatories, which meant that Russia was not bound by it. An appeal of this judgment is currently pending. Russia has also resisted the enforcement of the *Yukos* awards in many other jurisdictions.[133]

The attitude of the Russian Government towards investment treaty arbitration may confuse many practitioners. On the one hand, Russia has ignited several investment treaty claims, some of which involve highly political sensitivity, for instance, such as the *Yukos* saga.[134] Russian officials have condemned the

---

Holdings, incorporated in the Netherlands and Cyprus respectively, filed a request for ICSID arbitration against Ukraine under art. 9 of the Netherlands-Ukraine BIT.

130 *Russian Federation v. RosInvestCo Ltd.*, SVEA Court Ruling, 5 September 2013.

131 *Sedelmayer v Russian Federation*, Decision of the Supreme Court of Sweden, 1 July 2011; *Sedelmayer v Russian Federation*, Decision of the Supreme Court of Germany, 4 October 2005.

132 See *Yukos Universal Ltd v Russian Federation*, PCA Case No. AA 227, UNCITRAL ad hoc arbitration, Final Award, 18 July 2014; *Veteran Petroleum Ltd v Russian Federation*, PCA Case No. AA 228, UNCITRAL ad hoc arbitration, Final Award, 18 July 2014; *Hulley Enterprises Ltd v Russian Federation*, PCA Case No. AA 226, UNCITRAL ad hoc arbitration, Final Award, 18 July 2014.

133 Russia, Overview of Investment Treaty Programme, Global Arbitration Review (2018), available at https://globalarbitrationreview.com/jurisdiction/1005360/russia (visited May 1, 2019).

134 See *Yukos Universal Ltd v Russian Federation*, PCA Case No. AA 227, UNCITRAL ad hoc arbitration, Final Award, 18 July 2014; *Veteran Petroleum Ltd v Russian Federation*, PCA Case No. AA 228, UNCITRAL ad hoc arbitration, Final Award, 18 July 2014; *Hulley Enterprises Ltd v Russian Federation*, PCA Case No. AA 226, UNCITRAL ad hoc arbitration, Final Award, 18 July 2014.

enforcement of such awards against Russian state assets.[135] Most recently, the Russian Government has disparaged the *Yukos* awards as politically motivated.[136] Given all the current and past activity surrounding Russia's investment treaty and arbitration, it comes as no surprise that Russia has refused to ratify the BIT with Cyprus and the ECT in light of huge risk of potential claims under these treaties.[137] On the other hand, the Russian Government "has recognised the importance of investment treaty arbitration in protecting the rights of Russian investors abroad,"[138] and has continued to actively negotiate treaties with robust investment protection with those countries it views as target locations for Russian investment.[139] The Guidelines (2016) also prioritise the conclusion of BITs with countries where Russian investors have significant commercial interests.[140]

Arguably, Russia's reluctance to accept any modifications to its investment treaty reform stems from the scholarly-backed preference for private international law over public international law. Russia's tendency to favour commercial arbitration originates from a long-life characterisation of international investment law as a form of private international law rather than public international law, which explains Russia's reluctance to join the efforts toward a public international law-oriented reform.[141] The existing ISDS system

135 For example, Russian government reaction to Mr Sedelmayer attaching Russian government assets in Germany and Sweden: The Ministry of Foreign Affairs of the Russian Federation, Press Release, Russian MFA Spokesman Andrei Nesterenko Response to Media Query on Situation around Russian House Building in Berlin, 22 September 2009; The Ministry of Foreign Affairs of the Russian Federation, Press Release, Swedish Charge d'Affaires Summoned to the Foreign Ministry, 7 July 2011; The Ministry of Foreign Affairs of the Russian Federation, Press Release, On call of the Swedish Ambassador to the Russian Federation to the Russian Ministry of Foreign Affairs, 20 April 2012.

136 "The Ministry of Finance found 13 flaws in the court's decision on Yukos", Vedomosti, 28 July 2014, available at https://www.vedomosti.ru/politics/news/2014/07/28/minfin-rossii-nashel-izyany-v-reshenii-suda-po-isku-eks (visited May 3, 2019).

137 On 20 August 2009, Russia officially informed the Depository of the Energy Charter Treaty that it did not intend to become a contracting party to it. Available at www.encharter.org/index.php?id=414. See also "Russia has protected itself from investors", Kommersant, 12 January 2006.

138 Russia, Overview of Investment Treaty Programme, Global Arbitration Review (2018), available at https://globalarbitrationreview.com/jurisdiction/1005360/russia (visited May 1, 2019).

139 For example, Press Release by the Ministry of Economic Development, 26 January 2012 (in relation to the signing of a BIT with Nicaragua); Protective measures in foreign trade discussed in the Ministry of Economic Development, 28 July 2009.

140 See Guidelines (2016), Enclosure No. 1.

141 For more details, see Dmitry Labin, Alena Soloveva, International Investment Law as International Law: Russian and Western Approaches, 112 *AJIL Unbound* 202 (2018) 202–206.

is built predominantly on international commercial arbitration, which has traditionally rejected public-law elements of dispute settlement, such as higher transparency of arbitral proceedings. This can also explain why the Guidelines (2016) expressly excludes the application of the UNCITRAL Rules on Transparency but underscores the significance of a duty of confidentiality.

As discussed above, Russian BITs concluded in the 1990s generally provide for SCC arbitration and UNCITRAL ad hoc arbitration. In this regard, Russia urged[142] the UNCITRAL Secretariat to solicit, for the benefits of the ISDS reform discussion, comments on the dispute settlement procedures from the major arbitration centres in London, Stockholm, Singapore, and Hong Kong. As important commercial arbitration centres which administer numerous arbitrations and have acquired high prestige, they can benefit much the improvement of the ISDS mechanism.[143]

These references to commercial arbitration signal a private law paradigm. Historically, the rise of investment treaty arbitration attracted not only those active in the field but also practitioners "who did not have a background in public international law, but in international commercial arbitration"[144] largely because applicable procedural law was "either the same as that applicable to commercial arbitrations, as in the case of investment arbitrations under UNCITRAL Arbitration Rules, ⟨…⟩ the SCC Rules, or the Rules of the International Chamber of Commerce (ICC Rules), or modelled on commercial arbitration procedure, as in the case of ICSID arbitrations."[145]

Accordingly, international investment law is more characterized by the division of private commercial law and arbitration on the one hand, and between public international law and inter-state dispute settlement on the other.[146]

142 Recording: United Nations Commission on International Trade Law, 35th Sess. (Apr. 23–27 2018), available at http://www.uncitral.org/uncitral/en/commission/working_groups/3Investor_State.html (visited August 10, 2018). In particular, Russia's delegation said that "We believe we need a similar commentary from commercial arbitrations (including Hong Kong, London and Singapore) in order to ensure that the further discussion is all-around and objective."

143 For more details, please refer to the 2018 International Arbitration Survey: The Evolution of International Arbitration conducted by the School of International Arbitration, Queen Mary University of London (QMUL) in partnership with White & Case LLP, available at http://www.arbitration.qmul.ac.uk/media/arbitration/docs/2018-International-Arbitration-Survey-report.pdf (visited April 21, 2019).

144 Stephan W. Schill, W(h)ither Fragmentation? On the Literature and Sociology of International Investment Law, 22 *European Journal of International Law* 875 (2001) 887.

145 Id.

146 See Joseph Weiler, The Rule of Lawyers and the Ethos of Diplomats, 35 *Journal of World Trade* 191 (2001) 194–197.

Private commercial and public international lawyers are known to have different perspectives on the function of dispute resolution mechanism. Whereas public international lawyers "embed international investment law firmly in general international law, commercial arbitration lawyers see investment treaty arbitration as a subset of international (commercial) arbitration."[147] Certainly, the classification of certain provisions into public international law and commercial arbitration approaches is "no more than a blueprint or archetype."[148] in the chosen reasoning and preferred methods of interpretations,[149] and in their respective understanding of the role of arbitrators and dispute settlement.[150]

Of particular note on this subject is that Russian courts have never had to deal with an investment treaty arbitration seated in Russia. Continuing in this vein, on 27 June, 2017 the Arbitrazh Court of Moscow refused Tatneft's bid to enforce an investment arbitration award against the Ukrainian Government property in Russia (the Ukrainian Embassy and Cultural Centre buildings), "primarily on the grounds of sovereign immunity."[151] The Court held that under the Russia-Ukraine BIT, Ukraine had not waived its immunity in relation to the enforcement of an award under the relevant BIT. That was the first time that a Russian court had been called upon to enforce an investment treaty award. On a related note, Russian courts have never been asked to enforce an award against the Russian Federation.

6 Concluding Remarks

The small number of publications addressing Russia's investment treaty and arbitration programme is conspicuous in light of the noticeable contribution

147 Barton Legum, Investment Treaty Arbitration's Contribution to International Commercial Arbitration, 60 *Dispute Resolution Journal* 70 (2005) 73; Andrea K. Bjorklund, Private Rights and Public International Law: Why Competition Among International Economic Law Tribunals Is Not Working, 59 *Hastings Law Journal* 241 (2007) 251.

148 Stephan W. Schill, *supra* note 144, at 889.

149 For example, Thomas W. Wälde, Interpreting Investment Treaties: Experiences and Examples, in C. Binder et al. (eds.), *International Investment Law for the 21st Century – Essays in Honour of Christoph Schreuer* (Oxford: Oxford University Press, 2009) 724.

150 Stephan W. Schill, Crafting the International Economic Order: The Public Function of Investment Treaty Arbitration and Its Significance for the Role of the Arbitrator, 23 *Leiden Journal of International Law* 401 (2010) 401.

151 Russia, Overview of Investment Treaty Programme, Global Arbitration Review (2018), available at https://globalarbitrationreview.com/jurisdiction/1005360/russia (visited May 1, 2019).

of the Russian doctrine and practice to the development of international investment law.

It can be seen from the historical explorations in this chapter that international investment treaty practice developed as a mechanism with a major aim of protecting the interests of capital-importing states. History provides evidence that economic downturns in Russia have often corresponded with periods of greater cooperation. Economic stagnation in the late 1980s was associated with the end of the Cold War, and the contraction of the early 1990s correlated with a more accommodating foreign investment policy. This chapter has argued that Russian BITs generally do not cover pre-establishment issues,[152] and that they have embraced the so-called "controlled entry" approach.[153] An apt example is the USSR-Germany BIT (1989), which provides that each Contracting Party shall permit investments "in accordance with its legislation," which means that the admission of foreign investment is subject to domestic laws of the host State. There are hardly any Russian BITs which go beyond this.[154] The only BIT which contains some tangible pre-establishment commitments is the Russia-US BIT, which was discussed above.

The Russian (Model) BITs have always contained a standard formulation of the protection against unlawful expropriation. Also, the interpretation and application of the expropriation provisions in Russian BITs by arbitral tribunals have not unearthed any specific characteristics in comparison to the interpretation of such clauses in other BITs.[155]

Arguably, Russian Model BIT (2001) scaled back the level of substantive investment protection. The limitations placed on the MFN, national treatment and FET can hardly be reconciled with the aspiration of the developed states, for instance EU Member States, which base their BITs on the "best practices".[156]

---

152 David Collins, *The BRIC States and Outward Foreign Direct Investment* (Oxford: Oxford University Press, 2013) 62.

153 See Ignacio Gómez-Palacio and Peter Muchlinski, Admission and Establishment, in Peter Muchlinski, Frederico Ortino and Christoph Schreuer (eds.), *The Oxford Handbook of International Investment Law* (Oxford: Oxford University Press, 2008) 240–242.

154 Tilman Dralle, *supra* note 29, at 33.

155 Tilman Dralle, *supra* note 29, at 37–38.

156 European Parliament resolution of 6 April 2011 on the future European international investment policy, Official Journal of the European Union (2012/ C 296 E/05) para. 19, P. 37; Council Negotiating Directives for Canada, India and Singapore, 3109th Council meeting Press Release (Brussels, 12 September 2011) P. 13; Council of the European Union, Conclusions on a comprehensive European international investment policy, 3041st Foreign Affairs Council meeting (Luxembourg, 25 October 2010) para 15. P. 3; European Commission, Towards a comprehensive European international investment policy (Brussels, 7 July 2010) P. 8.

Russian Model BIT (2001) highlights an underlying difference in the appreciation by Russia of the international investment regime. In light of this distance, and the deep-rooted divergences between the Russian and Western approaches to treaty practice, it is not surprising that Russian BIT drafters are generally reluctant to accord significant weight to both "relative treatment" and "absolute treatment" provisions in investment treaties. Because of this, the use of such standards is often considered as "a political choice that enables the responsible parties to adopt the language of deliberate indeterminacy in order to secure the agreement."[157]

However, the Guidelines (2016) represents certain seeds of change, which may signify more willingness on the part of Russia to negotiate international agreements from the perspective of a capital-exporting state rather than a capital-importing state. The existence of such variable treaty norms corresponds with Russia's political and economic transformations, from being an inexperienced newcomer to a powerful heavyweight in international investment relations. Therefore, the Guidelines (2016) does not envisage that future BITs should contain a FET clause or a full protection and security guarantee. The Guidelines (2016) provides for the possibility of both institutional and ad hoc arbitration, but they do not specify which international arbitration rules are to be included in new investment treaties. Such an approach can certainly be framed as another illustration of how Russia reproduces itself as an innovative and forward-looking bilateral investor leaving the treaty essentials to be discussed individually with each BIT partner.

---

157 N. Jansen Calamita, International human rights and the interpretation of international investment treaties: constitutional considerations in Freya Baetens (ed.), *Investment Law within International Law: Integrationist Perspectives* (Cambridge: Cambridge University Press, 2013) 169.

CHAPTER 4

India's Investment Treaties: How an Emerging Economic Giant Makes International Commitments

Xiaoxia Lin

1 Introduction

The Indian economy is growing strongly and remains a bright spot in the global landscape. It is one of the fastest growing economies in the world. According to the latest forecasts released by the International Monetary Fund (IMF), India's growth forecast will be 7.5 per cent for 2019.[1] As the survey by the United Nations Conference on Trade and Development (UNCTAD) suggests, India remains amongst the most favourite foreign direct investment (FDI) destinations, just after the US and China.[2] Arguably, India's economic success is largely attributed to India's efforts to improve its regulatory framework to attract FDIs, including its acceleration of structural reform and its extensive investment treaty network.[3]

Due to the adverse *White Industries–India* award issued in November 2011,[4] India decided to reorient its investment treaty practice in spite of the exponential increase in FDIs and the huge number of already existing BITs. Actually, India had frozen its on-going BIT negotiations shortly after *White Industries–India* award and began a thorough review of the 2003 India Model BIT.[5]

---

1 International Monetary Fund, For India, Strong Growth Persists Despite New Challenges (February 22, 2017), available at https://www.imf.org/en/News/Articles/2017/02/21/NA022217-For-India-strong-growth-persists-despite-new-challenges (visited June 18, 2019).

2 *See* UNCTAD, World Investment Report 2017, 7 June 2017, at 8.

3 *See e.g.*, Nagesh Kumar, Liberalisation and Changing Patterns of Foreign Direct Investments. Has India's Relative Attractiveness as a Host of FDI Improved? 33 (22) *Economic and Political Weekly* 1321 (1998); Sreenivasa Rao, Bilateral Investment Protection Agreements: A Legal Framework for the Protection of Foreign Investments, 26(1) *Commonwealth Law Bulletin* 623 (2000).

4 *White Industries Australia Limited v. Republic of India*, UNCITRAL, Final Award (30 November 2011).

5 Sujay Mehdudia, BIPA Talks Put on Hold (January 22, 2013), available at https://www.thehindu.com/business/Economy/bipa-talks-put-on-hold/article4329332.ece (visited May 22, 2019).

 | DOI:10.1163/9789004376991_005

In March 2015, the Indian government released a new draft model BIT[6] and on 28 December 2015 it unveiled its considerably revised final version (the Model BIT (2015)).[7] According to the Indian government, the new Model BIT "will provide appropriate protection to foreign investors in India and Indian investors in the foreign country,.... while maintaining a balance between the investor's rights and the Government obligations".[8]

Against this background, this chapter is structured around different periods of India's investment policy and strategy with a focus on recent treaty developments. The Introduction is followed by Section 2, which provides a brief overview of the history of India's investment policy and strategy. The chapter tracks the observations of Ranjan, who observed that India's investment strategies underwent the phases of "rejection", "embracement" and "hesitance".[9] Section 3 focuses on the most recent treaty model and examines its particular features as well as its implication for India's future trajectory on investment treaties with other countries. A close examination reveals that they extensively strengthen India's regulatory authority on foreign investments. Section 4 proceeds to examine how Indian Model BIT (2015) will affect the treaty negotiation and FDI flows between India and China. This chapter concludes with the suggestion that India's new investment treaty practice should aim to achieve the balance between investment protection and the host state's right to regulate.

2 Evolution of Investment Treaties of India

Over the past several decades, Indian policy toward foreign investment has undergone fluctuation from one phase to another.[10] Three distinct phases in the evolution of India's investment regulation framework can be identified. The first phase started from 1947 following the independence of India, with

6 Ministry of Finance (India), Draft Indian Model Bilateral Investment Treaty Text, available at https://www.mygov.in/group-issue/draft-indian-model-bilateral-investment-treaty-text/ (visited May 14, 2019).

7 "Bilateral Investment Treaty between the Government of the Republic of India and –", available at https://investmentpolicy.unctad.org/international-investment-agreements/countries/96/india (visited June 5, 2019).

8 Press Information Bureau, Government of India, Model Text for the Indian Bilateral Investment Treaty (16 December 2015), available at http://pib.nic.in/newsite/PrintRelease.aspx?relid=133411 (visited May 23, 2019).

9 Prabhash Ranjan, India and Bilateral Investment Treaties: From Rejection to Embracement to Hesitance?, in Srinivas Burra and R. Rajesh Babu eds., *Locating India in the Contemporary International Legal Order* (India: Springer, 2018) 101–126.

10 Aniruddha Rajput, *Protection of Foreign Investment in India and Investment Treaty Arbitration* (London: Kluwer Law International, 2017) 10.

four decades of a cautious attitude toward FDI.[11] The second phase started with India's opening of its economy in the early 1990s, along with the progressive economic policies of liberalization, the proliferation of international investment treaties, and the dramatic FDI upsurge. This phase ended with the unfavourable award of the first investment arbitration case against India, *White Industries v. India*. This case brought a significant change in India's approach toward international treaty practice as well as foreign investment protection. The adoption of Indian Model BIT (2015) is emblematic of India's new approach to investment treaties.

2.1 *1947–1991*

India's policy toward foreign investment has evolved since the country gained its independence in 1947. In the immediate aftermath of India's independence, it embarked on a strategy of import substitution and placed the priority on the development of indigenous industries.[12] This inward policy rejected the internationalization of industrialization.[13] The political ideology underlying the aforementioned policy was to achieve the self-sufficiency by way of nonalignment.[14]

However, acknowledging that foreign investment would be important for industrialization of the country,[15] the Indian government gradually adopted relevant laws for this purpose. The 1948 Industrial Policy Resolution conceded that "participation of foreign capital and enterprise ... will be of value to the rapid industrialisation of the country", but emphasized that in the meantime the major interest in ownership and control should be in Indian hands.[16] On April 6, 1949, the then-Prime Minister Jawaharlal Nehru articulated this foreign investment policy in his statement to the Constituent Assembly, taking a step further in liberalization of foreign investment. In this statement, foreign capital was recognized as an important supplement to domestic savings for

---

11 Nagesh Kumar, *supra* note 3, at 1321.

12 For a detailed discussion on India's domestic policy toward foreign investment during this period of time, *see* Michael Kidron, *Foreign Investment in India* (London: Oxford University Press, 1965) 45–112.

13 Devashish Krishan, India and International Investment Law, in Bimal N. Patel (ed.), *India and International law* (Leiden: Brill, 2008, Volume 2) 291.

14 Jawaharlal Nehrus Speeches Vol. 3 (March 1951–August 1957), available at: https://archive.org/stream/in.ernet.dli.2015.98837/2015.98837.Jawaharlal-Nehrus-Speeches-Vol-3march-1953-august-1957_djvu.txt (visited May 17, 2019).

15 In the first two years after 1947, the direct investment of multinational companies turned to be the dominant form of private foreign investment. *See* Tomlinson, B.R., Foreign Private Investment in India 1920–1950, 12(4) *Modern Asian Studies* 655 (1978) 660.

16 Industrial Policy Resolution New Delhi, 6 April, 1948, available at http://www.dcmsme.gov.in/policies/iip.htm#Indus1 (visited April 20, 2019).

facilitating national economic and technological progress.[17] In particular, the statement announced several important principles, including: existing foreign interests would be accorded "national treatment"; new foreign capital would be encouraged on a mutually advantageous basis; fair compensation would be paid "if and when foreign enterprises are compulsorily acquired"; government would not object to foreign capital having control of a concern for a limited period with certain conditions, and others.[18]

India's attitude toward FDI became more friendly after 1956 when India started its second five-year plan. Due to India's fragile Balance of Payment (BOP) position, India carried out comprehensive FDI scrutiny until the middle of the 1950s, thereby causing scarce foreign exchange resources.[19] India was hence encouraged to liberalize its investment regime for attracting foreign investments to bring in more foreign exchange.[20] In 1960, India established the India Investment Center with some branches in major capital-exporting countries including the UK, Singapore, the US, and Germany, disseminating information and guidance on the investment policies and investment opportunities in India.[21]

Unlike its newly founded neighbouring country, the People's of Republic of China (hereinafter "China") which adhered to the self-sufficiency development strategy during this period, India was active in building economic relationship with other countries, mainly from the Western world. For instance, India concluded trade agreements with Austria, Finland, Switzerland and West Germany in 1949, with Sweden in 1950, with Norway in 1951, and the Soviet Union in 1953.[22] Negotiations regarding investment agreements came thereafter. While India failed to negotiate with the US a comprehensive treaty of friendship, commerce, and navigation, the two countries successfully reached some practical arrangements to expand commercial exchanges and facilitate industrial collaboration.[23] In 1957 India entered into an investment protection agreement

17 Amitendu Palit, India's Foreign Investment Policy: Achievements and Inadequacies. Asie Visions, Institut Français des Relations Internationales (IFRI), Vol. 18, July 2009, available at https://ssrn.com/abstract=2019897 (visited June 3, 2019).

18 Michael Kidron, *Foreign Investment in India* (London: Oxford University Press, 1965) 100–101.

19 Amitendu Palit, *supra* note 17.

20 *Id.*

21 Aniruddha Rajput, Protection of Foreign Investment in India and International Rule of Law: Rise or Decline?, KFG Working Paper Series, 2017, No. 10, available at https://ssrn.com/abstract=3135261 (visited July 8, 2019).

22 K.B. Lall, India and The New International Economic Order, 17 *International Studies* 435 (1978) 436.

23 *Id.*

with the United States,[24] which was amended in 1959[25] and again in 1966.[26] American investments in India were accorded with substantial protection under these arrangements. In addition to the compensation against expropriation, war or insurrection, the Indian government also provided protection towards losses arising from risks of a non-commercial nature, including non-convertibility of currency, profits and capital repatriation.[27]

At the international level, however, India rejected the doctrine of state responsibility for injuries to aliens associated with foreign investment. India argued at the United Nations International Law Commission (ILC) that doctrine of state responsibility was "a completely different ideology of social justice, involving completely different social and economic systems which endanger, among other things, the existing conception of private property".[28] Likewise, an Indian scholar suggested that, "the law of responsibility then, is not founded on any universal principles of law or morality. Its sole foundation is custom, which is binding only among states where it either grew up or came to be adopted."[29] Concurrently, India did not accept the Convention on the Settlement of Investment Disputes between States and Nationals of Other States (ICSID Convention).[30] According to India, if it would become a Party to the ICSID Convention, it would subject itself to the ICSID jurisdiction and enforce the unfavourable ICSID awards against India; otherwise, it would be deprived of credit support by the World Bank.[31]

24 Exchange of Notes Constituting an Agreement Between the United States of America and India Relating to the Guarantee of Private Investments, Washington, 19 September 1957, India Bilateral Treaties and Agreements, Volume 2: 1951–1957, 634–636.

25 Agreement Supplementing the Agreement of September 19, 1957, Washington, 7 December 1959, United States Treaties and Other International Agreements, Volume 10: 1997–2000.

26 Exchange of Notes Between the Government of India and the Government of the United States of America Regarding the Agreement Supplementing the Agreement of 19 September 1957 on Investment Guarantees, New Delhi, 2 February 1966, India Bilateral Treaties and Agreements, Volume 5: 1964–1966, 328–334.

27 Sreenivasa Rao, *supra* note 3, at 624.

28 Devashish Krishan, *supra* note 13, at 293. (Citing the 9th Session of International Law Commission Yearbook, 157–158).

29 S.N. Guha Roy, Is the Law of Responsibility of States for Injuries to Aliens a Part of Universal International Law, 55 *American Journal of International Law* 863 (1961) 888.

30 Convention on the Settlement of Investment Disputes Between States and Nationals of Other States (Signed at Washington 18 March 1965, entered into force 14 October 1966) 575 U.N.T.S. 159.

31 S.R. Subramanian, BITs and Pieces in International Investment Law: Enforcement of Investment Treaty Arbitration Awards in the Non-ICSID States: The case of India, 14 *Journal of World Investment & Trade* 198 (2013) 199–200.

However, special efforts were made by India to work with other developing and socialist countries in crafting an international legal order that would not merely in favour of the Western economies, but benefit all nations based upon the principle of equality of sovereignty. A major step was to support the movement of New International Economic Order (NIEO) vigorously.[32] India was a major leading state in the NIEO movement.[33] In 1974, the General Assembly adopted the Declaration on the Establishment of a New International Economic Order[34] and the accompanying Programme of Action,[35] followed in the same year by the adoption of the Charter of Economic Rights and Duties of States.[36] These resolutions affirmed the sovereign right of developing countries over their natural resources and all economic activities as well as the right to nationalization.[37]

India's leading role in the NIEO movement reversed its relatively open foreign investment regime along with a number of yet quite restrictive legislations towards foreign investment.[38] The Monopolies and Restrictive Trade Practices Act 1969 (MRTP), for instance, was introduced to control monopolies by defining monopoly merely in terms of size.[39] Also, general insurance companies and the 14 largest banks were nationalized in 1971 and 1972 respectively.

---

32 For discussion and developments on establishment of a new international economic order, *see* Question Concerning Establishment of a New International Economic Order, 28 Yearbook of the United Nations 1974, Section 1, Chapter 1, 305–357. *See also* A. Caesar Espiritu, The New International Economic Order and the Emerging International Obligations in International Investments, 11 *Philippine Yearbook of International Law* 29 (1985).

33 Prabhash Ranjan, India's International Investment Agreements and India's Regulatory Power as a Host Nation (DPhil thesis, King's College London 2012) 39. *See also* K.B. Lall, *supra* note at 22, at 449–450.

34 Resolution 3201 (S-VI), 1 May 1974.

35 Resolution 3202 (S-VI), 1 May 1974.

36 Resolution 3281 (XXIX), 12 December 1974.

37 Kenneth J. Vandevelde, A Brief History of International Investment Agreements, 12(1) *U.C. Davis Journal of International Law & Policy* 157 (2005) 167–168. Prabhash Ranjan, India and Bilateral Investment Treaties-A Changing Landscape, 29 *ICSID Review* 419 (2014) 424–425.

38 *See e.g.*, K.S. Chalapati Rao and Biswajit Dhar, India's FDI Inflows – Trends and Concept (The Research and Information System for Developing Countries (RIS) and Institute for Studies in Industrial Development, 2011), available at https://ris.org.in/sites/default/files/FDI_Book-Final.pdf (visited April 23, 2019). *See also* Vishal Shah and Alka Parikh, Trends, Changing Composition and Impact of Foreign Direct investment in India, *International Journal of Economic Research* 134 (2012) 135. For the details of the government strategy during the period from 1965 to early 1980s, *see* Arvind Panagariya, *India: The Emerging Giant* (Oxford: Oxford University Press, 2008) 47–81.

39 *See* Nitya Nanda, The Indian Growth Story: Myths and Realities, 44 (6) *Journal of Asian and African Studies* 750 (2009).

Furthermore, the Industrial Policy Resolution (IPR) in 1973 limited foreign investments in export-oriented industries that were deemed with strategical importance for long-term growth prospect of the country.[40] Foreign Exchange Regulation Act (FERA) of 1973 imposed most significant restriction on the use of foreign exchange.[41] The Industry Policy Statement (1977) further provided that only if the process of dilution in line with the FERA was completed, would companies with direct non-resident investment not exceeding 40 percent be accorded national treatment.[42] This period was therefore considered "the dearest in the post-independence economic history of India", although some of the restrictions posed a long-term negative impact on the growth.[43]

The 1980s kicked off a transition phase with prudential liberalization of the investment regime. In order to revitalize its stagnant economy, India decided to start economic reforms. Some foreign investment-friendly measures were taken. For instance, greenfield investments were gradually de-licensed, export production was exempted from investment licensing, and export obligation of companies was reduced. Companies were thus free to produce based on market demands.[44] In addition, a "fast channel" was set up in 1988 to speed up the approval of FDI proposals from major investing countries.[45]

2.2 *Early 1990s to 2011*

2.2.1 India's Economic Reforms

The liberal yet lukewarm economic reforms in the 1980s were transformed into drastic and systematic liberalization reforms beginning in 1991. The transition started with a new industrial policy announced on July 24, 1991.[46] In a single stroke, the industrial policy did away with the prior restrictions on foreign investment. The requirement for prior approval in cases of less than 51% foreign equity in 34 industries had been replaced with automatic approval.[47]

---

40 Amitendu Palit, *supra* note 17, at 7.

41 Sudip Chaudhary, FERA: Appearance and Reality, 14(16) *Economic and Political Weekly* 734 (1979).

42 Ministry of Micro, Small & Medium Enterprises, Government of India, Industrial Policy Statement, Foreign Investment (23rd December, 1977), available at http://www.dcmsme.gov.in/policies/iip.htm#Indus3 (visited June 4, 2019).

43 Arvind Panagariya, *supra* note 38, Introduction.

44 *See generally* Arvind Virmani, Policy Regimes, Growth and Poverty in India: Lessons on Government Failure and Entrepreneurial Success, at 29–31, available at http://icrier.org/pdf/WP170GrPov11.pdf (visited June 16, 2019).

45 Nagesh Kumar, *supra* note 3, at 1323.

46 Ministry of Industry, Government of India, Statement of Industrial Policy, July 24, 1991, available at http://www.dcmsme.gov.in/policies/iip.htm#Indus3 (visited May 24, 2019).

47 *Id.*

Investment licensing and myriad entry restrictions on the monopoly and restrictive trade firms were also abandoned.[48]

The economic reforms unleashed in 1991 brought about a series of subsequent calibrated macroeconomic policies and actions. The Foreign Investment Promotion Board (FIPB) was established to deal with foreign investment affairs, including granting approval to investment in which foreign investors hold more than 51% equity on a case-by-case basis.[49] Until 1997 nine industries were further allowed to increase the equity investment up to 74% under an automatic approval route.[50] In the meantime, the Indian government, for the time first ever, announced guidelines as to how to give special consideration of FDI projects in areas where automatic approval procedure did not apply (the so-called "priority areas").[51] Eligible FDI within these priority areas was also granted with expeditious approval.[52]

At the international level, India stepped up its efforts to participate in the international investment legal regime. In January 1994, India became a member of the Multilateral Investment Guarantee Agreement (MIGA). On 20 December 1992, India signed with the European Union (EU) the third generation Cooperation Agreement on Partnership and Development. Article 11 of the Cooperation Agreement stated that Contracting Parties should "encourage an increase in mutually beneficial investment by establishing a favourable climate for private investment including better conditions for the transfer of capital and exchange of information on investment opportunities."[53] More

48 For the full articulation of these two policies see Arvind Panagariya, Growth and Reforms During 1980s and 1990s, 39 (25) *Economic and Political Weekly* 2581 (2004) 2590.

49 Kumar, *supra* note 3, at 1323. The Indian government abolished the FIPB in 2017. *See* Sumit Chakraborty, What is FIPB? The 25-year-old Foreign Investment Promotion Board that the government has decided to abolish, 24 May 2017, *Financial Express*, available at https://www.financialexpress.com/economy/what-is-fipb-the-25-year-old-foreign-investment-promotion-board-that-the-government-has-decided-to-abolish/683826/ (visited May 20, 2019).

50 Part C, Press Note No. 2 (1997 Series), DIPP, Government of India, available at http://dipp.nic.in/sites/default/files/chap008_1.pdf (visited May 24, 2019).

51 Guidelines for the Consideration of Foreign Direct Investment Proposals by the Foreign Investment Promotion Board, Press Note No. 3 (1997 Series), DIPP, Government of India, available at http://dipp.nic.in/sites/default/files/chap008_1.pdf (visited May 25, 2019). Other listed items for the FDI proposals include infrastructure, export potential, large scale employment potential and especially for rural people, items linked with farm sector, items with greater social relevance, and proposals that result in induction of technology or infusion of capital.

52 Nirupam Bajpai and Jeffery D. Sachs, Foreign Direct Investment in India: Issues and Problems, Development Discussion Paper No. 759, March 2000, available at https://academiccommons.columbia.edu/doi/10.7916/D8F195J2 (visited July 20, 2019).

53 Text of the Agreement, available at http://trade.ec.europa.eu/doclib/docs/2007/june/tradoc_135123.pdf (visited April 18, 2019).

importantly, India embarked upon a trajectory of negotiating BITs with many countries.

2.2.2 India's Investment Treaty Framework

India signed its first BIT with the United Kingdom (UK) in 1994.[54] The India–UK BIT (1994) explicitly encouraged and incentivized investment.[55] The BIT was premised on the 1974 UK Model BIT, which aimed to facilitate and encourage British FDI into other countries, providing high standards of investor protection.[56] Importantly, the India–UK BIT (1994) served as the template for India's negotiations of BITs with other countries until India developed its own Model BIT in 2003. Indian Model BIT (2003) resembled with India–UK BIT (1994) to some degree, both in structure and content.[57] India first negotiated investment treaties with developed countries, and later with developing countries. By the time India released its Model BIT (2003), India had already entered into 56 BITs.[58] Therefore, the Model BIT (2003) was more of a "retrospective" statement based on its treaty-making practice.[59] As of December 2013 India had signed more than 80 BITs, making it one of the largest BIT signatories over the world.[60] In the single year of 1997, India concluded ten BITs.[61]

Generally speaking, Indian BITs around this period placed priority on offering substantial protection to foreign investments. This can be discerned by the

54 Full text of India–UK BIT, available at: http://investmentpolicyhub.unctad.org/Download/TreatyFile/1613 (visited May 15, 2019).

55 It is addressed in the preamble of the India–UK BIT that the BIT was "desir(ing) to create conditions favorable for fostering greater investment by investor of one State in the territory of the other State".

56 For the discussion of British BIT practice during this period, *see* Andrew Walter, British Investment Treaties in South Asia: Current Statement and Future Trends (Report Prepared for the International Development Center of Japan), January 2000, available at http://personal.lse.ac.uk/wyattwal/images/British.pdf (visited June 11, 2019).

57 Full Text of 2003 India Model BIT, available at https://www.italaw.com/sites/default/files/archive/ita1026.pdf (visited March 5, 2019).

58 "Investment Policy Hub: India", available at https://investmentpolicy.unctad.org/international-investment-agreements/countries/96/india?type=tips (visited March 11, 2019).

59 Aniruddha Rajput, India's Treaty Practice: A Comparative Analysis of the 2003 and 2015 Model BITs, 7 *Jindal Global Law Revive* 201 (2016) 204.

60 Department of Economic Affairs, Ministry of Finance, Government of India, List of Countries with Whom Bilateral Investment Promotion And Protection Agreements (BIPA) Has been Signed (As on December, 2013), available at https://www.finmin.nic.in/list-countries-whom-bilateral-investment-promotion-and-protection-agreements-bipa-has-been-signed (visited April 10, 2019).

61 "Investment Policy Hub: India", available at https://investmentpolicy.unctad.org/international-investment-agreements/countries/96/india?type=tips (visited March 11, 2019).

preamble of BITs.[62] All BITs concluded by India during this period highlight the objectives of promotion and protection of investment in the preamble. Article 3(1) of Indian Model BIT (2003) reads that, "*each Contracting Party shall encourage and create favourable conditions for investors of the other Contracting Party to make investments in its territory, and admit such investments in accordance with its laws and policy*".

India's BITs include many liberal substantive rules. Most of the BITs include a broad asset-based definition of investment.[63] Likewise, substantive investment treatment and protection, such as twin standards of treatments (national treatment and most-favoured-nation treatment),[64] fair and equitable treatment standard (FET),[65] prohibition of expropriation without compensation,[66] and free transfer of capital, were included. India, however, was reluctant to make liberal commitment in terms of investor-state dispute settlement as demonstrated by the fact that India did not sign the ICSID Convention. As a result, foreign investors cannot challenge India before the ISCID, where most investor-state investment disputes are heard. Nevertheless, foreign investors

62 *See* Prabhash Ranjan, The "object and purpose" of Indian International Investment Agreement: Failing to Balance Investment Protection and Regulatory Power, in Vivienne Bath and Luke Nottage (eds.), *Foreign Investment and Dispute Resolution Law and Practice in Asia* (London: Routledge, 2011) 192–209.

63 For instance, India-UK BIT Article 1(b) provides that investment includes, though not exclusively, movable and immoveable property, rights in mortgage or similar rights, shares, intellectual property rights, goodwill, technical process, know how, business concession, and rightful claims to money or to any performances under contract with value. The 2003 India Model BIT follows almost the same categories of India-UK BIT, with some exceptions in the intellectual property right. However, some BITs signed after the India 2003 Model BIT (for instance, India-Sweden BIT, India-Saudi Arabia BIT) came back to the board categories in terms of intellectual property right.

64 These two standards of treatments are usually combined in one provision with simply and broadly defined language, which is a distinguishing feature of many Indian BITs. *See* Prabhash Ranjan, International Investment Agreements and Regulatory Discretion: Case Study of India, 9 *Journal of World Investment & Trade* 209 (2008) 232.

65 A majority number of Indian BITs do not define the normative content of the FET standard.

66 Expropriation is broadly defined in India's BITs, including nationalization, expropriation and measures having effect equivalent to nationalization and expropriation. All of India's BITs provide that the expropriation shall be subject to compensation. The differences lie in the standard of compensation assessed. The 2003 India Model BIT and numerous later BITs provide that the host state shall undertake fair and equitable compensation amounting to genuine value of the investment expropriated. Terms of "fair market value" (See BITs with Austria; Denmark; Spain) or as vague as "value of investment" (See BITs with Germany; Czech Republic) are also seen. Few BITs offer an even higher compensation standard, equivalent to the Hull formula which advocates "prompt, adequate and effective compensation" (See BITs with Republic of Korea; Italy).

under India's BITs are allowed to bring claims against India before an international tribunal established in accordance with the ICSID Additional Facility rules or the United Nations Commission on International Trade Law (UNCITRAL) Arbitration Rules.[67]

From 2004 onwards, India, in addition to BITs, began to negotiate bilateral and regional free trade agreements (FTAs)[68] that contain separate investment chapters. As of August 2019, India has signed bilateral FTAs with Singapore, Korea, Malaysia and Japan.[69] Since 2008, India has been negotiating an FTA with the EU, including an investment chapter, though the final deal is yet to be reached.[70]

Unlike its BITs practice which is heavily based either on the India–UK BIT (1994) or on the Indian Model BIT (2003), India's FTAs have not followed a one-size-fits-all template. For instance, these FTAs contain different provisions of national treatment, MFN treatment, and the investor-state investment dispute settlement. More significantly, as observed by Ranjan, India's FTAs strike a better balance between the protection of foreign investment and that of regulatory authority than its BITs have done.[71] Such a balance can be found in the provisions of the definition of investment, monetary transfer, and non-precluded measures.[72] Thus, it has been argued that India's FTA were more carefully drafted than the BITs[73] because the latter left less space for India to exercise regulatory freedom.[74]

India has also negotiated regional comprehensive economic partnerships with investment chapter. For instance, India entered into a framework agreement on economic cooperation with the Association of South-East Asian Nations (ASEAN) in 2014.[75]

---

67 See for example India-Thailand BIT (2000), art. 9.

68 These agreements are known as FTA (Free Trade Agreement), EPA (Economic Partnership), CEPA (Comprehensive Economic Partnership Agreement), or CECA (Comprehensive Economic Cooperation Agreement).

69 For a full list of India's FTAs, available at https://investmentpolicy.unctad.org/international-investment-agreements/countries/96/india (visited March 11, 2019).

70 "India-EU free trade pact not possible without lowering tariffs for cars", *The Hindu Business Line*, March 1, 2019, available at https://www.thehindubusinessline.com/economy/india-eu-free-trade-pact-not-possible-without-lowering-tariffs-for-cars/article26409471.ece (visited April 18, 2019).

71 Prabhash Ranjan, Comparing Investment Provisions in India's FTAs with India's Stand-Alone BITs: Contributing to the Evolution of New Indian BIT Practice, 16 *Journal of World Investment & Trade* 899 (2015) 928.

72 For a detailed discussion, see Ranjan, *supra* note 71, at 899–930.

73 Rajput, *supra* note 10, at 18.

74 Ranjan, *supra* note 71, at 901.

75 Available at https://www.asean.org/wp-content/uploads/2016/04/ASEAN-India-Investment-Agreement-ASEAN-version.pdf (visited May 3, 2019).

It seems that India's BITs practice in the 1990s and in the 2010s was conducted on the premise that the investment treaties could effectively enhance FDI inflow.[76] However, a key question is whether BITs could really work as expected. Some observers suggest that there is a correlation between Indian BITs and FDI inflows, namely that India's BITs contribute to the growth of FDI inflows to India.[77] However, a comparison of the shares of FDI from countries who have concluded BITs with India with those who have not may disappoint observers. The comparison shows that during 2000–2006 the share of FDI inflows from Contracting Parties of India's BITs relative to the total investment flow to India.[78] A more supportable argument presumably is that investment treaties may make a difference in promoting investment flow to India, but they by themselves could not do so. Indeed, such a finding has been suggested by many empirical surveys.[79] In other words, an affirmative conclusion as to the effect of BITs on FDI flow could not be arbitrarily drawn merely by the fact that investment flows to India increase, say, from $4,029 million in 2000–2001 to $60,220 million in 2016–2017.[80]

---

76 The Ministry of Finance states that "[A]s part of the Economic Reforms Programme initiated in 1991, the foreign investment policy of the Government of India was liberalized and negotiations undertaken with a number of countries to enter into Bilateral Investment Promotion and Protection Agreement (BIPAs) in order to promote and protect on reciprocal basis investment of the investors". Pranhash Ranjan et al., India's Model Bilateral Investment Treaty: Is India Too Risk Averse?, Brookings India Impact Series, 2018, available at https://www.brookings.edu/wp-content/uploads/2018/08/India's-Model-Bilateral-Investment-Treaty-2018.pdf (visited March 22, 2019). (Citing the "Forewords" written by various Indian Finance Ministers on the BIT programme available in Ministry of Finance, Government of India Compendiums on BIPAs (Finance Ministry 1996–2011)).

77 Niti Bhasin and Rinku Manocha, Do Bilateral Investment Treaties Promote FDI Inflows? Evidences from India, 41 (4) *Vikalpa* 275(2016) 275 (By using an augmented gravity model and estimating both under static and dynamic conditions, this article argues that BITs are playing their desired role). *See also*, Luke Nottage and Jaivir Singh, Does ISDS Promote FDI? Asia-Pacific Insights from and for Australia and India (AFIA), available at http://afia.asia/2016/11/does-isds-promote-fdi-asia-pacific-insights-from-and-for-australia-and-india/ (visited April 4, 2019). ("[A]lthough the signing of individual BITs had an insignificant impact on FDI inflows into India, the *cumulative* effect of signing BITs is significant and so is the coefficient associated with the signing of FTAs. Since almost all of India's investment treaties provide for full ISDS protections, these preliminary results suggest that ISDS can have a positive influence on foreign investment, albeit in a non-obvious compound manner.")

78 *See generally* Jitender Singh, Do Bilateral Investment Promotion & Protection Agreements (BIPAs) Attract Foreign Direct Investment (FDI) Inflows into India? 3 (1) *Interdisciplinary Journal of Management and Behavioral Sciences* 8 (2014).

79 *See* Karl P. Sauvant and Lisa E. Sachs (eds.), *The Effect of Treaties on Foreign Direct Investment: Bilateral Investment Treaties, Double Taxation Treaties, and Investment Flows* (Oxford: Oxford University Press, 2009).

80 Quarterly Fact Sheet, Fact Sheet on Foreign Direct Investment from April 2000 to March 2018, Department of Industrial Policy and Promotion, Ministry of Commerce and

2.3 *2011 Onwards*

The third phase started with *White Industries v India* in which India for the first time was held in violation of its treaty obligations against an Australian investor under the India–Australia BIT (1999) which was signed in 1999 and came into effect in 2001. *White Industries v India* is significant because it not only ushered a wave of treaty-based investment claims against India,[81] but also – and presumably more important – inspired the process of India's BITs reform.

2.3.1 *White Industries v. India*

White Industries v India is the first case in which international tribunal found India in violation of its BIT obligations.[82] An Australian investor, White Industries, initiated an arbitration proceeding against India under the India–Australia BIT (1999).[83] White Industries claimed that the judicial delays in India in enforcing an International Chamber of Commerce (ICC) award concerning a contractual dispute between White Industries and Coal India, a state-owned mining company in India, violated several provisions of the India–Australia BIT. According to White Industries, these BIT provisions involve the right to fair and equitable treatment, free transfer of funds, protection against expropriation, and the guarantee of effective means to enforce rights and assert claims. The tribunal held that, among other issues, the delay of Indian courts in enforcing that ICC award deprived White Industries of "effective means of asserting claims and enforcing rights".[84] Although the India-Australia BIT (1999) contained no clause "guaranteeing investor an effective means of enforcement", the tribunal held that White industries could "import" such an obligation from Article 4(5) of the India-Kuwait BIT which was signed in 2001 and came into

Industry, Government of India, available at https://dipp.gov.in/sites/default/files/FDI_FactSheet_29June2018.pdf (visited March 10, 2019).

81 As of August 2019, India has been a respondent state in 24 cases. *See* "Investment Policy Hub: India-Cases as Respondent State", available at https://investmentpolicy.unctad.org/investment-dispute-settlement/country/96/india (visited September 16, 2019).

82 *White Industries v India*, In the Matter of an UNCITRAL Arbitration in Singapore, Final Award, 30 November 2011. Before *White Industries v India*, there were some other treaty-based investment disputes with India, all of which involved the Dabhol power project. Those disputes, however, were amicably settled and thus no award was made. For details of the *Dabhol* episodes, *see* Ronald J. Bettauer, India and International Arbitration: The Dabhol Experience, 41(2) *George Washington International Law Review* 381 (2009); P. Kundra, Looking Beyond the Dabhol Debacle: Examining its Causes and Understanding its Lessons, 41 *Vanderbilt Journal of Transnational Law* 907 (2008).

83 Agreement between the Government of the Republic of India and the Government of Australia on the Promotion and Protection of Investments (signed on 26th February 1999, entered into force 4 May 2000) (hereinafter "India-Australia BIT").

84 *White Industries v India*, Final Award, para. 11.4.19.

effect in 2003,[85] by relying on the MFN provision of the India-Australia BIT (1999),[86] which entitles a foreign investor to invoke more favourable treatment provided in another BIT that India concluded with a third state.[87]

With regard to the interpretation of "effective means", the *White Industries* tribunal heavily relied on *Chevron–Texaco v Ecuador* award,[88] in which the tribunal *inter alia* was of the opinion that an undue delay of the domestic courts in dealing with an investors' claim could amount to a breach of the "effective means" standard or "*Chevron* standard".[89] By applying the *Chevron* standard and evaluating the timeline of domestic litigation proceedings in India, the *White Industries* tribunal concluded that the failure of the Indian judiciary to deal with the claim of White Industries in over nine years had constituted a breach of India's obligation of providing White Industries with "effective means" of asserting claims and enforcing rights.[90]

The *White Industries* decision had several important implications for India.

First, this case involves how the MFN clause should be applied. The MFN clause, which can be found in most investment treaties, has been included in international economic treaties for centuries.[91] The very purpose of the MFN treatment clause in an investment treaty is to ensure equality of treatment between foreign investors.[92] However, the past two decades have seen incoherent applications of the MFN provision both in substantive and procedural matters.[93] While it has been commonly acknowledged that an investor under the

85 Art. 4(5) of India-Kuwait BIT provides that "Each Contracting State shall maintain a favourble environment for investments in its territory by investors of the other Contracting State. Each Contracting State shall, in accordance with its applicable laws and regulations, provide effective means of asserting claims and enforcing rights with respect to investments ..." (Agreement between the State of Kuwait and the Republic of India for the Encouragement and Reciprocal Protection of Investment (signed on November 27, 2001 and entered into force on June 28, 2003)).

86 Article 4 (2) of India-Australia BIT provides that "a contracting party shall at all times treat investments in its territory on a basis no less favourable than that accorded to investments or investors of any third country".

87 *White Industries v India*, Final Award, para. 11.2.3.

88 *Chevron Corporation and Texaco Petroleum Corporation v Ecuador*, UNCITRAL, PCA Case No. 34877, Partial Award on Merits (30 March 2010).

89 *Id.*, para. 250.

90 *White Industries v India*, Final Award, para. 11.4.19.

91 Rudolf Dolzer and Christoph Schreuer, *Principles of International Investment Law* (2nd Edition, London: Oxford University Press, 2012) 207.

92 UNCTAD, Most-Favoured-Nation Treatment, UNCTAD Series on Issues in International Investment Agreements II, UNCTAD/DIAE/IA/2010/1.

93 Yannic Radi, The Application of the Most Favoured Nation Clause to the Dispute Settlement Provisions of Bilateral Investment Treaties: Domesticating the Trojan Horse, 18(4) *European Journal of International Law* 757 (2007); Facundo Perez-Aznar, The Fictions and Realities of MFN Clauses in International Investment Agreements, 112 *AJIL Unbound* 55(2018); Tanjina Sharmin, Should the MFN within Investment Treaties exclude

MFN provision is entitled to a more favourable substantive treatment granted by the host state under another BIT,[94] there are debates as to whether and to what extent any limits exist for the application of the MFN provision.[95] According to the UNCTAD, the borrowing or importing of substantive provisions from another treaty by invoking a MFN provision is "difficult and must be done carefully".[96]

In order to prevent the MFN provision being interpreted too broadly, many newly signed investment treaties seek to define the MFN in a clearer manner, for instance, explicitly confining it to the post-establishment phase, listing the substantive matters to which it apply, and carving out the MFN from the ISDS mechanism. However, for a majority of BITS in force, the MFN clause was prescribed generally, without clarifying the scope of its applications. This is also the case of India.[97]

It is through reliance on the MFN provision in the India-Australia BIT (1999) that White Industries successfully "borrowed" the provisions of Art. 4 (5) of India-Kuwait BIT (2001), which were absent in the basic India-Australia BIT (1999). Such automatic importation brought about great concern among scholars, practitioners and governmental officials alike in India who became concerned that there may be foreign investors inclined to borrow more favourable treatment from another treaty to challenge different Indian investment measures, given the fact that all early Indian BITs included a broad provision of the MFN.[98] An Indian Parliamentarian thus warned that India would be at risk of being sued by any investor.[99]

Dispute Resolution: An Evaluation of the Australian Approach, 35 *Australian Yearbook of International Law* 123 (2017).

94 Batifort and Heath describe this a "top-down" approach, which imposes presumptions about the nature of MFN clauses on the wording of the treaty, however "this perspective obscures the variation among MFN clauses in investment agreements and other treaties, and leads interprets to adopt an unduly uniform approach to the function of MFN provision". *See* Simon Batifort and J. Benton Heath, The New Debate on the Interpretation on MFN Clauses in Investment Treaties: Putting the Brakes on Multilateralization, 111 *American Journal of International Law* 873 (2018) 874.

95 Dolzer and Schreuer, *supra* note 91, at 211.

96 UNCTAD, *supra* note 92, at 101.

97 The tribunal in *White Industries v India* affirmatively ruled that "there is no express carve-out or limitation to Article 4(5)...". *White Industries v India*, Final Award, para. 11.2.7. For the details of MFN provision in all Indian BITs, *see* Prabhash Ranjan, Most favoured nation provision in Indian Bilateral Investment Treaties: A Case for Reform, 55 *Indian Journal of International Law* 39 (2015).

98 Rajput, *supra* note 21, at 25. *See also* Prabhash Ranjan, The White Industries arbitration: Implication for India's Investment Treaty Program, available at https://www.iisd.org/itn/2012/04/13/the-white-industries-arbitration-implications-for-indias-investment-treaty-program/ (visited March 22, 2019).

99 Statement by P. Rajeeve, Member of Indian Parliament (Transcript of the Proceedings of the Rajya Sabha, 22 May 2012) (Uncorrected Debates), available at http://164.100.47.5/newdebate/225/22052012/Fullday.pdf (visited March 17, 2019).

Second, the ruling of the *White Industries* tribunal on "effective means" increases the risk of BITs intruding into Indian judicial system.[100] Obviously, the application of *White Industries* to enforce a monetary award in India, which finally let White Industries bring an international claim against India, should be reviewed and enforced by Indian courts. The *White Industries* tribunal, by making an unfavourable award against India that India is obliged to comply with, arguably "replac[ed] the function of Indian courts".[101] It came as no surprise that the *White Industries* award ignited anger in the Parliament of India. The Parliament condemned the decision and stated that: "this is an attack on the sovereignty of the India Judiciary ... as well as an attack on the sovereignty of the country".[102] The Parliament thus urged that the Government of India should review all of its investment treaties.[103]

The *White Industries* award opened a "Pandora's Box". From then on, India, as a respondent state, has been involved in at least twenty-four known investment cases as of August 2019.[104] Of the twenty-four cases, nine have been settled,[105] two have been decided with final awards,[106] and thirteen are still pending.

2.3.2 India's BITs Reform

The Indian government began to review its BITs practice when the *White Industries* case was pending. In 2011, the Ministry of Commerce prepared an unpublished discussion paper, suggesting that India reconsider the effectiveness of BITs in attracting foreign investments.[107] For the first time, the paper acknowledged that Indian BITs had failed to strike a balance between the protection of foreign investment and the maintenance of regulatory power of India's government, mainly because of many poorly written BIT provisions.[108]

---

100 Manu Sanan, The White Industries Award – Shades of Grey, 12 *Journal of World Investment & Trade* 661 (2012) 683.

101 Rajput, *supra* note 21, at 25.

102 Statement by P. Rajeeve, Member of Parliament (India), Transcript of the Proceedings of the Rajya Sabha (Uncorrected Debates) (22 May 2012), p. 54, available at http://164.100.47.5/newdebate/225/22052012/Fullday.pdf (visited March 17, 2019).

103 *Id.*

104 For a full list of investment disputes against India, *see* UNCTAD, India as Respondent State, available at https://investmentpolicyhubold.unctad.org/ISDS/CountryCases/96?partyRole=2 (visited April 2, 2019).

105 All these settled cases involve the Dabhol Project.

106 One is *White Industries* and the other is *Louis Dreyfus Armateurs SAS v. The Republic of India* in which claims of French investor were finally denied.

107 The excerpt of that document is cited from Ranjan, *supra* note 37, at 439–441.

108 *Id.*

In July 2012, the Government of India initiated a thorough evaluation of each BIT it had signed.[109] In particular, in a statement addressed to the World Investment Forum (2014), Indian representative especially referred to the FET and MFN provisions of Indian BITS, suggesting that they could be susceptible to misinterpretation due to the vague definitions.[110] Also, in that statement, India expressed its intentions to revise the Model BIT and terminate or renegotiate investment treaties.[111]

3 Salient Features of Indian Model BIT (2015)

The Indian Model BIT (2015) was approved by the Cabinet in December 2015, following the circulation of a draft Model BIT in March 2015 soliciting public comment and suggestion. The Law Commission of India (LCI) conducted a thorough analysis of each BIT provision and suggested revisions,[112] seeking a balance between the protection of investor rights and the maintenance of the interests of the state.[113] It should be noted that the Model BIT (draft) radically departed from the previous Indian BIT approach, and while almost exclusively focusing on the maintenance of regulatory power of host state, the final Model BIT made some compromises. For instance, the Model BIT (draft) did not allow a tribunal to review a determination by the host State of whether a measure is "taken for a public purpose or in compliance with its Law", but the final Model BIT did not include a similar provision, thus permitting a tribunal to decide if a state's measure is really taken for public purpose.[114] Nonetheless, many provisions of the final Model BIT, as analyzed below, still are written

109 For the details of reviewing process, *see* Saurabh Garg, Ishita Tripathy and Sudhanshu Roy, The Indian Model Bilateral Investment Treaty: Continuity and Change, in Kavaljit Singh & Burghard Ilge eds., *Rethinking Bilateral Investment Treaties: Critical Issues and Policy Choices* (Both Ends, Madhyam & SOMO, 2016), available at https://ssrn.com/abstract=2763222 (visited June 6, 2019).

110 "Statement of India", available at http://worldinvestmentforum.unctad.org/wp-content/uploads/2014/10/Mayaram.pdf (visited August 3, 2019).

111 *Id.*

112 Government of India, Law Commission of India, Report No. 260, Analysis of the Draft Model Indian Bilateral Investment (August 2015), available at http://lawcommissionofindia.nic.in/reports/Report260.pdf (visited March 14, 2019).

113 Anirudh Krishnan, "A Bit for the State, a Bit for the Investor", *The Hindu* (8 September 2015), available at https://www.thehindu.com/opinion/op-ed/a-bit-for-the-state-a-bit-for-the-investor/article7625893.ece (visited March 2, 2019).

114 For a comparative analysis of Draft Model BIT and Draft Model BIT, *see generally* Grant Hanessian and Habir Duggal, The Final 2015 Indian Model BIT: Is This the Change the World Wishes to See? 32 *ICSID Review* 216 (2017) 219.

with the aim of protecting the regulatory discretion of host State and to control potential misinterpretation of international tribunals.[115]

3.1 *Substantive Rules*

Moving away from the broad asset-based definition of investment in the Indian Model BIT (2003), the Model BIT (2015) narrows the notion of investment and investor in various ways. Investment is defined as "an enterprise constituted, organized and operated in good faith by an investor in accordance with the law of the party in whose territory the investment is made, has the characteristic of an investment such as …".[116] The *bona fide* requirement translates to the extension of protection only to genuine enterprises. This requirement is reflected in other provisions of the Model BIT as well. For example, investors and their investment must comply with domestic laws and regulations;[117] and investments made by way of fraudulent misrepresentation, concealment, corruption, money laundering or similar conducts are excluded from the right to arbitration.[118] The Model BIT (2015) also adds a list items that are not considered assets of an enterprise.[119]

In particular, the Model BIT (2015) requires that certain characteristics for identifying the existence of an "investment", such as: (i) "commitment of capital or other resources", (ii) "certain duration", (iii) "expectation of gain or profit", (iv) "assumption of risk", and (v) "significance for the development of the Party".[120] Obviously, they largely follow the four characteristics of "investment" laid down in the *Salini v. Morocco* award.[121] Accordingly, an investment, despite being lawful, could still be excluded from treaty protection if it fails to significantly contribute to the development of the host state. This criterion, however, is arguably subjective in the absence of benchmarks to assess the "significance" or "contribution" of an investment.[122]

---

115 Rajput, *supra* note 59, at 224–226.

116 Indian Model BIT (2015), art. 1.4.

117 Indian Model BIT (2015), art. 11 (i).

118 Indian Model BIT (2015), art. 13.4.

119 These items include, *inter alia*, portfolio investments, debt securities, pre-operational expenditure, pure commercial contract claims, good will or similar intangible rights, orders or judgments from judicial, administrative or arbitral proceedings. Indian Model BIT (2015), art. 1.4 (i)–(viii).

120 Indian Model BIT (2015), art. 1.4.

121 In *Salini v. Morocco*, the Tribunal held that "investment" generally infers contribution, a certain duration of performance of the contract, a participation in the risks of the transaction and contribution to the economic development of the host state of the investment (as an additional condition). *Salini Costruttori S.p.A. and Italstrade S.p.A. v. Kingdom of Morocco [I]*, ICSID Case No. ARB/00/4, Decision on Jurisdiction, 31 July 2001, para. 52.

122 Rudolf Dolzer and Christoph Schreuer, *super* note 93, at 75.

In order to enjoy protection under the Model BIT (2015), an investor who is a juridical person must have "substantial business activities" in the territory of host state.[123] Concurrently, the Model BIT (2015) removes the requirement provided in the Model BIT (draft), that is, an investor shall "control" a host state enterprise or "own an enterprise".[124]

The Model BIT (2015) reconceptualizes the standard of protection. First, the FET standard is replaced with customary international law. The application of customary international law is limited to these situations: (i) denial of justice; (ii) fundamental breach of due process; (iii) targeted discrimination on manifestly unjustified grounds; and (iv) manifestly abusive treatment.[125] The standard of "customary international law" is explicitly defined as "a general and consistent practice of States that they follow from a sense of legal obligation",[126] which has been firmly established in international law,[127] rather than by broadly referring to the minimum standard of treatment of aliens as some other investment treaties, especially the U.S. BIT, did.[128] Second, the Model BIT (2015) introduces a "full protection and security" standard that only applies to "the physical security" of investors and investments, but "not to any other obligation whatsoever".[129] By doing so, the "full protection and security" is prevented from being extended to apply to commercial and legal security as some arbitral awards have done.[130] Third, the Model BIT (2015) excludes the MFN treatment. Arguably, this is a strong Indian response to the *White Industries* award. Finally, the Model BIT (2015) maintains the national treatment standard; however, it applies only to the post-establishment stage of investments by referring to "management, conduct, operations, sale or other disposition of investments in its territory".[131]

---

123 Indian Model BIT (2015), art. 1.5.

124 India Law Commission suggested that the requirement of "control" would unduly interfere with the investment freedom of investors and also run against India's foreign investment policy. Law Commission of India, *super* note 112, at 10.

125 Indian Model BIT (2015), art. 3.1.

126 *See* footnote of art. 3.1. of the Indian Model BIT (2015).

127 The Statute of International Court of Justice, art. 38 (1)(b).

128 *See, e.g.*, the *North American Free Trade Agreement* (NAFTA), art. 1105.

129 Indian Model BIT (2015), art. 3.2.

130 "[W]hen the terms 'protection' and 'security' are qualified by 'full', the content of the standard may extend to matters other than physical security. It implies a State's guarantee of stability in a secure environment, both physical, commercial and legal." *Biwater Gauff (Tanzania) Ltd. v. United Republic of Tanzania*, ICSID Case No. ARB/05/22, Award, 26 July 2008, para. 729. "[T]he protection provided for by Article 5(1) [of the BIT] to covered investors and their assets is not limited to physical protection but includes also legal security." *Total SA v. Argentina Republic*, ICSID Case No. ARB/04/01, Decision on Liability, 27 December 2010, para. 343.

131 Indian Model BIT (2015), art. 4.1.

Article 5 of the Model BIT (2015) allows a host state to expropriate or nationalize an investment: (i) for public purpose; (ii) in accordance with the due process of law and (iii) on payment of "adequate compensation".[132] In contrast to the broadly-defined compensation standard in India's previous BIT practice, the standard of compensation in the new Model BIT is specified by the elements of "adequate", "at least equivalent to the fair market value of the expropriated investment immediately on the day before the expropriation takes place", and "not reflect(ing) any change in value occurring because the intended expropriation had become known earlier".[133] The new Model BIT clarifies that "an action taken by a Party in its commercial capacity" would not constitute an expropriation.[134] Also, the exercise of "non-discriminatory" regulatory measures or judicial decisions being designed and applied to "protect legitimate public interest or public purpose objectives", for instance, public health, safety and the environment, shall not considered an expropriation.[135]

In addition, the Indian Model BIT (2015) contains a separate chapter providing for "Exceptions", which include "general exceptions" (art. 32) and "security exceptions" (art. 33).

Another innovative element in the Indian Model BIT (2015) is that it imposes obligations on investors. The Model BIT (2015), in the preamble, first affirms "the right of Parties to regulate investments in their territory in accordance with their law and policy objectives". It further explicitly provides that investors have the obligation to comply with the domestic law, regulations, administrative guidelines and policies of the host State, especially referring to corruption and taxation.[136] Such compliance extends to the phases of "the establishment, acquisition, management, operation and disposition of investments".[137] Further, the Model BIT (2015) addresses corporate social responsibility (CSR), requiring that foreign investors "shall endeavor to voluntarily incorporate internationally recognized standards of corporate social responsibility in their practices and internal policies, such as statements of principle that have been endorsed or are supported by the Parties. These principles may address issues such as labour, the environment, human rights, community relations and anti-corruption."[138] Importantly, India's Company Act of 2013 requires that certain

132 Indian Model BIT (2015), art. 5.1.

133 *Id.*

134 Indian Model BIT (2015), art. 5.4.

135 Indian Model BIT (2015), art. 5.5.

136 Indian Model BIT (2015), art. 11.

137 Indian Model BIT (2015), art. 11(i).

138 Indian Model BIT (2015), art. 12.

corporations contribute at least 2% of their net profits to social activities.[139] These developments, as Choukroune suggests, represent that India is "at the forefront" of the implementation of sound CSR policies.[140] However, compared with the legalization of CSR in Indian domestic law, the CSR provision in the new Model BIT obviously is far weaker because it merely provides a voluntary obligation.[141]

3.2 *Procedural Rules*

The Indian Model BIT (2015) establishes a complicated procedural scheme for the resolution of investor-state disputes.[142] The most significant feature is that an investor should first exhaust local remedies for a period of at least five years before the initiation of international arbitration.[143] While the exhaustion of local remedies is a long established rule of customary international law, very few investment treaties expressly require it.[144] This is an entirely new approach adopted by the Indian government.[145] India stated in the 2016 UNCTAD Expert Meeting that the purpose of including exhaustion of local remedies in its new Model BIT is to ensure that "the investor will give

139 *See* Companies Act (2013), Key Highlights and Analysis, available at https://www.pwc.in/assets/pdfs/publications/2013/companies-act-2013-key-highlights-and-analysis.pdf (visited May 4, 2019).

140 Leïla Choukroune, Indian International Investment Agreements and "Non Investment Concerns": Time for a Right(s) Approach, 7(2) *Jindal Global Law Review* 157 (2016) 163.

141 Leïla Choukroune, Corporate Social Responsibility and Foreign Direct Investment – The Indian Investment Treaty Approach and Beyond, 15(2) 1 *Transnational Dispute Management* (2018) 16.

142 For a detailed commentary on the ISDS Chapter in the Indian new Model BIT, *see* Prabhash Ranjan and Pushkar Anand, Investor State Dispute Settlement in the 2016 Indian Model Bilateral Investment Treaty. Does it Go Too Far?, in Julien Chaisse and Luke Nottage (eds.), *International Investment Treaties and Arbitration Across Asia*, Leiden: Brill/Nijhoff, 2018) 579–611.

143 Indian Model BIT (2015), art. 15.1 & 15.2.

144 According to the IISD, requirement of exhaustion of local remedies only exist in some first-generation BITs and in more recent BITs concluded by Argentina, Romania, Turkey, the United Arab Emirates and Uruguay, among others. Martin Dietrich Brauch, Exhaustion of Local Remedies in International Investment Law, IISD Best Practices Series, January 2017, available at https://www.iisd.org/sites/default/files/publications/best-practices-exhaustion-local-remedies-law-investment-en.pdf (visited March 11, 2019).

145 India-UAE BIT and India–ASEAN Investment Agreement are the only two exceptions among the first-generation treaties concluded by India that contain a choice of forum clause (the so-called "fork-in-the-road" clause). According to this clause, a dispute may be submitted either to an international arbitral tribunal, an administrative tribunal (only in India-ASEAN Investment Agreement), or to the competent court of the host State. *See* India-UAE BIT (2013), art. 10.5.c and India-ASEAN Investment Agreement, art. 20.7.

precedence to the Indian domestic court system rather than invoke BITs for settling all types of disputes."[146]

The Indian Model BIT (2015) further establishes specific timeframes related to exhaustion of local remedies. An investor first must submit the dispute to the relevant domestic courts or administrative bodies within one year from the date on which the investor first acquired, or should have acquired knowledge of the measures taken by the host State.[147] Nevertheless, the Model BIT (2015) grants the investors the possibility to seek an exception to the rule based on the unavailability of remedies.[148] However, if such a futility exception does not apply, it is only after exhausting all judicial and administrative remedies for at least five years can the investor commence the international arbitration proceeding by serving a notice of the dispute to the host state.[149] The five-year period is counted from the date when the investor first acquired knowledge of the breach.[150]

The Indian Model BIT (2015) sets out additional qualifications before initiating international arbitration. After submitting the notice of dispute, an investor must wait for a "cooling-off" period of six months to resolve the dispute amicably.[151] After the six-month period elapses, the investor can start the arbitration proceeding subject to the following additional conditions: (i) not more than six years have elapsed from the date on which the investor first acquired or should have acquired knowledge of the measures in question;[152] (ii) not more than twelve months have elapsed from the conclusion of domestic proceedings;[153] (iii) at least ninety days before submitting a claim to arbitration, the investor has transmitted to the host state a written notice of arbitration;[154] and (iv) the investor has waived its right to initiate or continue

146 UNCTAD Expert Meeting on Taking Stock of IIA Reform, *Indian Model Bilateral Investment Treaty* (Geneva, 16 March 2016), available at https://worldinvestmentforum.unctad.org/wp-content/uploads/2016/03/Statement-Indian-Model-BIT.pdf (visited March 12, 2019).

147 Indian Model BIT (2015), art. 15.1.

148 Article 15.1 provides that, "the requirements to exhaust local remedies shall not be applicable if the investor or the locally established enterprise can demonstrate that there are no available domestic legal remedies capable of reasonably providing any relief in respect of the same measure or similar factual matters for which a breach of this Treaty is claimed by the investors."

149 Indian Model BIT (2015), art. 15.2.

150 Id.

151 Indian Model BIT (2015), art. 15.4.

152 Indian Model BIT (2015), art. 15.5 (i).

153 Indian Model BIT (2015), art. 15.5 (ii).

154 Indian Model BIT (2015), art. 15.5 (v).

before any administrative tribunal or court under the law of the host state, or other dispute settlement procedures.[155]

Notably, the Indian Model BIT (2015) includes some innovative elements that echo the trend of reforming international investment regime. For example, in order to enhance the coherence of treaty interpretation,[156] the new Model BIT contemplates the establishment of an appellate mechanism to review an award,[157] like the EU-Canada Comprehensive Economic Trade Agreement (CETA).[158] Also, the Model BIT introduces the rules of conflict of interest and disclosure for arbitrators,[159] codes of conduct for arbitrators,[160] and transparency.[161]

According to the Indian government, the Indian Model BIT (2015) will serve as the basis for renegotiating existing treaties and negotiating new investment treaties.[162] In early 2016, India proposed a Joint Interpretation Statement to more than twenty countries with whom India has existing investment treaties for which the initial period of validity had not expired.[163] The statement involves the clarification of almost all the significant treaty texts, including the definition of "investor" and "investment", the concept of FET, the meaning of full protection and security, the scope of MFN and national treatment, and the ISDS amongst others.[164] More importantly, in July 2016, India served notices to forty-seven countries (including the UK, Germany, France and Sweden) seeking termination of BITs of which initial duration either expired or was about to expire soon.[165]

---

155 Indian Model BIT (2015), art. 15.5 (iii) & (iv).

156 The current ISDS system has been subject to much criticism for the inconsistent arbitral awards. *See e.g.*, Susan D Franck, The Legitimacy Crisis in Investment Treaty Arbitration: Privatizing Public International Law Through Decisions, 73 *Fordham Law Review* 1521 (2005).

157 Indian Model BIT (2015), art. 29.

158 CETA, art. 8.28.

159 Indian Model BIT (2015), art. 19.

160 Indian Model BIT (2015), art. 20.

161 Indian Model BIT (2015), art. 22.

162 Press Information Bureau, Government of India, "Model Text for the Indian Bilateral Investment Treaty" (16 December 2015), available at http://pib.nic.in/newsite/PrintRelease.aspx?relid=133411 (visited March 11, 2019).

163 Ministry of Finance, Office Memorandum, Issuing joint interpretative statements for Indian Bilateral Investment Treaties, 8th February 2016, available at http://indiainbusiness.nic.in/newdesign/upload/Consolidated_Interpretive-Statement.pdf (visited March 11, 2019).

164 Kavaljit Singh and Burghard Ilge, Remodeling India's Investment Treaty Regime, available at https://thewire.in/trade/remodeling-indias-investment-treaty regime (visited April 3, 2019).

165 *See e.g.*, India overhauls its investment treaty regime, Financial Times, 15 July 2016, available at https://www.ft.com/content/53bd355c-8203-34af-9c27-7bf990a447dc (visited June 4, 2019); India's termination of BITs to begin, Global Arbitration Review,

3.3 *Indian Model BIT (2015): Swimming with the Ubiquitous Tide?*

Clearly, the Indian Model BIT (2015) is not as friendly as its 2003 predecessor in terms of investment treatment and protection accorded to foreign investors.[166] Arguably it represents a significant effort by India to pursue a more "balanced" investment treaty regime. However, does the 2015 Model BIT really achieve the desirable "balance", especially given the growing scale of Indian overseas investment? This issue remains open to debate.

First, the Indian Model BIT (2015) strategically ignores the fact that India has been an emerging capital-exporter. India's outward investment has increased from half a billion in 2000 to more than $11 billion in 2017.[167] In particular, India's overseas investment in developing region accounted for 56.2% of the cumulative outward FDI flows from 1980 to 2014.[168] The significant increase of outbound investment needs a better investment treaty project to offer proper protection to Indian overseas investors. Indian investors have resorted to the ISDS mechanism in six cases based on the respective BITs, modelling the investor-friendly India–UK BIT (1994) and the Model BIT (2003).[169] The Indian Model BIT (2015), however, departs significantly from the former scheme without arguably giving sufficient consideration of interests of Indian overseas investors. Obviously, the Indian government, in the Model BIT (2015), places the priority on the protection of regulatory authority. Thus, the Model BIT (2015) excludes the provisions of the MFN and FET, defines the terms of "investor" and "investment" in a narrower manner, and limits the access to the ISDS mechanism, amongst others. These provisions significantly restrict the protection accorded to the investment in India and Indian overseas

---

22 March 2017, available at https://globalarbitrationreview.com/article/1138510/indias-termination-of-bits-to-begin (visited May 13, 2019).

166 Ranjan argues that the 2016 Model BIT is "a complete departure from BITs India signed during the 'Embracement' phase [between early 1991 to 2010]". *See* Prabhash Ranjan, India and Bilateral Investment Treaties: From Rejection to Embracement to Hesitance?, in Srinivas Burra and R. Rajesh Babu eds., *Locating India in the Contemporary International Legal Order* (New Delhi: Springer, 2018) 121.

167 *See* UNCTAD, FDI Outflows, by region and economy, 1990–2017: India, published on 06 Jun 2018, available at https://unctad.org/en/Pages/DIAE/World%20Investment%20Report/Annex-Tables.aspx (visited March 23, 2019). *See also generally* Badar Alam Iqbal et al., India's Outward Foreign Direct Investment: Emerging Trends and Issues, 10(1) *Transnational Corporation Review* 98 (2018).

168 Jaya Prahash Pradhan, Indian Outward FDI: A Review of Recent Developments, 24 (2) *Transnational Corporations* 43 (2017).

169 The full list of treaty-based investment disputes in which India serves as the home state, available at https://investmentpolicyhubold.unctad.org/ISDS/CountryCases/96?partyRole=1 (visited June 12, 2019).

investment. In particular, the weak ISDS mechanism in the new Model BIT appears to especially disadvantage small-middle sized investors having lesser bargaining power in initiating an arbitration claim.

Second, the Indian Model BIT (2015) is flawed in achieving sustainable governance on investment. Indeed, the new Model BIT clearly seeks to align the objective of investment protection with those of sustainable development and public interest, as provided in its preamble and text. Provisions of the CSR, etc., are merely voluntary. Also, the right of the host State to bring counterclaims is not provided in the new Model BIT.[170] Hence, if an investor violates these obligations, the host State has no real sword to curb such breaches, except those breach actions that have been excluded from getting access to the arbitration under the BIT.[171] Excluding such measures from the enforcement mechanism, by debarring the counter-claim right of the state party, has made a major part of the investor obligations "largely unenforceable".[172]

However, some other (Model) BITs are aggressive in this aspect. According to the South African Development Community (SADC) Model BIT (2012), for instance, a host State may initiate a counterclaim against the investor for an alleged breach of the agreement.[173] Also, the Morocco-Nigeria BIT (2016) includes similar provisions of investor obligations as to those proposed in India's Model BIT (draft).[174] Indeed, the Morocco-Nigeria BIT (2016) does not allow the host State to initiate a counterclaim against investors, but it does introduce meaningful investor obligations in two ways: first, those measures addressing environmental and social concerns is only subject to the good-faith

170 Art. 14.11 of the Draft Model BIT provides that "a party may initiate a counterclaim against the Investor or Investment for a breach of the obligations set out under Articles 9 [Obligation against Corruption], 10 [Disclosures], 11 [Taxation] and 12 [Compliance with Laws of Host State]."

171 Article 13.4 of the Indian Model BIT (2015) provides that an investor may not submit a claim to arbitration if the investment has been made through "fraudulent misrepresentation, concealment, corruption, money laundering or conduct amounting to an abuse of process or similar illegal mechanisms". However, obligations of human rights and environmental protection are not included therein.

172 Eric Leikin, Stuti Gadobdia and Charles Loudon, The State Doesn't Strike Back After All: India's Final Model BIT Takes the Bite out of Investor Obligations and Eliminate State Counterclaims, 15(2) *Transnational Dispute Management* 1(2018) 2, 14–16.

173 SADC Model Bilateral Investment Treaty (2012), art. 19.2. The full text is available at https://www.iisd.org/itn/wp-content/uploads/2012/10/sadc-model-bit-template-final.pdf (visited May 22, 2019).

174 Reciprocal Investment Promotion and Protection Agreement between The Government of The Kingdom of Morocco and The Government of the Federal Republic of Nigeria (Signed on 12 March 2016), available at https://investmentpolicyhubold.unctad.org/Download/TreatyFile/5409 (visited March 11, 2019).

judgment of the host State ("any measure that it considers appropriate") (art. 13); second, investors shall be subject to civil liability for their wrongful doings before the tribunals of their home state (art. 20).[175]

Another concern stems from the demanding obligation requiring investors to exhaust local remedies in the Model BIT (2015). This requirement was considered by Sornarajah to be a "thrust" of the Model BIT (2015).[176] This requirement clearly was created in light of the notorious judicial delay in India,[177] which was evident in the *White Industries* case.[178] Indeed, a sovereign state, under general international law, has the jurisdiction over disputes in its territory. And the ICSID Convention also explicitly permits a Contracting Party to "require the exhaustion of local administrative or judicial remedies as a condition of its consent to arbitration under this Convention."[179] However, it is open to debate because the exhaustion of local remedies in defined in such a broad manner, namely, it may be required to last "for at least a period of five years" from the date on which the investor first acquired knowledge of the measure in question.[180] Arguably, what India should do is to improve its judicial system rather than to imposing too demanding obligations on investors.

Finally, there is a mixed picture regarding whether the Indian Model BIT (2015) would be accepted by India's potential negotiating partners, especially developed states. Indeed, in 2015, India signed a BIT with Cambodia, virtually basing it on the Model BIT (2015), including the requirement to exhaust local remedies. The India-Belarus BIT, which was signed in 2018, almost follows the Model BIT (2015).[181]

---

175 Tarcisio Gazzini, The 2016 Morocco-Nigeria BIT: An Important Contribution to the Reform of Investment Treaties, 26 September 2017, available at https://www.iisd.org/itn/2017/09/26/the-2016-morocco-nigeria-bit-an-important-contribution-to-the-reform-of-investment-treaties-tarcisio-gazzini/ (visited May 22, 2019).

176 M. Sornarajah, The Unworkability of "Balanced Treaties" and The Importance of Diversity of Approach Among the BRICs, 112 *AJIL Unbound* 223 (2018) 227.

177 Excessive caseloads is the most important factor that causes the judicial delay in India. Another reason is that Indian judiciary does not established effective case management system. *See* Rajput, *supra* note 10, at 105.

178 Sumeet Kachwaha, The White Industries Australia Limited – India BIT Award: A Critical Assessment, 29(2) *Arbitration International* 275 (2013) 293. ("Sadly, India does have a problem of judicial delays. To the extent, the White Award may help move the Indian State to address this problem, it would have served a laudable purpose – but other than that, I do not see it as a fit precedent.")

179 ICSID Convention, art. 26.

180 Indian Model BIT (2015), art. 15.2.

181 Full text of India-Belarus BIT, available at https://investmentpolicy.unctad.org/international-investment-agreements/treaty-files/5724/download (visited March 11, 2019).

At this stage, however, it appears unclear whether developed states would accept the Indian Model BIT (2015).[182] This is illustrated by the negotiations of Broad-based Trade and Investment Agreement (BTIA) between India and EU, which has now taken more than ten years without a final deal. It has been reported that the EU is complaining that the Model BIT (2015) includes too many provisions that protect the government and go against the interest of the investor.[183] Likewise, negotiations of a BIT between India and the US look dim, which were believed attributable primarily to the huge gap between Indian Model BIT (2015) and the US Model BIT (2012) especially as to the ISDS mechanism.[184]

Nevertheless, it is still possible that India may take a flexible approach to investment treaty. It was reported that in 2016 India signed a BIT with Brazil that was not totally based on the Indian Model BIT (2015). For example, it includes elements of investment cooperation and facilitation, and focuses on dispute prevention rather than providing for investor–state arbitration, which is provided in the Brazilian Model CFIA (2015). On the other hand, it does not include the FET provision and MFN clause, which reflects Indian approach.[185]

4 India-China BIT (2006) and Its Future

Both India and China play increasingly significant roles in the international economy.[186] Martin Wolf described the economic development of China and India as "the most important story of our age. It heralds the end, in the not too

182 Tejas Shiroor, India Revamps Its Bilateral Investment Treaty Regime, available at http://internationalarbitrationlaw.com/blog/india-revamps-its-bilateral-investment-treaty-regime/ (visited March 22, 2019).

183 Amiti Sen, India-EU Attempts to Restart Free Trade Talks Stumble on Old Issues, December 7, 2018, available at https://www.thehindubusinessline.com/economy/india-eu-attempts-to-re-start-free-trade-talks-stumble-on-old-issues/article25692022.ece (visited March 25, 2019).

184 Prabhash Ranjan, Bit of a bumpy ride, *The Hindu* (16 September 2016), available at https://www.thehindu.com/opinion/op-ed/Bit-of-a-bumpy-ride/article14378406.ece (visited May 10, 2019).

185 "Brazil and India initial bilateral investment treaty (BIT); text yet to be published", available at https://www.iisd.org/itn/2016/12/12/brazil-and-india-initial-bilateral-investment-treaty-bit-text-yet-to-be-published/ (visited March 23, 2019).

186 Amelia U. Santos-Paulino and Guandhua Wan (eds.), *The Rise of China and India: Impacts, Prospects and Implications* (Basingstoke: Palgrave Macmillan, 2010), xvi; Matthew Sweeney, Foreign Direct Investment in India and China: The Creation of a Balanced Regime in a Globalized Economy, 43 *Cornell International Law Journal* 207 (2010) 208.

distant future, of as much as five centuries of domination by the European and their colonial offshoots".[187]

India began to develop mutual relations with China shortly after the People's Republic of China (PRC) was founded in 1949. Actually, India was the first non-socialist country establishing diplomatic relations with the socialist China. For decades, India and China, as two major developing states, have coordinated and cooperated in various international forums to fight for the New International Economic Order (NIEO) which was perceived to be more sensitive to the development needs of developing states. For instance, India and China contributed to the adoption of the Declaration of the Establishment of the New International Economic Order, as well as the Charter of Economic Rights and Duties of States within the UN framework in the 1970s. Unfortunately, their mutual relations are often discouraged by territorial disputes, which brought about military confrontations and war in the 1960s.[188] Although the two states restarted friendly mutual relations during the 1980s, it seems that they have begun to identify as strategic competitors with each other as they emerge as global power, which presumably discourages mutual cooperation.[189]

Presumably because of the complexity of their mutual relationship, China obviously is not a state that India considers a priority to negotiate a BIT with, and vice versa. India and China finally signed a BIT on November 21, 2006,[190] twenty-four years since China signed its first BIT with Sweden and twelve years after India signed its first BIT with the UK A BIT was finally concluded between India and China because the mutual relationship in the 2010s developed smoothly and because both states were quite open to liberal investment treaties.

The India-China BIT (2006) includes several provisions in favor of investors. In particular, it allows "any dispute ... in relation to an investment" to be submitted to international arbitration.[191] Also, it includes the FET in broad manner, providing that foreign investments and returns of investors "shall at all times be accorded fair and equitable treatment",[192] without further

187 Muthucumaraswamy Sornarajah, Jiangyu Wang, Introduction and Overview, in Muthucumaraswamy Sornarajah, Jiangyu Wang (eds.), *China, India and the International Economic Order* (Cambridge: Cambridge University Press, 2010) 1.

188 *See, e.g.*, Surya P. Sharma, The India-China Border Dispute: An Indian Perspective, 59 *American Journal of International Law* 16 (1965).

189 Surjit Mansingh and Steven I. Levine, China and India: Moving beyond Confrontation, 38 *Problems of Communism* 30 (1989); Rong Ying, The Modi Doctrine and the Future of China-India Relations, 68 *China International Studies* 26(2018).

190 India-China BIT (2006) came into effect on January 8, 2007.

191 India-China BIT (2006), art. 9.

192 India-China BIT (2006), art. 3(2).

clarification. However, as developing states, India and China are sensitive to the protection of their economic sovereignty, thereby imposing several important limitations on the commitments. In particular, although the India-China BIT (2006) permits an investor access to international arbitration, it states that a respondent state may require the investor to exhaust the domestic review procedure before the dispute is submitted for international arbitration.[193] Interestingly, the India-China BIT (2006) shows that the US somewhat influences developing states in investment treaties. For instance, the provision of indirect expropriation in the India-China BIT (2006) is virtually the same as that of the US investment treaties.[194]

According to Article 16 of the India-China BIT (2006), that BIT shall remain in force for a period of ten years and thereafter it shall be deemed to have been automatically extended unless either Contracting Party gives to the other Contracting Party a written notice of its intention to terminate the BIT, which would make it no longer apply one year after the date of such written notice. As noted above, in 2006, as a step to reform its investment treaty regime, India sent notices to its twenty-five BIT partners hoping to sign joint statement to clarify the relevant BIT provisions. China was one of the twenty-five states. Since the two states did not sign such a statement, the India-China BIT (2006) was thus terminated on July 31, 2017.

Given the steady increase of Chinese investment in India,[195] it was reported that China expressed strong interest in negotiating a new BIT with India and

---

193 India-China BIT (2006), art. 9(4).

194 The determination of whether a measure or a series of measures of a Party in a specific situation, constitute indirect expropriation requires "a case by case, fact based inquiry that considers, among other factors: i. the economic impact of the measure or a series of measures, although the fact that a measure or series of measures by a Party has an adverse effect on the economic value of an investment, standing alone, does not establish that expropriation or nationalization, has occurred; ii. the extent to which the measures are discriminatory either in scope or in application with respect to a Party or an investor or an enterprise; iii. the extent to which the measures or series of measures interfere with distinct, reasonable, investment-backed expectations; iv. the character and intent of the measures or series of measures, whether they are for bona fide public interest purposes or not and whether there is a reasonable nexus between them and the intention to expropriate." Furthermore, it is provided that "[e]xcept in rare circumstances, non-discriminatory regulatory measures adopted by a Contracting Party in pursuit of public interest, including measures pursuant to awards of general application rendered by judicial bodies, do not constitute indirect expropriation or nationalization." India-China BIT (2006), Protocol. *See also* the US Model BIT (2004), Annex B: Expropriation.

195 Suparna Dutt D'Cunha, "How China is Positioning Itself Among India's Top 10 Investors Despite Bilateral Differences", *Forbes* (1 May 2018), available at https://www.forbes.com/sites/suparnadutt/2018/05/01/how-china-is-positioning-itself-among-the

preliminary discussions were conducted.[196] A new BIT obviously is helpful to increase the confidence of Chinese investors in the Indian investment climate, promoting Chinese investment inflow to India. It is not likely, however, that a BIT will be successfully negotiated between the two states in the near future. A major legal reason is that, although China supports a balanced investment treaty and thus it can find many commonalities with India in investment treaty regime, it also pursues BITs that are meaningful to Chinese investors, especially in the ISDS.[197] Therefore, China presumably could not accept India's position on several important issues, especially the MFN and the exhaustion of local remedies.

5 Concluding Remarks

The investment treaty regime has experienced a profound transformation in the past decade. The general approach among States to investment treaty regimes is that any regime should be more balanced than before. However, an important thing is that States have different conceptions of "balance". This is why States are divergent as to how to reform the current investment treaty regime, especially the ISDS.[198] According to the UNCTAD, the strategy that a State takes to reform investment treaties depends on which perspective that State prefers, host State, or home State, or both.[199]

Historically, India was a leading developing state that advocated the NIEO. As a result, was not until the mid-1990s that India began its investment treaty program by signing the first BIT with the UK in 1994, which was far behind other major developing states, namely, China. Generally speaking, India tended to make more commitments to investors, even though it remained reluctant to subject itself to international scrutiny in several important matters, especially the pre-establishment national treatment. The trend appears to have been reversed with the *White Industries–India*, which prompted India to

-top-10-investors-in-india-despite-bilateral-differences/#287b81b71dac (visited March 2, 2019).

196 "China keen on bilateral investment pact with India", available at https://economictimes.indiatimes.com/news/economy/foreign-trade/china-keen-on-bilateral-investment-pact-with-india/articleshow/63523147.cms?from=mdr (visited May 4, 2019).

197 *See* Norah Gallagher and Wenhua Shan, *Chinese Investment Treaties: Policies and Practice* (Oxford: Oxford University Press, 2009) Chapter 8.

198 Anthea Roberts, Incremental, Systemic, and Paradigmatic Reform of Investor-State Arbitration, 112 *American Journal of International Law* 410 (2018).

199 UNCTAD, 2015 World Investment Report, at 131.

reorient its investment treaty policy culminating in the adoption of the Model BIT (2015). Arguably, the Indian Model BIT (2015) represents India's effort to pursue a more balanced investment treaty regime, which indeed also happens in many other states. However, it seems that India goes too far by, for instance, excluding the MFN and providing demanding requirement of exhausting local remedies. Given the huge political and economic potential that India steadily acquires, this state arguably should be more open to investment treaties.

CHAPTER 5

The Belt & Road Initiative and the New Landscape of China's ISDS Policy and Practice

Huiping Chen

1 Introduction

The Belt & Road Initiative (BRI or Initiative) was proposed by China's President Xi Jinping in 2013. In September of that year, President Xi, in his speech delivered in Kazakhstan, proposed to build a "Silk Road Economic Belt".[1] In October 2013, President Xi also called for building a "Maritime Silk Road" in Indonesia.[2] The BRI has now been established by China's government as a fundamental national policy. A variety of policy instruments have been taken to enhance the BRI. For instance, in 2017, China's government issued a blueprint of Vision and Actions on Jointly Building Silk Road Economic Belt and 21st-Century Maritime Silk Road.[3] China also makes various efforts to win international support for the BRI.[4] The primary purpose and spirit that the BRI embraces is to build "a human community with a shared future".[5] Such an innovative conception of world order has been included in China's Constitution since 2018[6] and in several international documents.[7]

1 "President Xi Jinping Delivers Important Speech and Proposes to Build a Silk Road Economic Belt with Central Asian Countries" (2013/09/07), available at https://www.fmprc.gov.cn/mfa_eng/topics_665678/xjpfwzysiesgjtfhshzzfh_665686/t1076334.shtml (visited March 2, 2019).

2 "Xi in Call for Building of New Maritime Silk Road", available at http://usa.chinadaily.com.cn/china/2013-10/04/content_17008940.htm (visited February 20, 2019).

3 National Development and Reform Commission, Ministry of Foreign Affairs, and Ministry of Commerce of the People's Republic of China, Vision and Actions on Jointly Building Silk Road Economic Belt and 21st-Century Maritime Silk Road, May 12, 2017, available at http://en.ndrc.gov.cn/newsrelease/201503/t20150330_669367.html (visited March 23, 2019).

4 *See, e.g.*, Liu Yuxi, Sino-Africa Cooperation Should Give Full Play to Advantage, China Daily Global, April 29, 2019, available at http://www.chinadaily.com.cn/a/201904/29/WS5cc64e3ba3104842260b8fed.html (visited May 22, 2019).

5 *See, e.g.*, Xi Jinping, Working Together to Forge a New Partnership of Win-win Cooperation and Create a Community of Shared Future for Mankind, New York, 28 September 2015, available at https://www.fmprc.gov.cn/mfa_eng/topics_665678/xjpdmgjxgsfwbcxlhgcl70znxlfh/t1305051.shtml (visited March 2, 2019).

6 China's Constitution (1982, as amended in 2018).

7 For example, the Resolution 2344 (2017) adopted by the Security Council at the 7902nd meeting, on March 17, 2017, available at https://undocs.org/S/RES/2344 (2017) (visited April 14, 2019).

 | DOI:10.1163/9789004376991_006

The "Belt" means the "Silk Road Economic Belt", which is land-based routes focusing on bringing together China, Asia, Russia and Europe. The "Road" means the "21st-Century Maritime Silk Road", which is an ocean-based route designed to go from China's coast to Europe through the South China Sea, the Indian Ocean and the South Pacific. The Belt and Road domain involves geographically more than 70 countries in various regions and economic groupings. However, China does not geographically confine the BRI practice since the BRI over time has been established by China as a broader initiative for international cooperation and thus open to any country which agrees with its goals. Thus, the BRI also covers such states as Argentina, Panama and Chile in South America.

The BRI aims to further integrate China into the global economy through trade, investment, infrastructure construction, connectivity, and other development projects. The BRI may facilitate the market access of Chinese companies in BRI participating countries. On the other hand, the BRI also helps to enhance regional economic growth, development, and integration. Therefore, the BRI is a win-win cooperation policy. Investment and trade cooperation are two significant components of the BRI practice.

The BRI brings about significant implications for China's foreign investment law and policy both at the national level and at the international level. In particular, given the fact that China is a leading state, both as host State and as home State, and China's government and Chinese investors have become involved in the investor-state dispute settlement (ISDS), and in light of the efforts that many states and several international organizations have made to improve the ISDS, China seeks to reform its own ISDS, which is of significance for the BRI practice.

2 Implications of the BRI on Chinese Foreign Investment Law and Policy

The BRI has substantial implications for Chinese overseas investment, Chinese foreign investment law and policy as well as Chinese attitude toward the undergoing international ISDS reform.

2.1 *Impacts of BRI on Chinese Overseas Investment*

As an international economic cooperation initiative that seeks the building of mutual connectivity and has aspirations of mutual benefits and win-win scenarios, the BRI is expected to enhance the prosperity of participating countries and to sustain global economic growth. The Initiative intends to promote infrastructure construction, trade and investment, among other activities, between

China and other BRI participating countries and regions. Surely, the BRI is very helpful to promote Chinese investment in BRI countries. Currently, China has become the second-largest country for both capital-import and capital-export in the world. Since 2016, the total amount of China's outward investment has exceeded the amount of its inward investment.[8]

In terms of investment, the BRI will significantly promote Chinese outward foreign direct investment in developing countries. Investment dynamism has built up rapidly in recent years, and Chinese outward FDI has surged. In 2016, it rose 44 percent to $183 billion, and made China the second-largest home country for FDI flow for the first time. China also became a net outward direct investor in that year.[9] In 2017, China was the third-largest home country for FDI flows next to the US and Japan, and the second-largest home country for FDI stock next to only the US.[10] China's total outward FDI flows to the 63 countries along the Belt and Road in 2017 was more than 20 billion USD.[11] Some BRI countries such as Singapore, Kazakhstan, Malaysia, Indonesia, have started to attract a significant amount of FDI flows from China as a result of their active participation in the BRI.[12]

Most BRI countries are developing countries who face a shortage of capital for economic development. Therefore, they welcome Chinese investment gladly. It is a win-win policy since foreign countries receive the capital they need, and Chinese enterprises find projects to invest. Indeed, China has been the largest home economy investing in the least-developed countries (LDCs) for years.[13]

2.2 *Impacts of BRI on Chinese Foreign Investment Policy and Law*

The BRI also incentivizes China to reform its foreign investment policy and law both at the national level and at the international level.

---

8 "China becomes world's second-largest source of outward FDI: report", available at http://www.xinhuanet.com/english/2017-06/08/c_136350164.htm (visited March 13, 2019).

9 UNCTAD, *2017 World Investment Report*, at 14.

10 China's Ministry of Commerce, National Bureau of Statistics & State Administration of Foreign Exchange, 2017 Statistical Bulletin of China's Outward Foreign Direct Investment, China Statistics Press, at 83–85.

11 China's Ministry of Commerce, National Bureau of Statistics & State Administration of Foreign Exchange, *2017 Statistical Bulletin of China's Outward Foreign Direct Investment*, (Beijing: China Statistics Press, 2018) 153.

12 World Investment Report 2017, at 19; China's Ministry of Commerce, National Bureau of Statistics & State Administration of Foreign Exchange, 2017 Statistical Bulletin of China's Outward Foreign Direct Investment, (Beijing: China Statistics Press, 2018) 153.

13 UNCTAD, World Investment Report 2017, at 80.

On the national level, China has adopted new national investment laws and policies to carry out the Initiative, aiming to promote Chinese outward investment on the one hand and to regulate and protect Chinese outward investment on the other hand.

For two decades after China embarked on the Opening-up and Reforming policy in the late 1970, China's priority was to attract foreign investment to fuel its economy. The promotion of outward investment was not listed as an agenda of China's government. On the other hand, Chinese companies were not strong and competitive enough to manage their own investment abroad. Therefore, before 2000, outward investment was not supported by China's government. Actually, many of China's laws and policy instruments discouraged outward investment.[14] Since 2000, however, as the Chinese economy rapidly expanded and Chinese companies became more competitive, China established the "Going Abroad" strategy as its new economic strategy, a major component of which was to promote outward investment. As a result, many laws and policy instruments on financing and approval, etc. were newly adopted or updated to facilitate Chinese outward investment.[15]

In order to carry out the BRI, China's authorities, for instance the Ministry of Commerce (MOFCOM), the National Development and Reform Commission (NDRC), and the State Administration of Foreign Exchange (SAFE), have made various efforts to promote Chinese outward investment, including adopting new laws and policies, revising or repealing those laws and policies unfavorable to the outward investment.

For instance, in December 2017, the NDRC issued China's new Administrative Measures for Overseas Investment by Enterprises, to replace the Administrative Measures for Verification and Filing of Overseas Investment Projects issued in 2014.[16] This new document cancels or relaxes many restraints on outward investment while strengthening supervision over outward investment. In early 2018, the NDRC also issued the Measures for the Interim and Ex Post Supervision of Enterprise Investment Projects.[17] In early 2018, the MOFCOM and the SAFE, together with other state organs, jointly issued the Interim

14 Congyan Cai, Outward Foreign Direct Investment Protection and the Effectiveness of Chinese BIT Practice, 7 *Journal of World Investment & Trade* 621 (2006) 626.

15 *Id.* 627–631.

16 NDRC, Administrative Measures for Overseas Investment by Enterprises, available at http://zfxxgk.ndrc.gov.cn/web/iteminfo.jsp?id=2948 (visited March 17, 2019).

17 NDRC, Measures for the Interim and Ex Post Supervision of Enterprise Investment Projects, available at http://www.ndrc.gov.cn/fzgggz/gdzctz/tzfg/201801/W020180115553562483487.pdf (visited March 17, 2019).

Measures for the Filing (Verification) and Reporting of Overseas Investment.[18] The MOFCOM is also working on new regulation measures to replace the Measures on the Administration of Overseas Investment issued in 2014.[19]

The NDRC, the MOFCOM and other authorities issued the Guidance on Further Directing and Regulating Overseas Investment Direction in 2017, listing the sectors for encouragement, restriction and prohibition with respect to investment.[20] The NDRC updated the List of Sensitive Sectors for Outbound Investment in 2018,[21] which deleted from the list telecoms and electricity while adding the arms industry, transboundary water resources and several other high-profile sectors. Investment in the sectors on the list is subject to additional regulation. More new and detailed regulations and rules on Chinese outward investment are expected.

China always stresses that, although the BRI was initiated by China, it is not a project that can be unilaterally conducted by China. Rather, it is an initiative of international cooperation and thus it requires joint efforts from other BRI countries. As a result, China has begun to seek more efficient international regimes and mechanisms aiming to facilitate the BRI. Because of this, the Chinese approach is of special significance in making international economic governance more efficient, fair and balanced.

First, to jointly build the Belt and Road requires increasing coordination and cooperation between China and other BRI countries. China is making great efforts to build the framework for this to happen. The Belt and Road Forum represents an important effort in this regard. The first Belt and Road Forum for International Cooperation was held in Beijing on May 2017, attracting leaders from over 60 countries and international organizations to attend. It was reported that more than 50 agreements have been signed between China and its partners, covering six major international economic corridors.[22] Until the end of 2018, more than 120 countries concluded various agreements, including joint statements with China concerning the joint building of the BRI.[23] The

18 MOFCOM, Interim Measures for the Filing (Verification) and Reporting of Overseas Investment, available at http://www.mofcom.gov.cn/article/i/jyjl/k/201801/20180102704125.shtml (visited March 3, 2019).

19 Sina Finance, MOFCOM is Modifying the Measures on the Administration of Overseas Investment, available at https://finance.sina.com.cn/roll/2018-05-04/doc-ifyuwqfa6496705.shtml (visited March 3, 2019).

20 163 News, Notice on the Guidance on Further Directing and Regulating Overseas Investment Direction, available at http://news.163.com/17/0818/18/CS516NHH00018AOQ.html (visited May 4, 2019).

21 Sohu Net, NDRC issued the List of Sensitive Sectors for Outbound Investment (2018), available at https://www.sohu.com/a/222434146_165665 (visited March 17, 2019).

22 UNCTAD, World Investment Report 2017, at 19.

23 For the list of countries in the BRI domain and the various agreements, *see* BRI website: available at https://www.yidaiyilu.gov.cn/ (visited March 12, 2019).

second Belt and Road Forum for International Cooperation was held in Beijing in April 2019, and it attracted participants from more than 150 countries and 90 international organizations to attend the event.[24]

Second, the Initiative and the increase of Chinese outward investment both require China to update its investment treaty regime. Concluding bilateral investment treaties (BIT) is an effective way to protect foreign investment. So far, China has concluded international treaties with 149 states.[25] China has concluded BITs with most of the countries and regions in the Belt and Road domain. However, as Chinese traditional investment treaties are quite conservative in both substantive treatment and protection and, in particular, the investor-state dispute settlement (ISDS), they are not effective in protecting Chinese investment and expanding market access for Chines investors.[26] Therefore, China recognizes that it must improve its investment treaties in light of the trend of investment treaty regimes, with the goal of maintaining the high standards of investment treatment and protection while also seeking to strike a better balance than before between foreign investors and host States, home States and host States, and economic concerns and non-economic concerns, etc.

Third, the BRI and the growing outward Chinese outward investment has inspired China to propose, individually or jointly, new regulation on foreign investment at both regional and global levels. An important effort was that in 2014 China and other BRICS countries jointly issued a statement of "A BRICS Perspective on International Investment Agreements", in which BRICS state that they will "continue to build a common approach" to investment treaties.[27] Then came the G20 Guiding Principles for Global Investment Policymaking, proposed by China and agreed on by the G20 in 2016 during the group's Shanghai Ministerial Meeting and at the Hangzhou Summit.[28] That was the first time that developed, developing and transition economies reached multilateral consensus on an investment matter, albeit non-binding.[29] Importantly, the Chinese Government still works to set up rules on investment facilitation and promotion. Based on the G20 Guiding Principles, China

24 Xi Focus: Xi opens up new horizons for high-quality B&R cooperation, available at http://www.xinhuanet.com/english/2019-04/26/c_138013041.htm (visited May 22, 2019).

25 The data is from UNCTAD International Investment Agreements Navigator, available at http://investmentpolicyhub.unctad.org/IIA/CountryBits/42#iiaInnerMenu (visited May 9, 2019).

26 Congyan Cai, supra note 14, at 637–629.

27 Available at https://www.ranepa.ru/images/media/brics/brazpresidency2/investmet.pdf (visited March 14, 2019).

28 The Guiding Principles is available at https://www.oecd.org/daf/inv/investment-policy/G20-Guiding-Principles-for-Global-Investment-Policymaking.pdf (visited March 11, 2019).

29 UNCTAD, *2017 World Investment Report*, at xii.

proposed a framework of investment facilitation in the WTO in 2016, which received substantial support. In December 2017, during the WTO Ministerial Meeting, China announced a joint ministerial declaration on investment facilitation with some other countries.[30] In August 2017, before the Xiamen BRICS Summit, China proposed the Outline for BRICS Investment Facilitation to the agenda.[31] China's efforts in proposing investment facilitation coincide with and support the similar efforts of the UNCTAD[32] and some other developing states, for instance, Brazil.[33]

Fourth, the principle and spirit of the BRI is expected to increase Chinese contribution to making current international economic governance more efficient, fair and balanced. It is widely acknowledged that the current international economic governance notoriously disadvantages developing states and fails to pay for sufficient substantial development of the world.[34] In contrast, as noted above, China ensures that the BRI is aimed to promote win-win cooperation, joint development and prosperity, peace and cooperation, openness and inclusiveness, and mutual understanding and trust. This principle and spirit of the BRI is conceptualized as "building a human community with shared future," an overall idea that China proposes in many areas. As a matter of fact, such a principle and spirit has been enshrined in recent Chinese international legal policies, for instance, the proposal of founding of the Asian Infrastructure Investment Bank (AIIB).[35]

2.3 *Impacts of BRI on Chinese Attitude toward the Ongoing ISDS Reform*

According to an empirical survey, the ISDS in Chinese traditional BITs is not effective in protecting Chinese outward investment because a number of

30 WTO, New initiatives on electronic commerce, investment facilitation and MSMEs, available at https://www.wto.org/english/news_e/news17_e/minis_13dec17_e.htm (visited April 2, 2019).

31 MOFCOM, the Outline for BRICS Investment Facilitation Will Promote Mechanistic, systemic and Substantive Economic Cooperation among BRICS Countries, available at http://news.cri.cn/20170823/b8c82c89-b68b-2ce2-5b1f-531f270cafcd.html (visited February 22, 2019).

32 UNCTAD, Global Action Menu for Investment Facilitation, TD/B/63/CRP.2, December 1, 2016.

33 See the Chapter 2 of Brazil's investment treaties of the book.

34 *See, e.g.*, Pierre de Senarclens and Ali Kazancigil eds., *Regulating Globalization: Critical Approached to Global Governance* (Tokyo: United Nation University Press, 2007); Richard Falk, Balakrishnan Rajagopal and Jacqueline Stevens eds., *International Law and the Third World: Reshaping Justice* (Florence: Routledge, 2008).

35 According to Bin Gu, China advocates in the AIIB a multilateralism which fairly balances interests of all AIIB member states rather than privileges China as a sponsoring state. *see* Bin Gu, Chinese Multilateralism in the AIIB, 20 *Journal of International Economic Law* 137 (2017).

major host States have not concluded BITs with China and because, under the ISDS, the investment disputes allowed to be submitted for international arbitration are very limited.[36] Given the fact that most BRI countries are developing states where foreign investors are more susceptible to non-commercial risks than in developed states, it is necessary for China to update the ISDS in investment treaties, making it meaningful to protect its overseas investors. On the other hand, the fact that China is the second largest host State and substantial deficiencies still exist in Chinese national governance makes the Government of China susceptible to international claims by foreign investors in China.

Therefore, China is deeply interested with the ISDS reform and thus, in particular, actively participates in the debates within the United Nations Commission on International Trade Law (UNCITRAL). The UNCITRAL entrusted its Working Group III to work on the possible reform of ISDS since 2017.[37] The work is government-led with high-level input from all governments.[38] The Chinese delegation attends all the meetings of the Working Group III and expressed its opinions in the meetings.

Currently, the UNCITRAL appears to prefer to an institutional and multilateral approach by establishing a permanent and stand-along appellate body, or a permanent international investment court with an appellate mechanism.[39] As far as China is concerned, the Government of China submitted a formal written submission to the Working Group III on July 18 2019, stating its opinions to the possible ISDS reform.[40] In the Submission, China welcomes the ISDS reform initiative of UNCITRAL, but points out that in general, the ISDS itself already makes investment treaties meaningful enough to protect foreign investment and to improve the rule of law in host States while not necessarily threatening their sovereignty. According to China, the reform should focus on how to improve the multilateral rules and mechanisms for the settlement of current investment disputes which can safeguard the legitimate regulatory power of the host State, protect foreign investors, and enhance the confidence of

36 Congyan Cai, supra note 14, at 646–648.

37 Official Records of the General Assembly, Seventy-second Session, Supplement No. 17 (A/72/17), paras. 263 and 264.

38 UN General Assembly, Possible Reform of Investor-State Dispute Settlement (ISDS): Note by the Secretariat, A/CN.9/WG.III/WP.142, 18 September 2017, para. 3.

39 UN General Assembly, Possible Future Work in the Field of Dispute Settlement: Reforms of Investor-State Dispute Settlement (ISDS): Note by the Secretariat, A/CN.9/917, 20 April 2017.

40 Possible Reform of Investor-State Disputes Settlement: China's Submission to the Working Group III of UNCITRAL, A/CN.9/WG.III/WP.177.

various parties on the ISDS by improving the rule of law in the operation of the ISDS. Importantly, China suggests conducting research on establishing permanent appellate mechanisms, proposes mediation as an alternative to arbitration, and suggests incorporating pre-arbitration consultation procedures, among other suggestions. In short, although China is of opinion that there are deficiencies in the ISDS, it supports improvement instead of repeal.

3 China-Involved ISDS Cases

China started to attract foreign investment during the end of the 1970s, and has become the second largest investment destination in 2017, behind the United States.[41] China started to encourage outbound investment since 2000, and has now become the third major home State in the world, behind the United States and Japan.[42] In addition, China is the second largest signer of investment treaties, next to Germany. As of December 31, 2018, it has concluded 127 BITs and other 22 treaties with investment provisions.[43] However, China is not a major country involved in ISDS cases. As of March 2019 China was involved in only eight ISDS case, among which in three cases that the Chinese government acts as Respondent before the ICSID, in five cases that Chinese investors bring international claims against host States.[44] Nevertheless, it is expected that the sharp growth of Chinese outward investment, which will be enhanced by the BRI, will make China more involved in ISDS cases. Furthermore, the Chinese approach to the ISDS since the late 1990s, that "any investment dispute" is allowed to be submitted to international arbitration instead of only "the dispute over the amount of compensation of expropriation",[45] has encouraged Chinese investors to resort to the ISDS. Although Chinese culture prefers harmony, which may discourage both China's government and Chinese investors from resorting to the ISDS mechanism, it is expected that China-involved cases will gradually increase in the future.

---

41 UNCTAD, *2018 World Investment Report*, at 4.

42 UNCTAD, *2018 World Investment Report*, at 6.

43 UNCTAD, International Investment Agreements Navigator, available at https://investmentpolicyhub.unctad.org/IIA/IiasByCountry#iiaInnerMenu (visited March 11, 2019).

44 UNCTAD, Investment Dispute Settlement Navigator, available at https://investmentpolicyhub.unctad.org/ISDS/FilterByCountry (visited March 11, 2019).

45 Norah Gallagher and Wenhua Shan, *Chinese Investment Treaties: Policies and Practice* (Oxford: Oxford University Press, 2009)313–322.

TABLE 5.1 Current ISDS disputes in which China is involved as a Respondent state

Year	Short case name	Forum	Outcomes of original proceedings	Home States of investors
2017	*Hela Schwarz v. China*	ICSID	Pending	Germany
2014	*Ansung Housing v. China*	ICSID	Decided in favor of State	Republic of Korea
2011	*Ekran v. China*	ICSID	Settled	Malaysia

3.1 *China as Respondent State*

Table 5.1 shows the current ISDS disputes in which China is involved as a Respondent state.

The basic facts and major legal issues involved in the above cases are discussed as follows:

3.1.1 *Ekran v. China* (ICSID Case No. ARB/11/15)

Ekran Berhad (hereinafter "Ekran") is a Malaysian company. On May 24, 2011, it initiated an arbitration proceeding before the ICSID against the Chinese government based on the China-Israel BIT (1995) and the Malaysia-China BIT (1988). That is the first case in which China was challenged as a Respondent, and thus, both the relevant Chinese officials and the government were uncomfortable and anxious about it. China seemed not yet ready for an investment arbitration case and thus negotiated with the Claimant for peaceful settlement of the case. The two parties agreed to suspend the arbitration proceedings in July 2011. In about two years of negotiation and bargaining, the two parties eventually came to a settlement agreement without disclosing details. On May 16, 2013, the parties filed a request to the ICSID for the discontinuance of the proceedings.

The claims arose out of the local government's revocation of Claimant's subsidiary rights to a leasehold land due to an alleged failure to develop the land as stipulated under local legislation. In 1993, Ekran registered a subsidiary, Sino-Malaysia Culture & Art Co. Ltd. (Culture Co.), in Wanning-Xian, Hainan Province in China, in which Ekran held a 70% equity interest. To develop its business of arts and cultural facilities, the Culture Co. entered into a land lease agreement involving 900 hectares of land with the Wanning local government of Hainan Province, which has a 70-year leasehold from 1993 to 2063. However, after over 15 years, the Culture Co. had not developed any project on that piece of land.

Around 2007, real estate rose very fast in China, and during those years the Chinese government issued several rules and regulations to regulate the development of real estate and the prices of real estate. Accordingly, Hainan Province also amended its Regulation on the Land Administration of the Hainan Special Economic Zone in 2008 (2008 Amended) (hereinafter "the Regulation"). Article 44(2) of the Regulation provides that the right to use the land will be taken back without any compensation when the land is kept idle for more than two years. Therefore, in 2009, the Hainan government revoked the Culture Co.'s rights to the leasehold land due to its failure to develop the land.

Ekran then brought the claim before the ICSID claiming for expropriation. In all the BITs that China concluded in the 1980s and 1990s, until the one with Barbados in 1998, China only consented to refer any dispute with a foreign investor over the amount of compensation for expropriation to international arbitration. Moreover, when the China-Malaysia BIT was concluded in 1988, China had not yet joined the ICSID Convention (China Signed the ICSID Convention in 1990, and it entered into force for China in 1993), therefore, the China-Malaysia BIT provides that an investor may request an international arbitral tribunal (not the ICSID) to review the amount of compensation. According to this, Ekran was not entitled to bring the case before the ICSID. Therefore, Ekran relied on the most-favoured nation (MFN) provisions of the China-Malaysia BIT and thus based its claim on the China-Israel BIT (1995), which allows a dispute over the amount of compensation in the case of expropriation to be submitted to the ICSID.

The case was eventually settled and thus no award or decision was made.

Ekran v. China was the first case in which China acted as a Respondent in the ICSID arbitration. This dispute was related to China's first generation of BITs, which only allowed the "dispute over the amount of compensation of expropriation" to be resolved by international arbitration. However, the Claimant asserted expropriation, which obviously exceeds the scope of dispute in the BIT. Although the Claimant relied on the MFN clause and invoked the China-Israel BIT (1995), this BIT also belonged to the first generation with the same scope of ISDS. The reason that the Claimant invoked the China-Israel BIT was to justify its submission of the case to the ICSID. Therefore, this case would not be a big deal for China, but since this was the first case of its kind, China showed too much worry and lacked confidence on the ISDS arbitration and so China decided to settle with the Claimant.

Though due to the discontinuance of the proceeding the merits were not determined, the case still has some crucial legal significance, especially concerning China's BITs. The critical question concerns arbitration jurisdiction, which involves the subject matter of the case and whether the MFN provision applies. Firstly, Ekran claimed expropriation of its investment, while the China-Malaysia BIT only permits disputes over the amount of compensation for the expropriation to be submitted for international arbitration. Secondly, the China-Malaysia BIT allows the MFN treatment to be given to the investment (substantive treatment), which raises the question of whether or not it could be expanded to disputes over the investment (procedural treatment). Moreover, the question remains whether or not referring a dispute to the ICSID is a better treatment than referring it to an international arbitral tribunal. These questions were not answered in this case since it was settled.

3.1.2 *Ansung Housing v. China* (ICSID Case No. ARB/14/25)

Ansung Housing Co., Ltd. is a Korean company. On November 4, 2014, it instituted an arbitration proceeding against China at the ICSID based on the China-Korea BIT (2007). That was the second case in which China was sued for an investment dispute. This time China showed more confidence. It did not negotiate at all with Ansung for settlement. The Tribunal was constituted on September 2, 2016. Then China filed preliminary objections to dismiss the claim, which it said was manifestly without legal merits pursuant to the ICSID Arbitration Rule 41(5), because Ansung instituted the ICSID arbitration more than three years after it first acquired the knowledge that it had incurred loss or damage, rendering the claim time-barred under Article 9(7) of the China-Korea BIT. Ansung responded that the China-Korea BIT's MFN clause applies and allows Ansung to take advantage of more favourable treatment in third-party BITs concerning the time requirement. Eventually, the Tribunal found Ansung's claim to be time-barred and not protected by operation of the MFN Clause. The Tribunal found the claim hence to be manifestly without legal merit. The Tribunal rendered its award in favour of China on March 9, 2017.

The claims arose out of the local government's alleged actions in relation to Ansung's investment in the construction of a golf and country club and luxury condominiums in Sheyang-Xian, Jiangsu province. On 12 December 2006, the South Korean company Ansung Housing entered into an investment agreement on a golf course and condominium development project in Sheyang-Xian with the Sheyang Harbor Industrial Zone Administration Committee (the Committee). The project construction consisted of two phases, each of which would occupy 1,500 mu (100 hectares) of land. After the commencement of the first phase of the project, Chinese policies on real estate development changed, and the Committee could no longer provide the 1500 mu of land for the second phase at the price agreed in the investment agreement, and so Ansung would have to apply for land use rights through a public sale at higher prices. After the completion of the first phase, the Committee didn't provide the additional land necessary for the second phase. At latest by October 2011, Ansung had knowledge of loss or damage incurred on the project. On December 17 2011, Ansung had to sell its shares in the golf business to a Chinese purchaser at a low price. Ansung sent its Request for Arbitration with the ICSID electronically on October 7 2014, and physically on October 8 2014, based on the China-Korea BIT that entered into force on 1 December 2007. On November 4, 2014, the ICSID Secretary-General registered the institution of arbitration proceedings. The Tribunal issued the award on 9 March 2017 in favour of China and rejected all the claims made by Ansung.

That was the second case in which China was challenged. With the experience that came from its deep thoughts after the above *Ekran* case, this time China showed more confidence and calm. It decided to appear before the arbitration proceeding and defend its rightful interests. Moreover, China's performance in the case showed that it had a sounder understanding of the arbitration rules and was more tactful than in the previous case. It invoked the time bar in the fast-track procedure in the jurisdiction issue and succeeded. Further, its interpretation of the MFN clauses to not cover procedural provisions was more accurate and was accepted by the Tribunal.

This dispute mainly focused on the following two legal issues: 1. Does the claim that beyond arbitration limitation period constitute "manifestly without legal merit"? and 2. Does the MFN clause apply to the question of time limitation?

For the first issue, since Article 9(7) of the China-Korea BIT explicitly sets up a three-year time limitation, so the Tribunal accepted the preliminary objection advanced by China by issuing a decision sustaining the objection that the case was manifestly without legal merit due to a lack of temporal jurisdiction according to Article 41(5) of the ICSID Convention. For the second issue, the Tribunal supported China's view that the wording of Article 3 limits MFN treatment to the host State's territory and covers only "investment and business activities" which is defined as "the expansion, operation, management, maintenance, use, enjoyment, and sale or other disposal of investments", and does not include dispute settlement.

3.1.3 *Hela Schwarz v. China* (ICSID Case No. ARB/17/19)

Hela Schwarz GmbH (Hela) is a German company. On June 21, 2017, it instituted an arbitration proceeding against China before the ICSID based on the China-Germany BIT (2003). That was the third case in which China was challenged as Respondent. Now China seemed to be accustomed to investment arbitration and responded accordingly. A Tribunal was constituted on

January 8, 2018. China filed a memorial on jurisdiction, including a request to address the objections to jurisdiction as a preliminary question on October 1, 2018. The Tribunal decided to join the objections to jurisdiction to the merits of the dispute. The case is pending, and no more data is available currently.

The claims arose out of the local government's alleged actions related to an investment in Jinan-city, Shangdong Province. Hela is a German-owned spice and food additive manufacturer. It has been operating in the city of Jinan since 1996, as a joint-venture with a local meat processing company. In 1999, it was transferred to German ownership. According to Hela, Jinan government deprived it of its investment by expropriating the land which was necessary for its operation. After losing domestic administrative proceedings in China, Hela brought the claim before the ICSID under the China-Germany BIT.

That case arose from the second generation of China's BITs. China showed experience with the ISDS now, though the award is yet to be made.

3.1.4 Summary

In the above cases that China was acting as Respondent, we can find some common features:

First, all three cases are related to expropriation and brought before the ICSID for arbitration.

Second, while the counsels representing China consist of both foreign lawyers and Chinese lawyers, the foreign lawyers play a major role. This is the model China used in its WTO cases, and in this way, Chinese lawyers get to practice and will eventually become more experienced and sophisticated.

Third, the actions challenged by foreign investors were conducted by local governments, instead of the Central Government. This gives pause to the Chinese government that the major risks of being challenged come from its vast amount of local governments. China is a vast country with 34 provincial governments and about 2800 local governments. Officials of these local governments lack the awareness of the rule of law and do not know much about BITs and ISDS.

Fourth, the subjects of all the three cases are related to land, especially a change of policy regarding real estate. Over the past ten years, the real estate sector has developed steadily in China and housing prices have been increasing very fast as well. This led dramatic changes of relevant policies at both the central government level and local government level, which caused the investment disputes discussed. Frequently changing its policy is a problem in China, and the ISDS cases should serve as a warning to China to keep stable policies and laws.

TABLE 5.2 Situations in which Chinese investors bring international claims against host States

Years	Short case name	Forums	Outcomes of original proceedings	Respondent states
2007	*Tza Yap Shum v. Peru*	ICSID	Decided in favour of investor	Peru
2010	*Beijing Shougang and others v. Mongolia*	PCA	Decided in favor of State	Mongolia
2012	*Ping An v. Belgium*	ICSID	Decided in favor of State	Belgium
2014	*Beijing UrbanConstruction v. Yemen*	ICSID	Discontinued	Yemen
2017	*Sanum Investments v. Laos (I)*	PCA	Discontinued	Laos
2018	*Sanum Investments v. Laos (II)*	ICSID	Pending	Laos

3.2 *China as Home State*

Table 5.2 shows the situations in which Chinese investors bring international claims against host States. In other words, China in these cases acts as home State.

There is a clear trend that Chinese investors have been more confident on the ISDS mechanism. The basic facts and major legal issues involved in these cases are examined as follows:

3.2.1 *Tza Yap Shum v. Peru* (ICSID Case No. ARB/07/6)

On February 12, 2007, Mr. Tza Yap Shum, a citizen of Hong Kong Special Administrative Region of China, instituted arbitration proceedings at the ICSID against Peru under the China-Peru BIT (1994). Peru challenged the jurisdiction but the Tribunal confirmed its jurisdiction and competence in the Decision on Jurisdiction and Competence dated June 19, 2009. On July 7, 2011, the Tribunal rendered its award in favour of the Claimant. On November 9, 2011, Peru applied for annulment of the decision and award, and on February 12, 2015, the ad hoc Committee issued its decision on annulment, dismissing Peru's claims in its entirety and upholding the original Tribunal's award.

The claims arose out of the seizure of the bank account of the Claimant's enterprise due to tax debt and other alleged actions undertaken by Peruvian tax authorities, that the Claimant alleged resulted in the substantive deprivation of Claimant's investment. Mr. Tza Yap Shum is the major shareholder of the Peruvian company TSG Perú S.A.C. company ("TSG") which engaged in the manufacturing of food products derived from fish. According to Mr. Tza Yap Shum, in 2004, the Peruvian National Superintendence of Tax Administration ("SUNAT") started to conduct a series of actions that destroyed the commercial operations and the economic viability of TSG. SUNAT considered TSG to be an industrial company rather than as a service company operating as a financing source for the Peruvian industrial fisheries.

The audit of TSG conducted by SUNAT in 2004 resulted in the issuance in 2005 of 95 retroactive taxation decisions, resolutions and fines arising from breaches of the income tax and general sales tax laws totaling approximately US$45 million. On 28 January 2005, SUNAT issued an Enforcement Resolution to freeze TSG's bank accounts up to the amount of S/. 3,535,791 and notified fifteen Peruvian banks of its decision. Under the circumstances described, on 29 September 2006, Mr. Tza Yap Shum together with TSG submitted a Request for Arbitration against the Republic of Peru before the ICSID. The Request for Arbitration claimed that Peru violated the fair and equitable treatment, expropriation, transfer of capital and returns, and other provisions provided in the Peru-China BIT.

Peru challenged the Tribunal's jurisdiction for two reasons: first, the China-Peru BIT was concluded in 1995 when Hong Kong was not yet returned to China. Therefore, it argued, the China-Peru BIT did not apply to Hong Kong and Hong Kong citizens. Second, the BIT only allows a dispute over the amount of compensation of expropriation to be resolved in arbitration. The Tribunal decided that the China-Peru BIT applied to Tza Yap Shum who was a Chinese national and thus falls into the definition of "investor" in the BIT, and that the dispute "involving" the amount of compensation of expropriation covered the dispute over expropriation, and therefore confirmed its jurisdiction over the dispute over expropriation but dismissed the other claims. Finally, the Tribunal decided that Peru violated its obligation under the China-Peru BIT by indirectly expropriating Mr. Tza Yap Shum's investment and awarded 0.78 million USD for compensation. Then Peru filed an application for annulment of the award claiming that the Arbitral Tribunal committed a manifest excess of powers, Failure to State Reasons and Serious Departure from a Fundamental Rule of Procedure, but the ad hoc Committee dismissed all the claims in its Decision on Annulment.

This is the first case in which Chinese investor challenged a host State under a Chinese BIT. However, this case also showed two serious problems in Chinese BITs: firstly, whether Chinese BITs apply to Hong Kong and Macao Special

Administrative Regions (SAR); and secondly, whether the dispute involving the amount of compensation of expropriation covers disputes over expropriation. The Tribunal's affirmative decision received criticisms. Professor An Chen, a high-profile Chinese scholar in the field of international economic law, asserted that the China-Peru BIT could not be directly applied to the Hong Kong Special Administrative Region because under China's "One Country, Two Systems" policy, Hong Kong has high autonomy and has concluded several its own BITS. The Tribunal's broad interpretation of the dispute "involving" the amount of compensation over expropriation showed its tendency to expand its jurisdiction. Nevertheless, the Tribunal's decision has had a profound impact on future cases related to Chinese BITS, such as the case of *Sanum v. Laos*, which will be discussed later on.

3.2.2 *Beijing Shougang and others v. Mongolia* (PCA Case No. 2010-20)

On February 12, 2010, three companies organized under Chinese laws, Beijing Shougang Mining Investment Company Ltd., China Heilongjiang International Economic & Technical Cooperative Corp., and Qinhuangdaoshi Qinlong International Industrial Co. Ltd, brought a case before the Permanent Court of Arbitration (PCA) against Mongolia for arbitration according to the UNCITRAL Arbitration Rules under the China-Mongolia BIT (1991). The Tribunal rendered an award in favour of the state on 30 June 2017 decided that it lacked jurisdiction over the dispute. On September 28, 2017, the Claimants filed a petition at the United States District Court Southern District of New York to vacate the Tribunal's arbitral award declining to exercise arbitral jurisdiction and compel arbitration. The petition was dismissed in the early 2020.

The claims arose out of Mongolian government's cancellation of licenses held by the claimants in the Tumurtei iron ore mine. In 2002, the Claimants formed a joint venture with a Mongolian company that held a license to exploit certain iron ore deposits located in Mongolia to develop these deposits commercially. In 2006, a new government took power in Mongolia. Due to the increased price of iron ore, the new Mongolian government ultimately revoked the license. The Claimants asserted that the revocation constituted expropriation and referred the case to PCA. The Tribunal interpreted the dispute "involving" the amount of compensation for expropriation as being a dispute over the amount and thus ruled it lacked jurisdiction over the dispute over expropriation.

In contrast to the Tza Yap Shum case, this Tribunal took a different approach to the interpretation of the scope of disputes and strictly restricted its jurisdiction to dispute only about the amount of expropriation.

3.2.3 *Ping An v. Belgium* (ICSID Case No. ARB/12/29)

On September 19, 2012, Ping An Life Insurance Company of China, Limited and Ping An Insurance (Group) Company of China, Limited (Ping An) instituted arbitration proceedings at the ICSID against Belgium under the Belgium-Luxembourg Economic Union (BLEU)-China BIT (1984) and the Belgium-Luxembourg Economic Union (BLEU)-China BIT (2005). On December 20, 2013, the Respondent filed a notice of intent to file objections to jurisdiction and later the proceeding on the merits was suspended. On April 30, 2015, the Tribunal rendered its award in favour of Belgium, declining to exercise its jurisdiction.

Ping An is the largest shareholder in the Belgian-Dutch financial institution Fortis. The claims arose out of the Belgium Government's bailout, and subsequent nationalisation and sale to a third party, of the financial institution in which the claimants had invested, in the context of the 2008 financial crisis. Between October 2007 and July 2008, the Claimants acquired shares in Fortis in the open market and became Fortis Bank's single largest shareholder. On September 15 2008, Lehman Brothers collapsed, and the interbank lending market dried up. On September 28 2008, Belgium acquired a 49.93% stake in Fortis Bank in return for a payment of €4.7 billion. Finally, Belgium transferred 75% of the shares in Fortis to BNP Paribas, which caused huge losses to Ping An. After failing in negotiations with Belgium, Ping An brought the case before the ICSID, alleging that Belgium's behaviour was a direct expropriation and violated other provisions of the 1984 BITs.

The Claimants relied on the BLEU-China BIT (1984) for the substance of their claim and on the BLEU-China BIT (2005) for the jurisdiction of this Tribunal, probably because the former BIT had a narrow scope regarding disputes while the latter had a broader scope for international arbitration. The BIT (1984) entered into force on October 5, 1986, while the BIT (2005) entered into force on December 1 2009. The BIT (1984) allowed a dispute on an amount of compensation for expropriation to be submitted for international arbitration, while the BIT (2005) allowed a legal dispute to be submitted to the ICSID for resolution. The BIT (2005) also provided for the "transition" of the two BITs, and stated that the new BIT would not apply to any dispute or any claim concerning an investment which was already under judicial or arbitral process before its entry into force. Such disputes and claims would continue to be settled according to the old BIT. Belgium challenged the jurisdiction of the Tribunal majorly based *on Ratione Temporis* and other reasons, because the dispute between the parties arose before the entry into force of the 2005 BIT. The Tribunal accepted the Respondent's argument and ruled it did not have jurisdiction.

Again, this case involved the first generation and the second generation of Chinese BITs, especially concerning the scope of dispute for international arbitration and the transition of the old and the new BITs.

3.2.4 *Beijing Urban Construction v. Yemen* (ICSID Case No. ARB/14/30)

On December 3, 2014, Beijing Urban Construction Group Co. Ltd. (Beijing Urban), a Chinese state-owned enterprise, instituted an arbitration proceeding at the ICSID against Yemen based on the China-Yemen BIT (1998). Yemen challenged the Tribunal's jurisdiction by asserting that state-owned enterprises cannot bring claims before the ICSID and that the dispute is not concerning the amount of compensation for expropriation. The Tribunal rendered a decision on jurisdiction dated 31 May 2017 in favour of the Claimant. Then the parties settled the case, and the arbitration proceedings were declared discontinued on 7 June 2018.

The claims arose out of the alleged forced deprivation of Claimant's assets and contract concerning a project for the construction of an airport terminal in Sana'a, Yemen. Beijing Urban won the tender by the Sana'a International Airport project (phase 2) for selection of the construction contractor for a new International Terminal Building. On 28 February 2006, Beijing Urban entered into a construction contract with the Yemen Civil Aviation and Meteorology Authority (CAMA). Beijing Urban alleged that in July 2009, the Yemeni government unlawfully deprived it of its investment in Yemen by employing its military forces and security apparatus to assault and detain its employees and forcibly deny it access to the Project site and thus its ability to perform its contractual obligations. On 22 July 2009, Beijing Urban alleged, following weeks of state-orchestrated harassment and intimidation, CAMA gave notice of its intention to terminate the Contract based on its failure to return to the site to complete the works. Beijing Urban said it was prevented from performing the Contract by CAMA and the Yemeni government.

Yemen challenged the Tribunal's jurisdiction by asserting that Beijing Urban was a state-owned entity and did not qualify as a "national of another Contracting State." Further, it asserted that the China-Yemen BIT only allows a dispute relating to the amount of compensation for expropriation be brought to the ICSID for resolution, and the MFN clause of the BIT did not apply to the dispute settlement provisions. Both Parties accepted the Broches test which was formulated by Aaron Broches, the first Secretary-General of the ICSID, that a government-owned corporation should not be disqualified as a 'national of another Contracting State' unless it acts as an agent for the government or is discharging an inherently governmental function. The Tribunal decided that Beijing Urban met the *Broches test*, took the broad interpretation approach as to the dispute concerning the amount of compensation, denied the application of MFN clause to dispute settlement, and finally affirmed its jurisdiction over those claims related to the Claimant's allegations of expropriation.

This case raised three critical issues for Chinese investors. First, it raised concerns about what the scope of the dispute is, whether the dispute involves the amount of compensation, or any dispute. Second it showed that the issue of whether the MFN clause applies to the dispute settlement provisions is settled. Moreover, and third, the question was raised whether a state-owned enterprise qualifies as national of another contracting state. China has a large number of state-owned enterprises accounting for 18% of the global total, and those state-owned enterprises have played a key role in China's outbound investment.[46]

3.2.5 *Sanum Investments v. Laos (I)* (PCA Case No. 2013-13) and *Sanum Investments v. Laos (II)* (ICSID Case No. ADHOC/17/1)

Sanum Investments Limited is involved in two cases based on interrelated facts.

3.2.5.1 *Sanum Investments v. Laos (I)*

The Claimant here is Sanum Investments Limited ("Sanum" or "Claimant"), an entity incorporated in the Macao Special Administrative Region of China ("Macao"). On 14 August 2013, the Claimant commenced arbitration proceedings using the UNCITRAL Arbitration Rules at PCA against the Laos based on the China-Laos BIT (1993). The Respondent challenged the Tribunal's jurisdiction by asserting among other issues that: first, the BIT does not apply to Macao which was handed over to China and established as a special administrative region in 1999, much later than the conclusion of the BIT; second, the BIT only allows a dispute involving the amount of compensation for expropriation be submitted to an ad hoc arbitral tribunal; and thirdly, the MFN clause does not apply to dispute settlement provisions. After analysis, the Tribunal concluded that the China-Laos BIT was applicable to the Macao SAR. The Tribunal also took a broad interpretation of the scope of dispute as covering disputes involving expropriation, not only the dispute over the amount of compensation for expropriation. Finally, the Tribunal rendered its award on December 13, 2013, in Singapore affirming its jurisdiction to arbitrate only the expropriation claims of Sanum.

On 7 January 2014, the Laotian Ministry of Foreign Affairs sent a letter to the PRC Embassy in Vientiane, Laos stating its view that the China-Laos BIT

46 UNCTAD, World Investment Report 2017, at 31, available at https://unctad.org/en/PublicationsLibrary/wir2017_en.pdf (visited March 27, 2019).

did not extend to Macau, and on 9 January 2014, received a letter from the PRC Embassy in Vientiane, Laos stating its view that the PRC-Laos BIT did not apply to Macau "unless both China and Laos make separate arrangements in the future".

On 10 January 2014, Laos applied to the Singapore High Court in Singapore, the seat of the arbitration. The application requested the court vacate the Tribunal's decision on jurisdiction. Laos' two submissions concerned the applicability of China-Laos BIT to the Macau SAR and the interpretation of the scope of dispute for international arbitration. Finally, the Singapore High Court made its judgement on 20 January 2015 concluding that the China-Laos BIT does not apply to Macau, and the Tribunal did not possess subject-matter jurisdiction over the defendant's expropriation claims because only disputes over the amount of compensation for expropriation can be submitted to arbitration.

On 20 July 2015, Sanum appealed against the judgment made by the Singapore High Court to the Court of Appeals of Singapore. During the proceedings, China's Ministry of Foreign Affairs (MFA) replied to Lao's letter on 18 November 2015, confirming the letter from the PRC Embassy in Vientiane, Laos stating that the previous letter had been sent with its authorization. However, the Court of Appeals of Singapore rendered its judgement on 29 September 2016 reversing the High Court's decision and concluding that the PRC-Laos BIT does apply to Macau and second, that the Tribunal has subject-matter jurisdiction over the claims brought by Sanum.

Less than one month after the judgement, on October 21, 2016, China's Foreign Ministry Spokesperson responded to the judgement in a Regular Press Conference. It stressed again that the geographical scope of application of the China-Laos investment agreement is a question of fact concerning acts of state, which is up to the contracting parties to decide. China has confirmed twice in diplomatic notes that the China-Laos investment agreement does not apply to Macao SAR. The ruling made by the Singaporean court on this question of fact is, in the Chinese view, incorrect.

The Chinese side handles the application of treaties to Hong Kong and Macao SARs in line with the "one country, two systems" policy and the Basic Laws in Hong Kong and Macao. To be specific, the Chinese central government decides whether or not the international treaties to which the People's Republic of China is or becomes a party apply to the SARs based on the circumstances and their needs after seeking the views of the governments of the SARs. The SARs can conclude agreements with foreign countries in their own in the appropriate fields, including economy, finance, trade and investment, following the Basic Laws or under the specific authorization of the central government.

Therefore, as a principle, the investment agreements between the central government and foreign countries do not apply to SARs, unless otherwise decided by the central government after seeking the views of the SAR governments and consulting with the other contracting parties of the agreement.[47]

Interestingly, on June 5 2014, Sanum and the Dutch company, Lao Holdings N.V. who challenged Laos at the ICSID for the same events (Case No. ARB(AF)/12/6) concluded a settlement agreement with Laos and terminated the arbitration proceedings.

3.2.5.2 *Sanum Investments v. Laos (II)*

Sanum alleged that the Laotian Government breached the settlement agreement concluded by the Claimant and Lao Holdings N.V. with the Government in 2014. On April 27 2017, the Tribunal was constituted under the ICSID Arbitration (Additional Facility) Rules because Laos is not a contracting state of the ICSID Convention. The Respondent challenged the Tribunal's jurisdiction. The case is pending and no more information is available currently.

3.2.6 Summary

In the above cases where Chinese investors acted as claimants, we can find some common features:

First, all cases are related to expropriation and brought before the ICSID or administered by PCA.

Second, the key issues are concerning: (1) the geographical application of Chinese BITs, i.e., whether they cover Hong Kong and Macau; (2) the scope of dispute for international arbitration, i.e., whether the dispute involving the amount of compensation for expropriation covers the dispute over expropriation; (3) the application of the MFN clauses, i.e., the MFN clause applies to the procedural provisions.

Third, the Tribunals in the above cases gave different interpretations as to the above issues.

Fourth, the Chinese government should learn lessons from the above cases and formulate its own consistent position as to the above three issues and incorporate them in future new BITs.

---

47 Embassy of the People's Republic of China in the United States of America, Foreign Ministry Spokesperson Hua Chunying's Regular Press Conference on October 21, 2016, available at http://www.china-embassy.org/eng/fyrth/t1407743.htm (visited April 20, 2019).

4 Innovations of China's ISDS Mechanisms at the Domestic Level[48]

In addition to actively participating in the UNCITRAL ISDS reform, China also recently has sought to innovate the ISDS mechanism at the domestic level for trial and experiment.

China has taken efforts to innovate the ISDS mechanism over the last few years. The first is to extend the jurisdiction of existing commercial arbitral institutions in China to cover foreign investment disputes. The second is the creation of new Chinese commercial courts to handle contractual investment disputes. The third is to establish joint arbitration centers with some states which are major of China's investment destinations, for instance, South Africa.

4.1 *Extension of Jurisdiction of Existing Commercial Arbitral Institutions in China*

There are many arbitral institutions in China which handle domestic and international commercial disputes involving Chinese businesses, but not investor-state disputes. In recent years, some of the Chinese commercial arbitration institutions have expanded their jurisdiction to cover investor-state disputes.

The Shenzhen Court of International Arbitration (SCIA) and the China International Economic Trade Arbitration Commission (CIETAC) pioneer this new approach. In 2016, the SCIA updated its arbitration rules enabling it to handle investor-state disputes.[49] The SCIA also formulated rules guiding the administration of investor-state disputes under the Arbitration Rules of the UNCITRAL.[50] Moreover, in 2017, the Shenzhen municipal government merged the Shenzhen Arbitration Commission into the SCIA to make the latter more competitive.[51] The SCIA is now working on building its capacity to attract

48 The major body of this part was one part of my separate article published in AJIL Unbound (Vol. 112, 2018).

49 The SCIA 2016 Arbitration Rules provide that the SCIA "accepts arbitration cases related to investment disputes between states and nationals of other states." SCIA Arbitration Rules, art. 2, ¶ 2. Available at http://www.sccietac.org/web/doc/view_rules/861.html, (visited September 5, 2018).

50 Guidelines for the Administration of Arbitration under the UNCITRAL Arbitration Rules, available at http://www.sccietac.org/web/doc/view_rules/863.html (visited September 20, 2018).

51 Herbert Smith Freehills, Arbitration Notes: SCIA and SAC Arbitration Institutions Merge to Form New Arbitration Centre in Shenzhen, available at https://hsfnotes.com/arbitration/2018/02/14/scia-and-sca-arbitration-institutions-merge-to-form-new-arbitration-centre-in-shenzhen/, (visited February 14, 2018).

more ISDS cases. Importantly, the SCIA entered into a Cooperation Agreement with the ICSID in June 2018.[52]

The reform of CIETAC – the oldest and largest arbitral institution in China – is no less significant. In 2017, the CIETAC for the first time adopted and implemented Arbitration Rules for International Investment Disputes.[53] The Rules explicitly provide that the CIETAC can exercise jurisdiction over international investment disputes arising out of contracts, treaties, laws, and regulations, or other instruments between an investor and a State.

4.2 *Creation of New Chinese Commercial Courts*

In June 2018, the Supreme People's Court (SPC) of China officially established First International Commercial Court in Shenzhen and Second International Commercial Court in Xi'an in late June 2018,[54] both under the supervision and coordination of the SPC's Fourth Civil Division.[55] These courts initially appeared to be designed with a focus on disputes concerned with BRI countries,[56] but they finally have been given more jurisdiction to handle disputes concerned with other countries as well.[57] Importantly, the courts were initially thought

52 SCIA Concludes Cooperation Agreement with ICSID in Washington, D.C., Shenzhen Court of International Arbitration, available at http://www.sccietac.org/web/news/detail/1745.html (visited June 27, 2018).

53 China International Economic and Trade Arbitration Commission International Investment Arbitration Rules (For Trial Implementation), China Council for the Promotion of International Trade (China Chamber of International Commerce), available at http://www.cietac.org/index.php?m=Page&a=index&id=390&l=en (visited July 1, 2018). The Rules entered into force on October 1, 2017.

54 The First International Commercial Court and the Second International Commercial Court of the Supreme People's Court Started to Operate Officially, China International Commercial Court, available at http://cicc.court.gov.cn/html/1/219/208/209/814.html (visited June 29, 2018).

55 Opinion Concerning the Establishment of the Belt and Road International Commercial Dispute Resolution Mechanism and Institutions, China International Commercial Court, available at http://cicc.court.gov.cn/html/1/219/208/210/819.html (visited June 27, 2018).

56 This much is apparent from the title of the most important document in the creation of the international commercial courts. *See* Opinion Concerning the Establishment of the Belt and Road International Commercial Dispute Resolution Mechanism and Institutions, China International Commercial Court, available at http://cicc.court.gov.cn/html/1/219/208/210/819.html (visited June 27, 2018). The opinion was reviewed and passed by the Central Leading Group for Comprehensively Deepening Reform on January 23, 2018, and officially issued by the General Office of the Communist Party Central Committee and the General Office of the State Council of the People's Republic of China on June 28, 2018.

57 Provisions of the Supreme People's Court on Several Issues Regarding the Establishment of the International Commercial Court, China International Commercial Court, available at http://cicc.court.gov.cn/html/1/219/199/201/817.html (visited June 27, 2018).

to possibly hear investor-state disputes. According to Judge Gao Xiaoli of the SPC, who now sits as a judge at First International Commercial Court in Shenzhen, the SPC considered the idea that the would-be commercial courts would have jurisdiction over three types of investment and trade disputes: state-state disputes; investor-state disputes; and disputes between commercial parties. According to Jude Gao, this followed the phenomenon that some states, for instance, Canada, had established courts to hear investor-state disputes. Therefore, the SPC considered the possibility that Chinese courts could do so as well.[58] On June 27, 2018 two days before the inauguration of the two commercial courts, the SPC released a judicial note regarding the two courts. At the press conference on June 28, 2018, a SPC judge explained that the courts would accept international commercial disputes between equal commercial entities.[59] This explanation clearly precludes newly established commercial courts from handling treaty-based investor-state disputes. However, they might still exercise jurisdiction over investment disputes between investors and host States arising out of state contracts.

Importantly, the newly established Chinese commercial courts are distinct from traditional courts or institutions of arbitration and mediation in that they aim to create a one-stop shop for dispute resolution, linking litigation, arbitration, and mediation. To realize this goal, the SPC established an International Commercial Expert Committee which comprises legal professionals in China and abroad. The commercial courts, when they deem necessary, invite the Committee to help handle disputes by, for instance, providing legal opinions for commercial courts or sitting as conciliator for the settlement of disputes.[60] The commercial courts will cooperate with international arbitration and conciliation institutions to build a one-stop shop for dispute resolution.[61] The idea of establishing a one-stop shop for dispute resolution draws inspiration from

58 *Update on China's International Commercial Court*, Supreme People's Court Monitor Blog, https://supremepeoplescourtmonitor.com/2018/03/11/update-on-chinas-international-commercial-court/ (visited March 11, 2018).

59 *See* The State Council Information Office Held a Press Conference on the "Opinion on the Establishment of 'The Belt and Road' International Commercial Dispute Settlement Mechanism and Institutions" available at http://cicc.court.gov.cn/html/1/219/208/210/769.html (visited June 28, 2018).

60 The SPC, Decision Regarding the Establishment of the International Commercial Expert Committee, August 24, 2018, available at http://cicc.court.gov.cn/html/1/219/199/201/817.html (visited June 27, 2018).

61 Provisions of the Supreme People's Court on Several Issues Regarding the Establishment of the International Commercial Court, Article 11, http://cicc.court.gov.cn/html/1/219/208/210/817.html (visited July 1, 2018).

the Singapore International Commercial Court,[62] the Singapore International Arbitration Centre,[63] and the Singapore International Mediation Centre,[64] which operate in tandem to provide a complete suite of options for the resolution of cross-border disputes.

4.3 *Formation of Joint Arbitration Centers*

The establishment of joint arbitration centers represents a very important innovation. At the China-Africa Johannesburg Summit and the 6th Ministerial Conference of the Forum on China-Africa Cooperation, China and fifty African countries accepted a proposal by China Law Society to establish the China-Africa Joint Arbitration Center (CAJAC).[65] Thus far, the CAJAC has set up five centers: three in China (Shanghai, Beijing, and Shenzhen) and two in Africa (Johannesburg and Nairobi). In these locations, the CAJAC will provide arbitration, mediation, and conciliation services[66] to commercial disputes between African and Chinese parties. The creation of CAJAC reflects not only Chinese interests, but also the desire of African countries, many of which are dissatisfied with the established international tribunals whose rulings have mostly gone against them.[67] In this sense, the new mechanism reflects a win-win strategy between China and Africa. Together these ISDS reforms offer a number of new options to Chinese investors. They were created primarily for the BRI, but are not limited to disputes arising from investments in that domain.

These innovations could be understood as reflecting an important facet of China's broader international strategy. In particular, the recent innovations aim to furnish adequate protection to Chinese investors in foreign countries,

---

62 SICC, Singapore International Chamber of Commerce, available at http://www.sicc.com.sg, (visited June 5, 2018).

63 SIAC, Singapore International Arbitration Centre, available at http://www.siac.org.sg (visited June 5, 2018).

64 SIMC, Singapore Mediation Centre, available at http://mediation.com.sg (visited June 5, 2018).

65 China-Africa Joint Arbitration Centre Shanghai, available at http://www.shiac.org/CAJAC/aboutus_E.aspx?page=3 (visited July 17, 2018); The Forum on China-Africa Cooperation Johannesburg Action Plan (2016–2018), available at http://www.focac.org/eng/ltda/dwjbzjjhys_1/t1327961.htm (visited July 17, 2018).

66 The China Africa Joint Arbitration Centre, available at http://dentons.com/en/insights/newsletters/2017/january/26/south-africa-newsletter/south-africanewsletter-january-edition/the-china-africa-joint-arbitration-centre (visited January 26, 2017).

67 Francis Kariuki, The Vision of Co-Building China-Africa Joint Arbitration Centres in Different Legal Systems, available at http://www.kmco.co.ke/attachments/article/195/Co-building%20China-Africa%20Joint%20Arbitration%20Centres%20in%20Different%20Legal%20Systems.pdf (visited June 15, 2018).

particularly developing states; actively shape international discourses on international investment law; and offer alternative, Chinese-initiated institutions that will break the monopoly of the West.

5 Concluding Remarks

The BRI has significant impacts on China's foreign investment law and policy. In particular, it enhances China's positive attitude toward ISDS reform, which is demonstrated by China's principled position expressed in debates concerning the ISDS reform within the UNCITRAL.

China's government and Chinese investors do not have much experience in handling the ISDS practice, but it is expected that the capability will improve over time. Nevertheless, the perception that China's government would face growing risk of being claimed or being threatened to claim by foreign investors is an important factor that has significant implication on China's ISDS policy. Therefore, it comes as no surprise that, while China is active in participating in the multilateral debates on the ISDS reform, it endeavors to develop new mechanisms to handle investor-state disputes both at the domestic level and at the regional level. In particular, China has an ambition to build itself into a major centre for the resolution of international economic disputes.

CHAPTER 6

Investor Protection in South Africa – Eroded Bit by Bit?

Engela C. Schlemmer

1 Introduction

South Africa officially joined the BRIC in April 2011[1] following which the BRICS Trade and Investment Cooperation Framework and Trade and Investment Facilitation Action Plan was endorsed. At that time South Africa had bilateral investment treaties with China[2] and the Russian Federation,[3] but merely a memorandum of understanding on the promotion of trade and investment with Brazil[4] and no agreement with India.[5] In 2015, the Strategy for the BRICS Economic Partnership was adopted, which was considered to be the fundamental guideline for expanding trade and investment within BRICS.[6]

---

1 Minutes of Proceedings of the National Assembly of 14 June 2011 *Unrevised Hansard*. At the time, strong relations already existed between India, Brazil and South Africa in the IBSA Dialogue Forum which continues. Available at https://pmg.org.za/hansard/18171/ (visited September 14, 2019).

2 The agreement was signed in 1997 entered into force on 1 April 1998. Available at https://treaties.dirco.gov.za/dbtw-wpd/images/19971230%20CHINA%20PROTECTION%20OF%20INVESTMENTS.pdf (visited September 14, 2019).

3 The agreement was signed in 1998 and came into force on 12 April 2000. Available at https://treaties.dirco.gov.za/dbtw-wpd/images/19981123RussiaProtectionofInvestments.PDF (visited September 14, 2019).

4 It was signed and came into force on 9 October 2009, available at https://treaties.dirco.gov.za/dbtw-wpd/images/20091009BrazilTradeandInvestment.pdf (visited September 14, 2019).

5 During this period, the South African government was busy reviewing its international investment policy framework. See the discussion in Section 2. An IBSA Trade and Investment Working Group was established in 2004 which has as one of its objectives the fostering of investment; the working group identified that "[e]fforts aimed at facilitating intra-IBSA investment" took place which included "business seminars as well as international trade and investment (ITI) initiatives." However, the areas it identified that still need to be explored included trade and Investment Promotion activities – IBSA Trade and Investment Working Group, available at http://www.ibsa-trilateral.org/images/stories/documents/IBSA%20Trade%20and%20Investment%20rev%20KM.pdf (visited December 14, 2018).

6 *See* "Outlines for BRICS Investment Facilitation", available at https://www.tralac.org/documents/resources/external-relations/brics/1612-outlines-for-brics-investment-facilitation-july-2017/file.html (visited September 14, 2019).

 | DOI:10.1163/9789004376991_007

Before the 2018 BRICS Summit in Johannesburg, Deloitte, in support of the South African Department of Trade and Industry, published *A Review of South Africa's Trade and Investment Relationship with BRIC*[7] which highlighted South Africa's trade and investment relations with BRIC countries. However, in this review, there is no reference to the existing bilateral investment treaties which is telling regarding the current fragmented and – to an extent – uncertain position relating to investor protection in South Africa.[8]

According to Deloitte, BRIC is hailed for 'together officially invest[ing] a total of US$17.8bn in 189 projects and creat[ing] 36,852 jobs in South Africa' between 2003 and 2017.[9] It is obvious that investor protection may play an important role in future relations between the BRICS countries and to that extent is important that investors from the BRIC who might need to rely on the legal protection of their investments in South Africa, other than through the normal remedies that apply to breaches of contract and the like, are informed of their potential legal position. Not all investors from the BRIC countries will fall under the protection of an investment agreement, there is thus no uniformity in the protection provided to investors, and this is not only in terms of the BRICS-grouping, but also in a broader context. In the following exposition, the focus will first be on South Africa's international investment treaties (Section 2); second on its policy change in relation to the dispute settlement mechanisms (Section 3); third on its current approach to BITs (Section 4); this is followed by the Protection of Investment Act (Section 5); efforts to seek a balance between investor protection and state sovereignty (Section 6); an assessment of the different bases of investor protection currently in South Africa (Section 7); and lastly investor protection in the SADC (Section 8).

Notwithstanding the call of the BRICS Trade and Investment Cooperation Framework published in 2013 for "mutually beneficial outcomes ... according to the principles of equality, transparency, efficiency, mutual understanding and consensus", "sharing policy practices"[10] and the Outlines for BRICS Investment

7 *See* Deloitte *A Review of South Africa's Trade and Investment Relationship with BRIC*, available at https://www.tralac.org/documents/resources/external-relations/brics/2105-brics-15-year-review-of-south-africas-trade-and-investment-relationship-with-bric-july-2018/file.html (visited September 14, 2019).

8 According to the South African Department of Trade and Industry, both these BITs are still in force (email communication on file with the author).

9 Deloitte, *supra* note 7, at 19.

10 "BRICS Trade and Investment Cooperation Framework", available at https://www.gov.za/brics-trade-and-investment-cooperation-framework (visited September 14, 2019).

Facilitation,[11] issues such as investor protection and investor-state dispute settlement mechanism are not at the forefront of discussions even though there are various permutations in the different BRICS countries and companies are urged to invest in BRICS. That the BRICS countries "fully preserve the right to regulate, national policy space, policy making and approaches to investment in other bilateral, plurilateral and multilateral frameworks and processes" should alert investors to the potential pitfalls that may lie ahead as can be seen from the South African example to be discussed.

2 An Overview of South Africa's Bilateral Investment Treaties and Investment Policy

2.1 *Introduction*

Since the early 1990s, South Africa has signed a number of BITs presumably to give comfort to investors, both existing and new, that their investments would be protected under the new dispensation.[12] It was still unclear at this stage what direction the economic policy of the new government would take, but the signing of investment promotion and protection agreements showed a measure of good faith on the side of the government. The protection of property, one of the cornerstones of the bill of rights, also added to the sense that investors and their investments would be protected.[13] But as will be seen, this is no longer the case. The South African parliament approved a proposal to amend its constitution to permit expropriation without compensation.[14] The process

11 See "Outlines for BRICS Investment Facilitation Annex II to the 7th Meeting of the BRICS Trade Ministers Statement August 31, 2017", available at http://www.brics.utoronto.ca/docs/170831-investment.html (visited September 14, 2019).

12 This section is based on a revision of myarticle that appeared in the 31 *ICSID Review* 167 (2016) 167–193 (Engela C. Schlemmer, An Overview of South Africa's Bilateral Investment Treaties and Investment Policy). See also Engela C. Schlemmer, Bilateral Investment Treaty Overview – South Africa, *Investment Claims* IC-OV 24 ZA (2015).

13 A bill of rights formed part of the interim Constitution (Constitution of the Republic of South Africa Act 200 of 1993; it entered into force 27 April 1994) and the current Constitution of the Republic of South Africa, 1996 (it entered into force 4 February 1997). The property clause is contained in Section 25 of the Constitution. "Property" is deemed to include *all* patrimonial rights and is not limited to real rights.

14 See "Review of Parliament 2018". It reads that "there was no unanimity on this and ultimately the majority view prevailed, *which recommended that Section 25 of the Constitution be amended to make it explicitly clear that expropriation of land without compensation by*

to amend the Constitution will take a while but once the amendment is done and it becomes constitutionally possible to expropriate without compensating the owner, the fate of nationals and foreign investors owning property in South Africa is not certain. A Draft Expropriation Bill[15] has since been published for public comment and it contains provisions which make it possible to expropriate land without having to pay compensation.[16]

The current political situation is in stark contrast to the position shortly after South Africa returned to the international scene in the early 1990s when many of the companies and corporations who disinvested from South Africa, returned, which signalled high investor confidence in the country.[17] The *World Investment Report 2018*[18] paints a less than rosy picture by reporting that foreign investment to South Africa declined by 41 per cent "as the country was beset by an underperforming commodity sector and political uncertainty".[19] The political uncertainty referred to may amongst others, relate to possible amendments to the Constitution and other legislation which may have a direct

the state in the public interest should be one mechanism to address the injustices of the past' ('Review of Parliament 2018", available at https://pmg.org.za/blog/Review%20of%20Parliament%202018.... visited October 1, 2019) – emphasis added.

15 Draft Expropriation Bill, 2019 published on 21 December 2018 for public comment – *Government Gazette* 42127 of 21 December 2018, available at https://pmg.org.za/bill/862/ (visited September 30, 2019).

16 Clause 12(3) of the draft bill reads as follows: "It may be just and equitable for nil compensation to be paid where land is expropriated in the public interest, having regard to all relevant circumstances, including but not limited to: (a) Where the land is occupied or used by a labour tenant, as defined in the Land Reform (Labour Tenants) Act, 1996 (Act No. 3 of 1996); (b) where the land is held for purely speculative purposes; (c) where the land is owned by a state-owned corporation or other state-owned entity; (d) where the owner of the land has abandoned the land; (e) where the market value of the land is equivalent to, or less than, the present value of direct state investment or subsidy in the acquisition and beneficial capital improvement of the land." It will take some time before the bill may become law and the whole process of land reform, amending the Constitution and expropriation without compensation which has already been the subject of litigation might see the inside of court rooms in the months to come.

17 See *South African Business Guidebook* (2006/2007) 19. This does not mean, however, that the return was due to the existence or conclusion of BITs – it remains a contentious issue whether foreign direct investment really increases with the existence of BITs. See in this regard Susan Franck, Foreign Direct Investment, Investment Treaty Arbitration, and the Rule of Law, 19 *Global Business and Development Law Journal* 338(2007) 354 ff; The Economist Intelligence Unit, *Risk and Return – Foreign Direct Investment and the Rule of Law* (2015).

18 UNCTAD, *World Investment Report 2018*, at 4.

19 UNCTAD, *World Investment Report 2018*, at 42 and the sources referred to.

impact on the legal position of foreign investments especially in relation to statements made on expropriation without compensation.

2.2 *The Constitutional Requirements*

The requirements that have to be complied with before an international agreement can bind South Africa are contained in the Constitution of the Republic of South Africa, 1996. For a treaty to bind South Africa at an international level Section 231 of the Constitution prescribes particular procedures to be followed and a distinction is also made between two types of agreement.[20] The first type of agreement binds the Republic only after it has been approved by resolution in both the National Assembly and the National Council of Provinces[21] and the second type, which is referred to as "technical, administrative or executive agreements, or agreements which do not require either ratification or accession", can be concluded by the executive alone and are exempt from the lengthy parliamentary procedure. Parliament merely needs to be notified of these agreements within a reasonable time.

The Constitution does not give any indication as to what type of agreements would be considered technical, administrative or executive but in the *Manual on Executive Acts* issued by the Presidency, practical guidelines are offered to government departments and the Office of the State Law Adviser. In terms of these guidelines, a few categories of international agreements would fall under this designation, namely agreements which are departmentally specific; agreements which are not of major political or other significance;[22] and agreements which have no financial consequences; and do not affect domestic law.[23] It is, however, not emphatically stated that if an agreement meets any one or more of these qualifiers, it will accordingly not be classifiable as a technical, administrative or executive agreement. This leaves us with uncertainty as

20 See in general Neville Botha, Treaty making in South Africa: A reassessment, 25 *South African Yearbook of International Law* (2000), 72; *Manual on Executive Acts of the President of the Republic of South Africa Revised Version* (2006) (hereinafter *The Manual*), chapter 5, available at http://www.dfa.gov.za/foreign/bilateral/conclusion_agreement0316.pdf (visited September 25, 2019) (this Manual serves as a guide to the practice of the Office of the Chief State Law Advisor).

21 This means that prior to signing the agreement, in essence, approval should be given by both houses of Parliament.

22 This particular aspect might be problematic when it comes to BITs especially when one looks at the potential impact that the obligations in a BIT may have for future policy changes and decisions of a government. The same may apply to the reference to 'no financial consequences' when one considers the severe financial consequences the government faced with the investment arbitrations that took place.

23 *The Manual*, *supra* note 20, at 5.5.

to whether the mere fact that any investment agreement that per definition has both financial consequences and may affect domestic law (for example an expropriation of foreign ownership which would (currently still) require compensation), will accordingly not be classifiable as a technical administrative or executive agreement. But for this uncertainty, bilateral investment treaties would thus seem to fall under technical, administrative and executive agreements;[24] these agreements also seldom require ratification[25] or accession. The absence of a ratification requirement is also a characteristic of most technical, administrative and executive agreements.[26] The negotiating parties normally decide during the negotiation phase when they would like a particular agreement to enter into force; the inclusion of a clause in a BIT to the effect that the BIT will only come into force once the parties have notified each other that their respective constitutional requirements have been complied with, does not affect this.[27]

It is thus clear that since the South African parliament was not required to grant permission for these agreements to be concluded and that these agreements were not required to be debated in parliament,[28] no barriers existed,

24 *The Manual* (*supra* note 20) states that technical, administrative and executive agreements are agreements "between two states" (at 5.5).

25 It is worthy to note that only the BITs with the UK, Austria and Germany required ratification (as a stated requirement in the treaty) and indeed were ratified.

26 Michele Emily Olivier, *International Law in South African Municipal Law: Human Rights Procedure, Policy and Practice* (doctoral thesis, University of South Africa 2002) 254.

27 *See* Olivier *id.*, at 183. See the Minutes of the "Appropriation Bill: Debate on Budget Vote No 35 – Trade and Industry" in the *Hansard* of 3 May 2010 (<https://pmg.org.za/hansard/18052/>) where reference is found to the South Africa-Zimbabwe BIT and the uncertainty surrounding ratification and the process to be followed in the conclusion of such treaties. The minutes of the proceedings of the national assembly of 1 June 2010 (*Hansard: Minister's Response / Member's Statements*, available at https://pmg.org.za/hansard/18127/ (visited September 30, 2019)). indicate approval being given by the National Assembly without any debate having taken place. The position in the National Council of Provinces (NCOP) is not clear. The NCOP committee on Trade and International Relations "ratified" the agreement at a meeting on 13 April 2010 (available at https://pmg.org.za/committee-meeting/11462/ (visited September 30, 2019)).

28 Little to no reference is found in the Parliamentary debates to any discussions that took place on bilateral investment treaties. The mere fact that these agreements were not discussed in Parliament (there is also little reference to discussions in the respective portfolio committees and even that does not really replace the rigorous debate of all members of parliament and the national council of provinces), might have played a role in the fact that knowledge of the contents of these agreements and the implications that they might have for future policy decisions and actions and inactions of the Government, did not filter through to all government departments and officials. See for example *Hansard*

no democratic control took place and a number of BITs were concluded in this way. This might have caused all relevant issues not to have been debated or raised and the real implications of entering into these BITs not to have been realised.[29]

As a result of the absence (literally) of democratic control over the process, the risks and pitfalls for the South African government apparently went by without being noticed or, if noticed, without the government thinking twice about them and without them being debated in an open setting.

Since bilateral investment treaties were also not incorporated into domestic law, investors cannot rely on the protection in terms of the BITs in proceedings before a domestic court and hence the only possibility for them to rely on this protection would be before international arbitration tribunals as provided for in a respective BIT.[30]

However, prior to the current constitution coming into operation, the Constitution of the Republic of South Africa[31] of 1993 governed the conclusion of international agreements and thus governed those BITs that were signed *prior* to 1997 when the final Constitution came into operation. The provision of the interim Constitution (1994) [32] required that the first few BITs up until 1997 had to be signed by the president and approved (agreed to) by parliament. Only three of these BITs explicitly required ratification[33] in terms of the agreement itself and these were only ratified after the new Constitution came into effect.[34]

26–28 August 1997 col. 4476 regarding the BITs with Austria, Switzerland, and Germany where it is reported in each instance "Order disposed of without debate"; the same applies to the BIT with the UK (*Hansard* 23–26 March 1998 col. 891).

29 There is an obvious downside to not require Parliament to discuss this type of agreement; unless proper notification of the signing and existence of the agreement is given at a later stage, the importance of these agreements and the fact that any type of governmental action (or action at the level of local government) may have consequences for the Government's international law obligations, are not given proper consideration. See also the confirmation to the lack of understanding and due regard being given to the importance of these agreements in Poulsen, *Sacrificing Sovereignty by Chance: Investment Treaties, Developing Countries, and Bounded Rationality* (PhD London School of Economics and Political Science 2011) chapter 9.

30 It was held by the Supreme Court of Appeal in *Progress Office Machines CC v South African Revenue Services* 2008 2 SA 13 (SCA) that parties can rely on the provisions of a treaty in a domestic court only if the treaty has been incorporated into South African law (17E–F).

31 Act 200 of 1993.

32 See Section 231 of the interim Constitution.

33 *See supra* note 17.

34 *See Hansard* 26–28 August 1997 col. 4476 and *Hansard* 23–26 March 1998 col. 891.

2.3 *South Africa's Bilateral Investment Treaties*

From the beginning of 1994[35] until the end of 1997, 14 bilateral investment treaties ranging from treaties with European countries,[36] countries from the Americas,[37] Africa,[38] the Middle East[39] and the Far East.[40]

Of these BITs, the ones concluded with the United Kingdom, the Netherlands, the Swiss Confederation, Korea, Germany, France, Cuba, Denmark, Austria, Italy and China came into operation during the course of 1997 and 1998. A number of other BITs, in the end totalling 49, were signed until 2009. Only twenty-one of these ever came into operation.[41]

An analysis of the provisions of the BITs concluded over the years clearly shows that there was no change or progression in the government's approach to the negotiation and signing of BITs. This is borne out by a comparison of the contents of the BITs and the protection provided in them. The provisions contained in these agreements are all more or less the same and have stayed the same through the years.[42] The only treaty that contains provisions fairly different from that of the other BITs concluded, is the one concluded with Canada.[43] However, since this treaty was signed in November 1995 it has become quite apparent that the different wording and the carve-outs contained in it did not emanate from South Africa and neither did it have anything to do with its policy position during the negotiations, but rather was due to Canada's insistence in including these clauses in the BIT because of its policy position.[44]

---

35 Thus, under the new governmental dispensation.

36 United Kingdom, the Netherlands, the Swiss Confederation, Germany, France, Denmark, Austria, Italy and the Czech Republic.

37 Canada, Chile, Cuba.

38 Egypt, Ghana, Mozambique, Iran.

39 Iran.

40 China and Korea.

41 For a detailed discussion see Schlemmer, An Overview of South Africa's Bilateral Investment Treaties and Investment Policy, 31 *ICSID Review* 167 (2016) 169 ff.

42 The duration of the treaties ranges between 10 and 20 years and the protection for investments after termination of the treaties extends anything between 10 and 20 years.

43 This treaty (Agreement between the Republic of South Africa and the Government of Canada for the Promotion and Protection of Investments; signed 27 November 1995, not yet entered into force) contains a number of exceptions regarding cultural goods; exceptions in relation to the environment and public health etc. See the text of the treaty, available at https://treaties.dirco.gov.za/dbtw-wpd/images/19951127CanadaInvestmests.PDF (visited September 30, 2019).

44 It is noteworthy that some of the provisions contained in this agreement grants the governments a fair amount of leeway with regard to its so-called policy space in terms of which the host state would be allowed to treat nationals (or some sections of its citizenry) different from foreign investors because it wants to achieve certain policy objectives. It is even more noteworthy when one reads the government's policy paper and other

However, before the analysis is commenced, a few things need to be said about the government's policies and enacted legislation that had, has or could potentially have a direct effect on foreign investors. It has been mentioned already that the constitution contains a property clause that provides for the protection of property rights as well as certain exceptions when it comes to expropriation. Furthermore, it is provided that

> [n]o provision of this section [the property clause] may impede the state from taking legislative and other measures to achieve land, water and related reform, in order to redress the results of past racial discrimination, provided that any departure from the provisions of this section is in accordance with the provisions of section 36 (1).[45]

This provision allows the government to introduce legislation such as the Broad Based Black Economic Empowerment Act (2003)[46] as well as the Preferential Procurement Policy Framework Act (2003)[47] in terms of which discrimination may take place in favour of particular South African nationals.[48] When these pieces of legislation were enacted, the Government did not necessarily consider the potential effect of these provisions on foreign investors and their investments and the resultant implications for South Africa's obligations in terms of the already concluded BITs.[49] As will be seen, the majority of the

pronouncements by government and government officials that a government needs to have the necessary policy space where they are allowed to treat nationals differently and where they are allowed to regulate and legislate without potentially breaching their international law obligations. With this in mind, it is quite strange that the government did not take heed of the contents of this BIT in the later BITs that were negotiated to enable them to use differentiated treatment in particular circumstances. This merely shows that there was no real plan or policy or uniform approach by the government when it comes to a number of policy issues.

45 Section 25 of the Constitution of the Republic of South Africa, 1996.

46 Act 53 of 2003.

47 Act 5 of 2000.

48 For example, for purposes of procurement a government department should have a preferential procurement policy and may award tenders according to a point system where particular points are awarded for specific goals such as "contracting with persons, or categories of persons, historically disadvantaged by unfair discrimination on the basis of race, gender or disability". See Section 2 of the Act as well as the regulations published in terms of the act (the latest are the Preferential Procurement Regulations, 2017, which came into effect on 1 April 2017 (GN R32 in *GG* 40553 of 20 January 2017); Geo Quinot, The third wave of preferential procurement regulations in South Africa, 2018 *TSAR* 856–867.

49 Which include all the BITs with Western states.

BITS do not contain any carve outs that make allowance for these policies and their implementation and neither was this taken into account in the negotiations and conclusion of the BITS that followed after the implementation of these policies and resultant legislation. This is now said to be addressed in the Protection of Investment Act.[50]

2.3.1 The Preamble

The preamble to a South African BIT has a fairly standard format which generally refers to the desire to intensify economic cooperation and to create and maintain favourable conditions for investments and investors.[51] They all refer to the advantages of creating an investor-friendly climate and mutual advantages of increasing the flow of investment between contracting states including stimulating individual business initiative and increasing the prosperity in the territory of both contracting states. The preamble to the Agreement between the Government of the Republic of South Africa and the Federal Democratic Republic of Ethiopia for the Promotion and Reciprocal Protection of Investment (South Africa-Ethiopia BIT)[52] signed in 2008 adds an additional element of 'securing an overall balance of rights and obligations between and among investors and host countries' which is different from all the other BITS. But all in all, the focus remains on the economic benefit for both countries.

However, since these BITS were all negotiated either during the transition period or by the newly elected ANC (African National Congress) government, that is, since 1992 until the end of 2009, one would have expected that at least some of the constitutional values and goals for social upliftment contained in the preamble to the South African Constitution (and the aims sought to be addressed by the black economic empowerment policy) would also have featured in the preambles to the BITS, at least in the ones that were signed after 1997, but this is not the case.

The fact that these goals, aims and values have not been included in the preambles means that when a dispute has to be decided by an arbitration tribunal who has to assess the actions of the South African government being

50 Protection of Investment Act 22 of 2015. It came into operation on 3 July 2018. See GenN 395 in *GG* 41766 of 13 July 2018. See the discussion below at para. 5.

51 Some of the preambles contains a reference to the transfer of capital as well. Agreement between the Republic of South Africa and the Republic of Chile for the Reciprocal Promotion and Protection of Investments; signed 12 November 1998, not yet entered into force, available at https://treaties.dirco.gov.za/dbtw-wpd/images/19981112ChileInvestment.pdf (visited September 30, 2019).

52 Signed 18 March 2008, not yet entered into force.

complained about and interpret the treaty provisions,[53] the tribunal does not have the benefit of measuring the governmental actions and its interpretation of the BIT against the backdrop of the values of the Constitution and the social upliftment goals mentioned in the preamble to the Constitution, and this can have no other result than giving an interpretation that is more investor-friendly than what could have been the position had the government's intentions to redress the wrongs of the past etcetera, been included in the preamble to the BIT.[54] The tribunal's power to interpret does not include taking such issues into account when it is not included in the preamble to the treaty or expressly provided for in its mandate. The omission of such qualifiers that would otherwise have ensured that provision is made for certain exceptions to national treatment (the carve-out referred to above), can cost a government dearly as South Africa had to experience.

2.3.2 Definition of "Investment"

South African BITs contain a relatively standard definition of investment that is broad in scope; it is not a 'closed' list. This definition has not changed over the years and this fact speaks against any unintended negative experience gained from the formulation as used in the earlier BITs. For example, both the very first South African BIT concluded with the United Kingdom[55] in 1994 as

53 The government's broad-based black economic empowerment (BBBEE) scheme comes to mind, as well as the Minerals and Petroleum Resources Development Act 28 of 2002 which had been complained about as resulting in the expropriation of mineral rights (see *Piero Foresti Laura de Carli v Republic of South Africa*, ICSID Case No. ARB(AF)/07/1 (Aug. 4, 2010); 2010 *Oxford Reports on International Investment Claims* IIC 445 as an example). See also the requirements of the Mining Charter and the government's land reform program (see *Green Paper on Land Reform, 2011*, available at https://www.gov.za/sites/default/files/gcis_document/201409/landreformgreenpaper.pdf (visited September 20, 2019)).

54 The mere termination of BITs which has taken place, instead of a renegotiation – many of the BITs do contain a clause that allows for amendment – seems strange if one looks at the possible changes that could have been made to existing BITs that could have allowed for policy matters to be considered (obviously depending on consensus being achieved). It is also not unheard of to amend a treaty with retrospective effect if one is prepared to take a look at compensatory measures to allow for amendments that might have a negative effect on existing investments. For a general discussion on whether BITs facilitate and contribute to a host country's development objectives, with particular reference to South Africa, see Nicole Yazbek, Bilateral investment treaties: the foreclosure of domestic policy space, 17(1) *South African Journal of International Affairs* 103 (2010) 103–120.

55 Agreement between the Government of the United Kingdom of Great Britain and Northern Ireland and the Government of the Republic of South Africa for the Promotion and Protection of Investments with Protocol to the Agreement; signed 20 September 1994, ratified 27 May 1998, entered into force 27 May 1998; terminated 31 August 2014, available at

well as the last BIT concluded with Zimbabwe[56] in 2009 defines "investment" along similar lines, to include:

> every kind of asset and in particular, though not exclusively …:
> a) movable and immovable property as well as other rights such as mortgages, liens or pledges;[57]
> b) shares, stock and debentures of a company and any other form of participation in a company;
> c) claims to money, or to any performance under contract having an economic value;
> d) intellectual property rights, in particular copyrights, patents, utility model patents, registered designs, trade-marks, trade-names, trade and business secrets, technical processes, know-how, and goodwill;
> and
> e) rights or permits conferred by law or under contract, including concessions to search for, cultivate, extract or exploit natural resources;
> and any change in the legal form in which assets are invested or reinvested shall not affect their character as investments under this Agreement.

The BIT with Ethiopia[58] defines "investment" as "assets invested or acquired by an investor of one Party in the territory of the other Party, through the total ownership of enterprise or the participation in the ownership of an enterprise which gives a significant amount of influence to the investors in the management of the enterprise"; even though this is a bit different from the previously quoted definition, it is merely an add-on since the rest of the provision includes the same wording as quoted above. The BIT does however expressly exclude certain assets from being considered as investments, namely those assets which were not acquired in the "expectation, or not used for the purpose of,

---

https://treaties.dirco.gov.za/dbtw-wpd/images/19940920%20UK%20PROTECTION%20OF%20INVESTMENTS.pdf (visited October 1, 2019).

56 Agreement between the Government of the Republic of South Africa and the Government of the Republic of Zimbabwe for the Promotion and Reciprocal Protection of Investments (South Africa-Zimbabwe BIT); signed 27 November 2009 entered into force 15 September 2010, available at https://treaties.dirco.gov.za/dbtw-wpd/images/20091127ZimbabweInvestments.pdf (visited October 1, 2019).

57 Whilst the rest of the examples contained in the definition can be defined as patrimonial rights that directly influence the sum of the holder of the rights' estate, mortgage bonds, pledges or liens are no assets and do not affect the value of the holder's estate with one single cent.

58 Not yet entered into force, available at https://treaties.dirco.gov.za/dbtw-wpd/images/20080318EthiopiaInvestment.pdf (visited October 1, 2019).

economic activity or other business purpose"; also portfolio investments such as stocks or shares of companies in a party acquired for speculative purposes and held for a short-term by investors of the other party are excluded as investments for purposes of protection in terms of the BIT.

One cannot, however, see a trend that the more recent BITs would exclude portfolio investments and assets not used for economic activity and other business purposes. This type of exclusion was already found in the BIT with Canada, one of the earliest BITs concluded[59] but that BIT also adds to the definition 'any direct or indirect contribution in cash, in kind or in services, invested or re-invested in any sector of economic activity'.[60]

That the investment must be made in conformity with the laws and regulations of the host state, irrespective of the legal form chosen as well as of the legal framework, is a requirement in many of the BITs which would then clearly indicate that any investment made in violation of domestic law does not fall under the protection of the BIT.[61]

The definition of investment in the South African BITs is uncontroversial and fairly standard.

2.3.3 Definition of "Investors"

The term "investor" includes both natural and juristic persons. Some of the BITs adopt a "separate approach" in terms of which the investors from the two contracting parties are defined separately.[62] In general, however, nationality is the relevant factor for "investors" who are natural persons, and this is determined under the domestic law of each party. For juristic persons, the definition normally used is that of "companies" of a Party, being any legal person, corporation, firm or association incorporated or constituted in accordance with the domestic law in force in the territory of that Party";[63] for corporate entities,

59 The BIT with Canada was concluded in 1995 but is not in operation yet.

60 The following is excluded: "real estate or other property, tangible or intangible, not acquired in the expectation or used for the purpose of economic benefit or other business purposes".

61 It is however noteworthy that South Africa currently does not have any legislation apart from the Protection of Investment Act, that is investor-specific and that could require the investors to comply with particular requirements, and neither does the Protection of Investment Act contain such provisions.

62 For example, the Agreement between the Government of the Republic of South Africa and the Government of the Republic of Austria on the Promotion and Reciprocal Protection of Investments (South Africa-Austria BIT) signed 28 November 1996, entered into force 1 January 2008, terminated 31 August 2014. Available at https://treaties.dirco.gov.za/dbtw-wpd/images/19961128AustriaInvestments.pdf (visited October 1, 2019).

63 For example, South Africa-Zimbabwe BIT, *supra* note 56.

the place of incorporation or sometimes also the 'central administration' and 'principal place of business' are the main factors used to determine the nationality of such investor.[64]

The issue of double nationality is raised in a few BITs and specifically in the BIT with Israel, where an investor with respect to South Africa is defined as a natural person who is a national of the Republic of South Africa who is not also a national or permanent resident of Israel and with respect to Israel a natural person who is a national or permanent resident of the State of Israel who is not also a national of the Republic of South Africa. This is, however, not a standard definition and reference to permanent residents being accepted as investors, or not, is not included in the majority of the BITs.[65]

2.3.4 Application and Duration of the BITs

The BITs all stipulate that the treaty will enter into force within a defined period of time (normally thirty days) after both contracting parties have notified each other in writing that their respective constitutional requirements for the entry into force of the agreement have been complied with. As indicated,

---

64 See for instance the South Africa-Austria BIT (n 62) where a third category of investors is added namely 'any juridical person, or partnership, constituted in accordance with the legislation of a third Party in which any natural person who is a citizen of the Republic of Austria or any juridical person or partnership constituted in accordance with the legislation of the Republic of Austria having its seat in the territory in the Republic of Austria exercises a dominant influence' (the same is repeated for purposes of South Africa); other BITs (Agreement between the Government of the Republic of South Africa and the Government of the Italian Republic on the Promotion and Protection of Investments (Italy-South Africa BIT) signed 9 June 1997, entered into force 16 March 1999, notice of termination has been given, (date of termination will be 15 March 2019), available at https://treaties.dirco.gov.za/dbtw-wpd/images/19970609%20ITALY%20PROTECTION%20OF%20INVESTMENTS.pdf (visited September 25, 2019); Agreement between the Government of the Republic of South Africa and the Swiss Federal Council on the Promotion and Reciprocal Protection of Investments (Switzerland-South Africa BIT) signed 27 June 1995, entered into force 30 November 1997, and termination date 31 August 2014, available at https://treaties.dirco.gov.za/dbtw-wpd/images/19950627SwitzerlandProtectionofInvestments.pdf (visited September 25, 2019); Agreement between the Government of the Republic of South Africa and the Government of the Republic of France on the Reciprocal Promotion and Protection of Investments (France-South Africa BIT, signed 11 October 1995, entered into force 22 June 1997 and terminated 31 August 2014, available at https://treaties.dirco.gov.za/dbtw-wpd/images/19951011FranceProtectionofInvestments.PDF (visited September 25, 2019)) refer to the element of control rather than dominance.

65 Investor and investment are defined in much different terms in the new act.

in the only three instances where explicit ratification was required, this was achieved, and the BITs entered into force.[66]

Most of the treaties provide for a definite duration, in general 10–20 years, renewable for an additional period. In most instances provision is made that after the expiry of the first period, the treaty will have an indefinite duration unless any one of the parties notifies the other before the date of expiry, that it wants to terminate the treaty.[67] And in all instances where the BITs are terminated, the protection granted by the relevant BIT will remain applicable to investments made prior to the termination and will continue for an additional period of 10–20 years after termination (all depending on the formulation used in the particular BIT).

The agreements are applicable to investments which are a) either made prior to its entry into force without any limitation;[68] or b) were made after a given date (for example 1 January 1957 in the case of the BIT with Tunisia; 18 August 1984 in the case of the BIT with Mozambique;[69] and 1 January 1987 in the case of the BIT with Russia;[70] or c) it is stated that the agreement will not apply to any property right or interest compulsorily acquired by either party in its own territory before the entry into force of the agreement.[71] All disputes

66 See *supra* note 17. The requirement for ratification was included in the wording of the respective treaties and is not related, it seems, to the fact that these BITs were negotiated and signed under the interim constitution. The ratification only took place much later, after the coming into operation of the final Constitution; see the discussion above.

67 As have been noted earlier, a number of the treaties that have almost reached the end of the application period, were terminated or notification of South Africa's intention to terminate has been sent to a number of countries.

68 For example the Treaty between the Federal Republic of Germany and the Republic of South Africa concerning the Reciprocal Encouragement and Protection of Investments (Germany-South Africa BIT) signed 11 September 1995, entered into force 10 April 1998 (ratified 10 March 1998), terminated 31 August 2014 (available at https://treaties.dirco.gov.za/dbtw-wpd/images/19950911GermanyInvestment.pdf (visited September 25, 2019)).

69 Both the BIT with Tunisia as well as the one with Mozambique is not in force yet.

70 Agreement between the Government of the Republic of South Africa and the Government of the Russian Federation on the Promotion and Reciprocal Protection of Investments (South Africa-Russia BIT) signed 23 November 1998, entered into force 12 April 2000, available at https://treaties.dirco.gov.za/dbtw-wpd/images/19981123RussiaProtectionofInvestments.PDF (visited September 25, 2019).

71 The South Africa-Zimbabwe BIT (*Supra* note 39) entered into force 15 September 2010. For a discussion of this BIT see E.C. Schlemmer, Agreement between the Governments of South Africa and Zimbabwe for the Reciprocal Protection of Investments: A BIT too late – if at all?, 34 *South African Yearbook of International Law* 183 (2009)183–200. Although the term 'compulsorily acquired' is not specially defined in the BIT's definition clause, it is, however, submitted to be a euphemism for expropriation without fair or adequate

regarding investments made prior to the coming into force of any one of the BITs, will not be covered by the provisions of the agreement.

2.3.5 The Admission and Encouragement of Investments

The parties to the BITs all have the general obligation to promote investments and this is coupled with an undertaking that each party will admit such investments in accordance with its laws and regulations (i.e. issuing of permits and carrying out of licensing agreements and contracts for technical, commercial or administrative assistance).[72] In order to assist investors even more, provisions are found in some BITs that relate to the granting of permission to nationals of either party to enter and remain in the territory of the other party for purposes of establishing, developing, administering or advising on the operation of an investment to which they, or an investor of the first party that employs them, have committed or are in the process of committing a substantial amount of capital or other resources. Each party should also, in compliance with its domestic law, consider favourably the requests concerning entry, stay, work and movement in its territory of the qualifying managerial and technical staff and consultants of the investors who carry out activities connected with investments and of their families forming part of their household regardless of their nationality.[73]

Almost a third of the BITs, and these are mostly with African countries, contain a provision that requires a party to permit, notwithstanding its own requirements for bookkeeping and auditing, the investments of investors to be subject also to bookkeeping and auditing according to standards which the investor is subjected to by his or its national requirements or according to internationally accepted standards (such as International Accountancy Standards (IAS) drawn up by the International Accountancy Standards Committee). This confirms that in instances where there may be doubt regarding the regulatory

---

compensation – no examples of legislation could be found compelling any legal subject to acquire particular assets, but rather the opposite: such as in the case of expropriation.

72 For example the South Africa-Ethiopia BIT, *supra* note 58; Agreement between the Government of the Republic of South Africa and the Government of the Republic of the Sudan for the Reciprocal Promotion and Protection of Investments (South Africa-Sudan BIT) signed 7 November 2007 (not yet entered into force), available at https://treaties.dirco.gov.za/dbtw-wpd/images/20071107SudanInvestments.pdf (visited September 25, 2019).

73 For example the Agreement between the Republic of South Africa and the Republic of Turkey concerning the Promotion and Reciprocal Protection of Investments (Turkey-South Africa BIT) signed 23 June 2000 (not yet entered into force), available at https://treaties.dirco.gov.za/dbtw-wpd/images/20000623TurkeyProtectionofInvestments.pdf (visited September 25, 2019).

framework concerning auditing and bookkeeping standards in the host state, the home state may assure that the companies/investors will still be subjected to the home state controls as well to ensure compliance with internationally accepted standards.[74]

2.3.6 Standards of Treatment

2.3.6.1 *Fair and Equitable Treatment*

The general standard of fair and equitable treatment is found in all the South African BITS. In some cases, this is coupled with a "full protection clause".[75] The language of these provisions is consistent with BIT practice worldwide and in general does not define the fair and equitable standard of treatment or link it specifically to the customary international law minimum standard.[76]

---

74 For example the Agreement between the Government of the Republic of South Africa and the Government of the Republic of Guinea for the Reciprocal Promotion and Protection of Investments (South Africa-Guinea BIT) signed 25 September 2007 (not yet entered into force), available at https://treaties.dirco.gov.za/dbtw-wpd/images/20070925Guinea Investments.pdf (visited September 25, 2019); Agreement between the Government of the Republic of South Africa and the Great Socialist People's Libyan Arab Jamahiriya for the Promotion and Reciprocal Protection of Investments (South Africa-Libya BIT) signed 14 June 2002 (not yet entered into force), available at https://treaties.dirco.gov.za /dbtw-wpd/images/20020614LibyaInvestment.pdf (visited September 25, 2019); and the South Africa-Zimbabwe BIT, *supra* note 39.

75 The wording is not always the same and sometimes, in about a third of the BITS, reference is found to "full protection and security" (Agreement between the Government of the Republic of South Africa and the Government of the Hellenic Republic on the Promotion and Reciprocal Protection of Investments (Greece-South Africa BIT) signed 19 November 1998, entered into force 6 September 2001, with a notice of termination given on 31 August 2013, available at https://treaties.dirco.gov.za/dbtw-wpd/images /19981119GreeceInvestment.pdf (visited June 15, 2019), and in two instances to 'full legal protection' (Agreement between the Government of the Republic of South Africa and the Government of the Argentine Republic on the Promotion and Reciprocal Protection of Investments (South Africa-Argentina BIT) signed 23 July 1998 and entered into force 1 January 2001, available at https://treaties.dirco.gov.za/dbtw-wpd/images/19980723 ArgentinaProtectionofInvestments.PDF (visited September 25, 2019); Agreement on Reciprocal Promotion and Protection of Investments between the Government of the Islamic Republic of Iran and the Government of the Republic of South Africa (Iran-South Africa BIT) signed 3 November 1997 (not yet entered into force)), available at https:// treaties.dirco.gov.za/dbtw-wpd/images/19971103%20IRAN%20PROTECTION%20OF%20 INVESTMENT.pdf (visited September 25, 2019).

76 Customary international law is considered part of South African law and is only subject to legislation and the Constitution and courts are obliged to interpret legislation in accordance with international law, Sections 232 and 233 of the Constitution of the Republic of South Africa, 1996.

2.3.6.2 *National and Most-Favoured Nation Treatment*

National treatment and most favoured nation treatment (MFN) are generally provided for in the South African BITs and apply to the investment and the activities of the investors in connection with the investment in general and also to the returns of investment. Certain exceptions to the most favoured-nation treatment are found, but this is not uniformly provided for in the BITs. What is uniformly provided for is that the MFN does not apply to benefits granted (currently as well as in the future) within the framework of a free trade area, customs and economic union, common market or to any similar international agreement; this also applies to any favourable treatment granted by any tax treaty.

In the BIT with Russia, the MFN is also excluded with reference to agreements which existed between Russia and the states which earlier formed part of the Union of Soviet Socialist Republics.

A number of BITs contains an exception to national treatment in favour of South Africa by virtue of any law or measure applied in South Africa for the purpose of the promotion of the achievement of equality in its territory, or designed to protect or advance natural or legal persons, or categories thereof, disadvantaged by unfair discrimination in its territory.[77] These exceptions seem to allow for preferential treatment of some of the local citizens and may be seen as giving effect to the constitutional values and the social upliftment goals of the South African government and thus the principles contained in the black economic empowerment policy. It remains unclear, however, why this has been included in some BITs but not in others since these aims and goals, perhaps not explicitly spelt out initially, have formed part of the government's policy stance since it came to power. It is thus not certain whether this was included as a result of the insistence of the South African government or rather by its co-contracting party, although everything points to the latter.

There is no progression to be seen in the drafting of the newer BITs. One thus cannot argue that although South Africa initially did not realise the need

77 For example Russia-South Africa BIT and in the protocol to the Iran-South Africa BIT (not yet entered into force) signed on the same date as the BIT); or in favour of both parties to the agreement (for example South Africa-Ethiopia BIT); Agreement between the Republic of South Africa and the Czech Republic for the Promotion and Reciprocal Protection of Investments (South Africa-Czech Republic BIT) signed 14 December 1998 (not yet entered into force), available at https://treaties.dirco.gov.za/dbtw-wpd/images/19981214CzechRepInvestments.pdf (visited September 25, 2019).

for this type of reservation (carve out) or exception to be included, the realisation came later on – it apparently never did.[78]

This, or similar, reservations or exceptions were not included in the BITs that formed the basis of the disputes in which South Africa had been involved and where the claims were made that South Africa's policy of broad based black economic empowerment and its implementation resulted in a breach of the treaty; had a carve out been included in the BIT, the outcome might have been totally different.

One also cannot argue that due to the fact that these BITs were concluded in the "early days" when the expertise were still being developed, these exceptions or carve outs were not included; other BITs concluded in the same time frame do indeed contain such exceptions causing the argument to falter. The BIT with Canada, signed in 1995, for example, makes provision for national treatment exceptions for South Africa that should be agreed upon before the coming into operation of the BIT – it was clearly something that was on the cards even though the details were not finalised at the time of signing the agreement.

Some BITs, such as the one with Russia, reserves the right to parties to determine economic fields and areas of activity where activities of foreign investors will be excluded or restricted; the BIT with Canada too, allows for the investment in cultural industries to be exempt from the provisions of the agreement and in the Annex to the BIT, a number of sectors or matters are identified where Canada reserves the right to make and maintain exceptions.

It thus seems clear that the South African government did not have a clear policy on how to approach bilateral investment treaties and this lack of policy and, it seems, understanding of the implications of not including reservations, carve outs, etcetera in a BIT, was only really brought to the fore and came under fire[79] when some investment arbitrations were instituted against the country. This became even more prevalent when the investment arbitration at the ICSID Additional Facility was initiated when the detail of the dispute, for the first time, was placed in the public domain. For the first time, the government's policies and actions which came under fire due to its alleged treaty

78 *See e.g.*, the statement in the Government Position Paper *Bilateral Investment Policy Framework Review* (2009) GN 961 of 2009 *GG* 32386 (7-07-2009) regarding the lack of understanding concerning the role and importance of BITs.

79 And recognised as such by the relevant government department – see the Government Position Paper (*supra* note 78) where it is stated that there was "no legal or economic analysis of the risk associated with the conclusion of BITs" and that there was "a lack of understanding regarding the real nature and consequences of BITs at that time. Cabinet was not fully apprised of the dangers inherent in BITs" (at 14).

breaches were now subject to public scrutiny and also subject to international scrutiny within the framework of international investment agreements.[80] The whole issue of whether the implementation of some of these policies and legislative provisions indeed amounted to expropriation was also raised but never decided.[81]

2.3.6.3 *Expropriation*

All the South African BITs contain an expropriation clause that covers not only actual expropriation but also measures tantamount to expropriation. Such clauses contain the classic requirements for an expropriation to be lawful, it must be in the public interest, done in accordance with procedure established by law, there must be no discrimination, and compensation must be given. Most of the BITs make provision for 'prompt, adequate and effective compensation', and some for "full compensation" and provision is also made for a right to prompt review of the case and the valuation of the investment under the domestic law of the expropriating country. Furthermore, some of the BITs[82] provide that when a contracting state expropriates the assets of a company or an enterprise in its territory, in which investors of the other contracting state have an investment, including through shareholding, the provisions concerning expropriation and compensation will apply to ensure prompt, adequate and effective compensation for those investors for any impairment or diminishment of the fair market value of such investment resulting from the expropriation.

It is important to note that the South African domestic law provisions regarding expropriation and the compensation to be paid are much less generous than the provisions of international law and those contained in the BITs. The undertaking in the BITs to pay market-related compensation is in line with international law and customary international law principles. However, the South African Constitution provides in Section 25 that expropriation must be in the public interest[83] and that when it comes to compensation, the amount of the compensation must be *just and equitable* and that things like the market value of the property may, amongst other things, be considered in

80 *See Piero Foresti, supra* note 53 and see the discussion at Section 3.

81 *See* Section 2.3.6.3.

82 *See* the Agreement between the Republic of South Africa and the Kingdom of Denmark concerning the Promotion and Reciprocal Protection of Investments (South Africa-Denmark BIT) signed 22 February 1996, entered into force 23 April 1997, but terminated 31 August 2014, available at https://treaties.dirco.gov.za/dbtw-wpd/images/19960222DernmarkProtectionofInvestments.PDF (visited September 25, 2019).

83 Which would mean something broader than for a "public purpose".

coming to the determination of the value of the compensation that needs to be paid out.[84] Although the Constitutional Court has not been called upon to deal with this particular subsection, academic writers and other courts are of the opinion that it is clear that the obligation, as worded in Section 25(3), does not require the compensation to be market-related and that compensation at less than market value can also be paid.[85] Thus, there is a disjuncture between the domestic law provisions and the provisions in the BITs.[86] This particular aspect puts foreign investors in a predicament. If their investments are covered by a BIT, even one that has been terminated, they might be entitled to larger amounts of compensation than another foreign investor who is not protected by any BIT. The Protection of Investment Act that is meant to replace the protection provided by BITs does not contain any reference to expropriation and as indicated, the new Draft Expropriation Bill which is meant to replace the current Expropriation Act,[87] provides that in certain circumstances "nil compensation" would be payable.[88] Until new legislation is enacted or clarity is given by the Constitutional Court on the issue of compensation, an investor who cannot rely on protection under a BIT, does not have much legal certainty regarding the issue of compensation in particular.[89]

2.3.7 Free Transfer of Payments

The free transfer of payments relating to an investor's investments and returns is guaranteed in all the BITs. Reference is sometimes made to the monetary transfer that guarantees the free transfer of the investor's investments and returns (sometimes referring to the local laws and regulations of the host state or the compensation paid in case of expropriation and also, the residual value of the investment). Some of the South African BITs guarantee the undelayed

84 *See also* E. du Plessis, Silence is golden: The lack of direction on compensation for expropriation in the 2011 Green Paper on Land Reform, 17(2) *Potchefstroomse Elektroniese Regsblad* 1 (2014) 1–35, available at http://www.scielo.org.za/scielo.php?script=sci_arttext&pid=S1727-37812014000200007&lng=en&nrm=iso (visited September 20, 2019).

85 *See* the detailed discussion and sources referred to by André van der Walt "Reconciling the state's duties to promote land reform and to pay 'just and equitable' compensation for expropriation". 2006 *SALJ* 23–40; the Constitutional Court has still not pronounced on this particular matter; *see also* Theunis Roux, "Property", in Stuart Woolman and Michael Bishop (eds.), *Constitutional Law of South Africa* (2 ed, Cape Town: Juta, 2014) chapters 46 34–36.

86 With a BIT in existence, the investor will be entitled to potentially higher compensation than what he would have been entitled to in the absence of a BIT and where the expropriation has taken place according to the constitutional provisions.

87 Act 63 of 1975.

88 Clause 12(3) quoted in *supra* note 16.

89 *See also* Section 2.3.6.3 and 6 below for the potential international law implications.

transfer of funds in connection with their investments and then provides a non-exhaustive list;[90] other BITs such as the one with Denmark, provides a list of the types of payments that are freely transferable.

The protocol to the South Africa-Chile BIT which was signed together with the BIT, provides that capital invested may only be transferred one year after it had entered the territory of a party unless its legislation provides for more favourable treatment.

In view of the South African foreign exchange control regulations, most of the South African BITs, or if not in the BIT itself then in the protocol that was signed simultaneously with the BIT, a clause is contained that provides that the provisions for transfers of investments and returns as contemplated in the agreement do not apply to foreign nationals who have resided in South Africa for more than five years and who, after having applied for permanent residency, completed the required exchange control formalities connected with immigration to South Africa, and are accordingly, deemed to have become a permanent resident in South Africa.[91] South Africa does undertake in these clauses to remove these restrictions that would otherwise apply to such investors as newly defined residents.[92]

2.3.8 Compensation for Losses Due to Armed Conflict or Internal Disorder

A clause dealing with compensation for losses due to armed conflict or internal disorder allowing the investor to the same restitution, compensation or other settlement as nationals and nationals of other nations is found in all of the BITs. The BIT with Angola[93] is the only BIT that also includes a provision that

90 For example, the South Africa-Chile BIT.

91 For example, Agreement between the Government of the Republic of South Africa and the Government of the United Republic of Tanzania for the Promotion and Reciprocal Protection of Investments (South Africa-Tanzania BIT), signed 22 September 2005 and not yet entered into force, available at https://treaties.dirco.gov.za/dbtw-wpd/images/20050922 TanzaniaInvestments.pdf (visited September 25, 2019); and the protocol to the South Africa-Zimbabwe BIT, *supra* note 3.

92 The Protection of Investment Act (2015) in turn merely provides in s 11 that a foreign investor may repatriate funds subject to taxation and other applicable legislation – no undertaking thus on the side of South Africa to remove any existing restrictions. The fact that is appears in the BITs does not place an enforceable obligation on South Africa but at least showed a positive intention which is cannot be replicated in a piece of domestic legislation.

93 Agreement between the Government of the Republic of Angola and the Government of the Republic of South Africa for the Reciprocal Promotion and Protection of Investments

the investor would be entitled to compensation for losses suffered as a result of a natural disaster as part of this article. It is unclear if this compensation refers to normal insurance payments as provided for by a private insurance policy covering such a risk or is intended to indicate a willing undertaking by the host state to act as an insurer without expecting the investors to make any contribution in the form of an insurance premium.

2.3.9 Subrogation

A subrogation clause is a standard in all the BITs providing that the parties will recognise any assignment of rights whether by law or by legal transaction (generally relating to a guarantee/insurance/indemnity given either by the home state or its designated agency) as well as the exercise of such rights and the enforcement of such claims by virtue of subrogation. In some of the BITs, it is provided that the party who is a party to a dispute may at no time during the procedure relating to the investment dispute invoke in its defence its immunity or the fact that the investor has received, pursuant to an insurance contract, an indemnity covering all or part of the damages or losses incurred.[94]

2.3.10 Other Relevant Provisions

Most of the South African BITs contain provisions to allow for the application of more favourable rules or treatment for investors and investments whether arising from domestic law or international law, to prevail over that contained in the BIT. Furthermore, most of the BITs contain an umbrella clause which casts the net for potential treaty breaches a bit wider. In none of the arbitrations against South Africa has this particular aspect yet played a role.

A few of the BITs contain a provision that allows the parties in the event of exceptional balance of payment difficulties, to exert restrictions on the free transfer of payments relating to their investments and returns for a limited period of time.[95]

(Angola-South Africa BIT) signed 17 February 2005 (not yet entered into force), available at https://treaties.dirco.gov.za/dbtw-wpd/images/20050217AngolaInvestments.pdf (visited September 25, 2019).

94 For example Agreement between the Republic of South Africa and the Government of the Democratic Republic of Congo for the Reciprocal Protection and Promotion of Investments (South Africa-Democratic Republic of Congo BIT) signed 31 August 2004 (not yet entered into force), available at https://treaties.dirco.gov.za/dbtw-wpd/images/20040831DRCInvestments.pdf (visited September 25, 2019).

95 For example Agreement between the Government of the Republic of South Africa and the Government of the Republic of Madagascar on the Promotion and Reciprocal Protection of Investments (South Africa-Madagascar BIT) signed 13 December 2006 (not yet

2.3.11 Dispute Settlement Clauses

2.3.11.1 *Disputes between Contracting Parties*

The provisions on the settlement of state-to-state investment disputes, that is disputes between the contracting parties regarding the interpretation and application of the BIT concerned are fairly standard in all the BITs. If an amicable settlement cannot be reached within six months, the dispute may be submitted to a three member ad hoc arbitral tribunal. The provisions vary as to the details regarding the appointment of the arbitrators and the arbitral procedures.

In a few of the BITs with African countries, no provision is made for arbitration, it is merely provided that any dispute between the parties arising out of the interpretation or application of the agreement will be settled amicably through consultation or negotiations.[96]

2.3.11.2 *Disputes between the Host State and the Foreign Investor*

All the bilateral investment treaties signed by South Africa, whether they are operational or not, contain a dispute resolution clause that allows for an investment dispute to be taken on arbitration. The wording of the dispute resolution clauses is more or less standard and consistent and in most of the treaties, the investor is given the option to decide whether it wants to make use of the court system or international arbitration. Although South Africa is not a member of the Washington Convention[97] and ICSID arbitration is thus not available to investors, many of the contracting parties to the BITs are ICSID contracting parties and because of the proliferation in BITs in the 2000s the general assumption existed that many new states might still join/accede to the convention. The result is thus that provision is made for ICSID arbitration in the expectation that it may become a possibility later on during the subsistence of the treaty.[98] Almost all the treaties that contain a reference to ICSID

---

entered into force), available at https://treaties.dirco.gov.za/dbtw-wpd/images/20061213 MadagascarInvestments.pdf (visited September 25, 2019).

96 For example, South Africa-Sudan BIT.

97 Convention on the Settlement of Investment Disputes between States and Nationals of Other States 575 *UNTS* 159, this convention came into force on 14 October 1966.

98 This does not currently seem to be a possibility even though in an earlier case where the South African government was taken to court by a South African citizen who requested diplomatic protection as a result of an expropriation of its investments that took place in Zimbabwe, and where he inter alia requested the SA government to accede to ICSID to give him the opportunity to make use of this avenue since Zimbabwe is a contracting state, the government turned a deaf ear to the request (see *Government of the Republic of South Africa v Von Abo* 2011 (5) SA 262 (SCA) and in fact stated emphatically after its BIT policy review that it has no intention to accede to the ICSID convention.

arbitration also as a matter of course allows disputes to be referred for resolution to the ICSID Additional Facility.[99] A third alternative means of dispute resolution is also allowed, namely, ad hoc arbitration – the majority of the BITs refers to arbitration subject to the UNCITRAL rules but in a few instances reference is made to the court of the Stockholm Chamber of Commerce and/or that of the International Chamber of Commerce.[100] Most probably as a result of legal certainty created by this, a number of the BITs contain a consent to arbitration undertaking in the BIT which enables any investor to take a dispute to arbitration without having to seek separate permission or consent from the host/respondent state to do so. The importance of having such a provision included becomes apparent when one looks at the arbitration awards which have dealt with this in the past. The majority of the arbitration awards available dealing with and interpreting BIT provisions relating to investment arbitration, especially in considering whether an undertaking to submit to arbitration can be considered consent to arbitration, emanate from the ICSID. Even though they do not have precedential value, they are considered persuasive within that particular framework. One could argue that it should also be the case for any other type of investment arbitration where a state party has agreed to it in a BIT, but it is always better to wear your braces and your belt rather than to be caught with your trousers down. By including such a clause in the BIT, the home states are ensuring that their investors will have the benefit of this type of dispute settlement.

Another clause which is most probably linked to South Africa not being an ICSID contracting state is the inclusion of a clause in which the home state agrees not to grant diplomatic protection to its investors in cases of disputes. A citizen does not have a right to diplomatic protection in terms of international

99 Article 11(2) Treaty concerning the Reciprocal Encouragement and Protection of Investments between South Africa and Germany signed 11 September 1995, prior to its cancellation. The treaty with Zimbabwe is an exception to the rule where no reference to arbitration at the Additional Facility is given as an option.

100 For example, Agreement between the Government of the Republic of South Africa and the Government of the People's Democratic Republic of Algeria on the Reciprocal Promotion and Protection of Investments (South Africa-Algeria BIT) signed 24 September 2000 (not yet entered into force), available at https://treaties.dirco.gov.za/dbtw-wpd/images/20000924%20ALGERIA%20PROTECTION%20OF%20INVESTMENTS.pdf (visited September 25, 2019); Russia-South Africa BIT; Agreement between the Republic of South Africa and the Belgo-Luxembourg Economic Union on the Reciprocal Promotion and Protection of Investments (South Africa-Belgium-Luxembourg-Economic Union BIT) signed 14 August 1998, came into operation 14 March 2003, and terminated 14 March 2013, available at https://treaties.dirco.gov.za/dbtw-wpd/images/19980814Belgo-Luxembouge(Investments).pdf (visited September 25, 2019).

law; if there is to be such a right it would be determined by the relevant national legislation. South African law does not grant a citizen a right to diplomatic protection, he/she has a right to request the government to provide diplomatic protection, and all that he/she may rely on, is the government's obligation to consider such a request.[101]

Some of the BITs contain as an alternative to international arbitration, a referral to the courts of the host State.[102] None of the South African BITs, however, contain an obligation to exhaust local remedies first but some of them contain a "fork-in-the-road" clause excluding international arbitration if the investor has had recourse to the courts of the host state or vice versa.[103]

A choice-of-law clause is found in some of the dispute settlement clauses indicating that the resolution of the dispute be derived by application of the domestic law, including the rules relating to conflicts of law, of the contracting party involved in the dispute in whose territory the investment has been made, the provisions of the agreement, the terms of the specific agreement which

101 The Constitutional Court held quite definitively that there is no right to diplomatic protection under South African law (and the Constitution and the Bill of Rights did not change this), the citizen has a right to approach the government, but it is absolutely in its discretion to decide whether it is going to grant the request or not. "[T]he provision of diplomatic protection at the request of a citizen whose rights are violated in and by a foreign State is a matter which forms part of the executive function of government. Thus, it is up to the government to decide whether protection should be given, and if so, what form the diplomatic intervention should take. This court stated that 'if government refuses to consider a legitimate request, or deals with it in bad faith or irrationally, a court could require government to deal with the matter properly'. This duty and function to give proper consideration to a legitimate request for diplomatic intervention by government is one carried out in terms of s 85(2) read together with Section 92(1) of the Constitution which makes it clear that the Minister concerned bears the constitutional responsibility to execute the assigned powers and functions. Thus, any failure of the national executive or one of its members to discharge its obligations must be remedied accordingly and a court is entitled to require the government, or the Minister concerned to fulfil its constitutional responsibilities" (*Von Abo v President of the RSA* 2009 (5) SA 345 (CC) 362G–363A). *See also* the decision by the Supreme Court of Appeal in *Government of the Republic of South Africa v Von Abo* 2011 (5) SA 262 (SCA).

102 See for example South Africa-Belgo-Luxembourg-Economic Union BIT, *supra* note 102.

103 For example, the South Africa-Tanzania BIT; South Africa-Zimbabwe BIT; and Bilateral Agreement between the Republic of South Africa and the Republic of Tunisia for the Promotion and Reciprocal Protection of Investments (South Africa-Tunisia BIT) signed 28 February 2002, not yet entered into force, available at https://treaties.dirco.gov.za/dbtw-wpd/images/20020228TunisiaInvestments.pdf (visited September 25, 2019).

may have been entered into regarding the investment as well as the principles of international law.[104]

In general, thus, South African bilateral investment treaties are fairly standard when it comes to their content other than what one could have expected of a State that was in a process of transformation when these treaties were signed and thus in a perfect situation to take its own domestic needs and policies into account whilst around the negotiating tables. This, as can clearly be seen, was not done and the resultant effect was that when an investment dispute arose and came into the public domain, there was a sudden awareness of the fact that the BITS perhaps could entail more harm than good. This particular aspect will be addressed in what follows.

3 South Africa's Concern with and Involvement in Investment Arbitration

As pointed out, all of the South African BITS make provision for investment arbitration, however, the government's approach to and stance on arbitration has changed since the time of signing the BITS. The government's concern with investment arbitration which seemed to be more of a concern with the fact that its policies and legislation were being exposed to *outside* (or foreign) scrutiny in international investment arbitrations than with the issue of arbitration itself, caused it to review its policy framework relating to its international investment agreements and in particular to do a comprehensive risk assessment of – even though not spelled out that clearly – the potential impact of investment arbitration.[105] It expressly stated that it needed to do damage control but neither the details of the damage nor of the proposed control were divulged. Reference, however, was made to an arbitration involving the Czech Republic (as defendant) where the Czech Republic lost a $350 million lawsuit. No detail is, however, given regarding the costs involved in the totality of arbitral proceedings instituted against South Africa. One can only come to the conclusion that it is the damage caused by the (two) arbitral proceedings that are referred to in the position paper that led the government on its path

104 For a general discussion of choice of law clauses in investment treaties and the applicable law, *see* Rudolf Dolzer and Christoph Schreuer, *Principles of Investment Treaties* (Oxford: Oxford University Press, 2012) 408 ff.

105 *See* the Position Paper published in June 2009 by the Department of Trade and Industry, *supra* note 78.

of review which in the end caused South Africa to cancel some of its investment agreements and to make the statement that it is not going to renew any of its existing treaties but will allow them to lapse. It is, however, not possible for the reader of this position paper to really appreciate the damage control that the government is referring to and one can merely assume what the position is. It does raise the question, though, of what is to be done if a host country finds itself in a position where, due to its behaviour, it feels the need to protect itself against the consequences of its behaviour with regard to imminent awards of damages.

At the time the position paper was published, the case of *Piero Foresti Laura de Carli v Republic of South Africa*[106] was imminent before the ICSID Additional Facility, but it was not finalised, and even though reference is made to it, no detail had been disclosed.[107] Yet, the value of the claim against the South African government in the *Piero Foresti* case was €260 million. The merits of the case[108] were eventually not argued because the department of mineral resources intervened in the background and the parties came to some or other settlement.[109] Irrespective of this settlement, the South African government insisted that the case should continue even though the claimants wanted to withdraw their claim. A costs order was given in favour of South Africa for €400 000 although their initial claim was €5 333 146,91.[110] It is thus fairly clear that this was merely a token award but if that was indeed the real costs involved, damage control was indeed necessary.

The other arbitration referred to in passing in the policy paper is not discussed or referred to anywhere else in the document. The reason for this is

---

106 *See supra* note 53.

107 *See* the Position Paper (*supra* note 78), at 31 where the nature of the claim is disclosed but not the value.

108 The Claimants in this case argued that some of the provisions of the Mineral and Petroleum Resources Development Act 28 of 2002 and some of the black economic empowerment requirements (as found in the mining charter), resulted in an expropriation of their investment.

109 Peter Leon is quoted as saying "The settlement with the Department of Mineral Resources involved the companies concerned being allowed to convert all their old order mining rights for 5% BEE by an offset against the companies' beneficiation activities ... This is obviously a rather different outcome from the 26% BEE ownership required by the Mining Charter ... No other mining company has been treated so generously or ... allowed to offset its beneficiation activities against the Mining Charter's ownership requirements." (Mark Allix, Economic sense "must override BEE" in foreign investing, *Business Day*, 8 November 2013 at 4).

110 No findings were made regarding the merits, only on the costs issue. It should be pointed out that the sum total of €5 333 146,91 claimed by the South African government did not include an additional €432 320,21, the costs of advocate Nthai SC who was accused of bribery – see para. 31 ff of the Award of *Piero Foresti* case.

that it was a confidential arbitration and obviously not handled by the ICSID Additional Facility. On investigation, it transpired that during 2001–2004, South Africa was involved in an investment arbitration which was held under the UNCITRAL rules and which made it possible for the parties to participate without any publicity being given of the case, the issues involved, or its outcome.

This arbitration concerned a violation of the bilateral investment treaty between Switzerland and South Africa. A Swiss investor invested in property in Acornhoek[111] intending to establish and develop a game farm and conference facilities on the property. South Africa was accused of breaching its obligation to provide police security/protection and to guarantee the safety of both the investor and his investment. The bilateral investment treaty contained a full protection and security clause.

> At the centre of the arbitration claim were two allegations: that South African police turned a blind-eye to the series of incursions visited upon the Swiss-owned property, and that the investment was subjected to an expropriation either by virtue of the cumulative destruction inflicted upon the property or, in the alternative, due to a domestic land-claims process under which several local residents were seeking all or parts of the property in question.[112]

South Africa lost the arbitration process regarding the allegations of not providing full protection and security, but the investor was not able to prove the alleged expropriation. Even though the amount of damages was split because the investor also did not take enough precautionary measures to secure and protect his property, the South African government nevertheless was ordered to pay R6,6 million plus interest and also to pay two thirds of the investor's legal costs.[113]

The amounts of money that had to be paid out of the coffers of South Africa in both these instances[114] are substantial and the taxpayer is the one

111 In the Limpopo province.

112 Luke Peterson, "3. Swiss investor prevailed in 2003 in confidential BIT arbitration over South Africa land dispute; award remains unpublished, but *IAReporter* investigation unearths significant details about arbitration outcome" *Investment Arbitration Reporter* (22-10-2008). *See also* Peter Leon, Balancing investor certainty and SA's legitimate interests, *Business Day*, 16 September 2009, at 13.

113 Even though that amount is not disclosed, taking the amount into account that was claimed in the *Foresti* case, the amount in this case would also have been substantial.

114 Not only due to the finding against it in the Swiss arbitration, but also for the legal costs involved.

that was ultimately on the losing end. In both of these cases, the taxpayer had to bear the brunt without necessarily being aware of the arbitration[115] or what caused it, furthermore, the government (or the recalcitrant sector of the government, the police or whatever department was involved) was not held accountable for its actions because Joe Citizen via its democratically elected members of Parliament was not aware of how his money was being wasted as a result of its government's (in)actions. One would prefer that the reasons for such uncalled-for expenditure be publicised in order to ensure that the principles of accountability and transparency are adhered to.

When one reads the rest of the discussion of this confidential award, it is very clear why the government did not want to disclose all the detail:

> As for the allegations of police failings, the tribunal would hold that there was no effective policing of the property – nor prosecution of those apprehended – during a period of several years. The tribunal noted that it was unclear whether this failing stemmed from a lack of resources or other systemic failures.[116]

Another point to note is that the tribunal apparently also looked into the obligation of national treatment

> which it interpreted as an invitation to explore the potential liability imposed on the government under South African law, in certain circumstances, for negligently failing to protect individuals from crime. Here, the tribunal singled out two South African cases in particular – *Carmichele v Minister of Safety* [*and Security*] and *Minister of Safety* [*and Security*] *v Van Duivenboden* – which were held to impose a similar duty of due diligence.[117]

At no stage was this arbitration award discussed in Parliament which means that the broader members of Parliament were not aware of its existence[118] and also the fact that due to the lack of proper policing and the exercise of governmental duties as identified in the *Carmichele* and *Van Duivenboden*

115 As is definitely the case regarding the Swiss arbitration.

116 *Investment Arbitration Reporter* (22-10-2008).

117 Luke Peterson, *supra* note 112.

118 Since then, mention has been made of this arbitration before some of the parliamentary committees, but this still does not mean that full disclosure had been made or that corrective actions were taken.

cases, a fairly big damages award and costs order were given against the state. The non-compliance with its international law obligations which was a result of its non-compliance with its constitutional obligations, had led to an expenditure that was not budgeted for and for which no accountability was required.[119] This links up with the point made earlier regarding the lack of parliamentary involvement in the decision to conclude and approve the final form of the BITs.

The *Piero Foresti* case was a different story, mainly because it took place under the auspices of the ICSID Additional Facility and because the parties disclosed the facts from the start. This led to the application of some non-governmental organisations to participate as *amici curiae* because the dispute dealt *inter alia* with the public interest and public policy issues.[120] Even though issues of public interest were also at stake in the Swiss arbitration, the complete opaqueness and confidentiality that surrounded the matter made it impossible for a similar intervention to take place. The mere fact that this dispute was not in the public eye creates an issue of public interest because there was no possibility of using the award to hold the government accountable and

119 The fact that the arbitration tribunal adjudicated on matters of public interest and interpreted the constitutional duties of the government, placed this arbitration in the public law realm (even though it dealt with international law obligations). Since this award is not in the public domain, it means that a future decision in an investment dispute based on similar actions and similar provisions of the same (or similar) bilateral investment treaty as well as the interpretation of the government's constitutional duties, will be looked at afresh. There would be no hindsight (or insight) that could have been provided by a published earlier award. The Government and all its departments (especially at local government level) are also not aware of how its actions were interpreted and classified and as a result, similar actions can continue without realising the consequences that may follow as a result of the existence of international investment agreements. Unless these awards are published and do not remain confidential, there cannot be any reassessment and correcting of governmental actions. There is thus a real need to have access to these awards. The possibility that the government may argue that the interpretation of its constitutional duties was wrong and against public policy also exists but in order to address these issues in a transparent manner, publicity needs to be given to these processes and more importantly, to these awards. The United Nations Convention on Transparency in Treaty-based Investor-State Arbitration may in future assist in this regard, but again, it will be dependent on the state to consent to apply the UNCITRAL Rules on Transparency in Treaty-based Investor-State Arbitration to its investment treaties signed before 1 April 2014. South Africa has not signed this treaty.

120 See in this regard *Petition for Limited Participation as Non-Disputing Parties International Centre for Settlement of Investment Disputes Case Number: ARB(AF)/07/01 Between Piero Foresti, Laura De Carli and the Republic of South Africa*, available at http://www.italaw.com/sites/default/files/case-documents/ita0333.pdf (visited September 25, 2019).

to ensure that service delivery or a violation of constitutional obligations was and could be corrected.[121]

The fact that the BITs involved did not include a carve-out or a national-treatment exception meant that the government's policy which culminated in the amendments to the relevant act which was in line with its social upliftment goals and the values enshrined in the Constitution, could not be considered. The fact that the *amici curiae* intervened might also not have had a big influence because matters of domestic policy may not as a rule be considered when it comes to the interpretation of treaties. A reliance on domestic law, as reason for transgressing your international law obligations, is also not a defence or an excuse.

South Africa's constitutional mandate seemingly requires the government to implement policies for purposes of socioeconomic reform and it is quite clear that they may sit at odds with its international investment obligations.

> These constitutionally sanctioned socioeconomic provisions are likely to sit at odds with the government's investment obligations, where a conflict of interests arises between the government's domestic mandate and a foreign investor's property rights. It is likely that the Constitution will give way to investor's rights in international investor arbitration.[122]

4 South Africa's Current Approach to BITs

The end result was that South Africa became very sceptical about investment arbitration and BITs in general. These challenges from investors of developed states that South Africa had to face when they sought to rely on BIT provisions to claim compensation for alleged breaches of the BITs[123] led to the

121 The International Arbitration Act 15 of 2017 which came into operation on 20 December 2017, provides that 'arbitration proceedings to which a public body is a party are held in public, unless for compelling reasons, the arbitral tribunal directs otherwise' (Section 11(1)). The positive impact of this provision is somewhat over-shadowed by the fact that investor-state arbitrations (apart from those that may still take place in terms of existing BITs or the sunset clauses of terminated or lapsed BITs) are no longer allowed.

122 *See* Nicole Yazbek, Bilateral investment treaties: the foreclosure of domestic policy space, 2010 *South African Journal of International Affairs* 113 (2010).

123 A confidential arbitration in terms of the Switzerland-South Africa BIT of 1995 and the arbitration in *Piero Foresti, supra* note 53.

comprehensive review of its Bilateral Investment Treaty Policy Framework already alluded to.[124]

The review process was based on the government's Position Paper (2009) which was not a comprehensive document that analysed all the different aspects of its own BITs; and neither did it provide a comprehensive picture of international investment law and potential possibilities available in connection with the renegotiation of BITs etc. An interim decision was taken to suspend all negotiations and conclusions of BITs pending the outcome of the review[125] and the finalisation of the litigation.

At the time of the initiation of the review, many of the BITs signed immediately after 1994 were fast approaching the end of their term of validity and it was felt that they should be revisited "with a view to ensuring that they incorporate measures which ensure that national developmental objectives may be pursued".[126] However, instead of pursuing this avenue, the South African government took a policy decision not to renew its existing BITs[127] and to rather develop a domestic framework for the promotion and protection of investment.[128] The initial position paper of the government was not followed up with any other document indicating to what extent the comments that were received, were taken into account or clearly setting out why it decided to follow the route on which it had embarked.

The development of a framework for the promotion and protection of investment was initiated and a draft Promotion and Protection of Investment Bill was published for comment late 2013, after a number of contracting parties were already notified that their BITs were being unilaterally terminated.[129] The Protection of Investment Act was promulgated in 2015 but only came into operation on 13 July 2018.

Even though it was reported that the South African government was to have consulted extensively on the issue of termination with governments with whom they had signed BITs following the Cabinet decision in July 2010 to terminate all BITs, this did not seem to reflect reality when reports from governments such

124 *Supra* note 60, at 19.

125 The review commenced in October 2008.

126 *See supra* note 101.

127 This was notified in the press through a Cabinet decision in July 2010.

128 ATC140331: Report of the Portfolio Committee on Trade and Industry on its activities undertaken during the 4th Parliament (May 2009–March 2014), adopted on 12 March 2014.

129 This led to the publication of the draft Promotion and Protection of Investment Bill, 2013 (General Notice 1087 *Government Gazette* 36995 of 1 November 2013) for comment.

as Germany and Switzerland are read.[130] The following BITs were terminated or notification of termination or notification of the intention to terminate was given: the United Kingdom, the Netherlands, Switzerland, Germany, France, Cuba, Denmark, Austria, Italy, Sweden, Argentina, Belgo-Luxembourg Economic Union, Finland, Spain, and Greece. The only contracting parties to BITs who apparently did not receive notices of termination, were Korea, China, Mauritius, Russia, Nigeria and Zimbabwe.[131]

Apart from the termination of the BITs, the Cabinet decision of July 2010 also contained the following: the development of a new Investment Act to codify and clarify typical BIT-provisions into domestic law, and to strengthen investor protection; to terminate "first generation" BITs and offer partners the possibility to renegotiate;[132] to refrain from entering into BITs in future, unless compelling economic and political reasons exist;[133] to develop a new Model BIT[134] as basis for (re-)negotiation; and to advance all decision-making in respect of BITs to an Inter-Ministerial Committee to oversee the process.[135]

130 *See also* Mark Allix, Economic sense "must override BEE" in foreign investing, *Business Day* 8 November 2013 4; Xavier Carim, Lessons from South Africa's BITs review, *Columbia FDI Perspectives*, No. 109, 25 November 2013.

131 This is the status of BITs in South Africa as at 19 August 2019. Information provided by the SA Treaty Register and the Department of Trade and Industry.

132 This apparently did not happen.

133 It should perhaps also be noted that the South Africa-Zimbabwe BIT (n 39) was signed during the period that the BIT policy review was underway. Apparently the permission to sign the BIT was already given by the South African government in 2004 but due to disagreement on the application of the BIT to existing South African investments, especially in the agricultural sector, reaching agreement was delayed until November 2009 when the parties agreed that the BIT would not apply to any property right or interest compulsorily acquired by either Party in its own territory before the entry into force. It would thus seem that in this one instance where the government experienced a fair amount of pressure from its own investors in Zimbabwe, it was still prepared to sign a BIT which contains in essence the same provisions as the ones that it has terminated. The only difference seems to lie in the fact that the other contracting party would most possibly be subjected to disputes based on treaty violations, and that the converse is not likely to happen (so it might seem) and that made it necessary to conclude a BIT on the same terms as all the others even though many similar BITs had already been terminated. This does not make logical sense.

134 According to officials of the Department of Trade and Industry, a Model BIT was being finalised, but it is not clear whether, in the light of the promulgation of the Promotion of Investment Act, there is any sense in having a Model BIT and whether work on it was completed.

135 *See* Rob Davies, South African Minister: New approach needed on investment treaties, 69 *South Bulletin* (2012); Mustaqeem Da Gama, International Experiences in Foreign Direct Investment (FDI): Lessons for South Africa (presentation given at a seminar entitled South Africa's Promotion and Protection of Investment Bill on 15 February 2015 in

This last-mentioned change in the approach to be followed when it comes to investment agreements is both important and concerning. Important, because the decision does not merely lie with one government department any longer, and concerning because it seems as if the South African parliament which has not been involved in this type of agreements under the new dispensation where some of the problems regarding the contents of the BITs could have been addressed and assessed at the outset had the process been different, is still being side-stepped. It is perhaps high time that the whole process concerning technical, administrative and executive agreements be considered in detail.

5 The Protection of Investment Act (2015)

A draft bill on the promotion and protection of investment was first published in 2013, which, according to officials, aimed to achieve a balance between the rights and obligations of investors and those of the government.[136] It tried to achieve a situation where the Government's decisions on beneficiation and black economic empowerment could not be challenged before foreign or international tribunals as encroaching on investments or expropriating[137] investments of foreign investors, thus striking a balance between protecting investor's rights and government's regulatory space to give effect to its constitutional obligations without having to answer to international tribunals and pay damages and/or compensation for actions taken that were seen to be totally legitimate within its internal policies to redress the inequalities of the past, ensure economic development for all its peoples etc. And thus, the Protection of Investment Act was promulgated in 2015 and came into operation in 2018.

The Act has several noteworthy features: First, it omits the investor-state dispute resolution mechanisms provided for in South Africa's BITs. Thus, for all practical purposes, dispute resolution is limited to mediation as the preferred

---

Cape Town), available at http://www.saiia.org.za/events/international-experiences-in-foreign-direct-investment-fdi-lessons-for-south-africa (visited September 25, 2019).

136 The concern related to the fact that the investors had no obligations in a BIT framework but only rights (and these rights were more comprehensive than that of local investors) and that all the obligations were laid at the door of the home state.

137 The provisions on expropriation that were contained in the 2013 draft did not reappear in the following drafts or the final act, however, a Draft Expropriation Bill was published. See *supra* note 15.

method[138] although an investor "is not precluded from approaching any competent court, independent tribunal or statutory body within the Republic for the resolution of a dispute relating to an investment".[139] Second, it significantly restricts the availability of international arbitration by allowing it after exhaustion of domestic remedies; if the government consents; *and only* "between [South Africa] and the home state of the applicable investor".[140]

The Act thus removes any possibility for investors to take any investment-related dispute with the government to arbitration.[141] In this way, the Act returns foreign investors to the arguably unsatisfactory position they held prior to the adoption of the Washington Convention,[142] which first recognised the importance of granting investors a right to appear before an international tribunal and to sue a host state for breaching obligations under international law.[143]

This puts a foreign investor in a predicament – the whole issue of reliance on diplomatic protection is now again brought to the fore. No government is obliged to take up its citizens' disputes with other states and for South Africa to provide for state-state arbitration in an act that is supposedly aimed at investor protection, does not help the foreign investor one bit. A foreign investor cannot be certain that if he has exhausted all local remedies and still feels aggrieved that his home state will feel it necessary to intervene, furthermore, South Africa may even decide that it is not inclined to consent to the arbitration.[144]

Thus, unlike the situation created with the BITs, where governmental actions[145] could be scrutinised and judged by tribunals that had no intimate knowledge of South Africa or the South African situation if these actions

138 Section 13(1)–(3), Protection of Investment Act and the Mediation Rules, 2018 RGN 712/41767/19 13 July 18.

139 Section 13(4), Protection of Investment Act (2015).

140 Section 13 (5), Protection of Investment Act (2015).

141 However, no such provision applies to other forms of international commercial arbitration. See Section 5 of International Arbitration Act 15 of 2017 which provides that "This Act, subject to the provisions of Section 13 of the Protection of Investment Act, 2015 (Act 22 of 2015), binds public bodies and applies to any international commercial arbitration in terms of an arbitration agreement to which a public body is a party."

142 Convention on the Settlement of Investment Disputes Between States and Nationals of Other States, 18 March 1965, 17 UST 1290, 575 UNTS 159.

143 Be that as it may, international arbitration before a tribunal like ICSID is off the cards and the South African government has made it quite clear that it is not considering acceding to the ICSID convention or allowing any further investor-state international arbitration in investment disputes.

144 Section 13 of the Protection of Investment Act (2015) is not prescriptive.

145 Undertaken to ensure compliance with its constitutional mandate and correcting the wrongs of the past.

were considered by foreign investors to be in violation of international law obligations contained in BITs, this is no longer the case for foreign investors who are not protected by an existing BIT.

It is said that the new act makes it possible within the domestic framework to ensure that the constitutional obligations of the government can be complied with without fear of litigation and in so doing the public interest can be safeguarded and the government retains its regulatory freedom. This may be so, but in the process the government created a legally untenable situation where there is no uniform way in which investors, both foreign and national are to be protected.

It is argued that the Act clarifies standards of protection for investors – both foreign and domestic – "by setting out provisions ordinarily found in BITs in a manner that is consistent with the Constitution and the existing legal framework".[146] There is a lot of criticism which indicates that the protections provided in the act do not replicate the same protection as those provided in BITs.[147]

Apart from the concerns that are raised in relation to the level and types of protection arguably offered to foreign investors, legal uncertainty in relation to the protection of foreign investors will continue as uniformity will only be achieved in the long run – when all the current BITs are terminated and the sunset periods have lapsed, but until then, a lot of legal uncertainty is clouding the protection of investors and this is particularly true in relation to the applicable legal principles. This uncertain situation is brought about through the termination of the BITs and the promulgation of the Protection of Investment Act and particularly in relation to the legal principles and protections applicable to investment disputes.

---

146 Da Gama, *supra* note 135; Xavier Carim, Lessons from South Africa's BITs Review, *Columbia FDI Perspectives*, No. 109, 25 November 2013.

147 See for example, Amy Farish, Protection of Investments Act – A balancing Act between policies and investments, 2016 (May) *De* Rebus 26; Richard Jansen van Vuuren Investment laws in South Africa – foreign investors take note' *Mining Review Africa*, 24 July 2018, available at https://www.miningreview.com/news/changes-investment-laws-south-africa-foreign-investors/ (visited August 20, 2019); Dreyer Swart *Legal Protection of Foreign Investment in South Africa* (LLM mini thesis UP 2016); and Sarah McKenzie *Resolving the Conflict between the Protection of International Investments and the State's Right and Responsibility to Regulate* (LLM thesis WITS 2017); Andile Sicetsha, South Africa's "Protection of Investment Act" may drive foreign investors away, *The South African*, 25 July 2018, available at https://www.thesouthafrican.com/business-finance/south-africas-protection-of-investment-act-may-drive-foreign-investors-away/ (visited August 20, 2019).

6 Efforts to Seek a Balance between Investor Protection and the Preservation of State Sovereignty in the Protection of Investment Act (2015)

The current landscape raises a series of questions about the future of investor-state dispute settlement in South Africa. First, to what extent will international law principles continue to govern the protection of investments under the new Act? BITs enabled foreign investors to pursue treaty-based claims and thus rely on principles of international law in arbitrations with South Africa. As fewer and fewer of those treaties remain operative, they lose significance as a source of law. In theory, foreign investors could continue to rely on treaty-based principles in South African courts and mediation, so long as those principles are part of South African domestic law. However, in reality, BIT principles are not incorporated.[148]

Nor is it clear that other forms of international law will apply. Section 3 of the Protection of Investment Act states that one must interpret and apply the Act in accordance with international law. Given that customary international law requires a state to provide compensation, typically at market value, in the event of an expropriation of private property, one might imagine investors using the Act to advance customary international law-based claims against expropriation. But this sort of argument remains untested.

The involvement of an investor's home state also raises difficulties. For example, what is the real reason for giving the home state standing in an arbitration with South Africa under the Protection of Investment Act? What will convince the home state to enter into arbitration with South Africa? What will the home state argue? Will it be acting as a representative of the foreign investor or on its own behalf? Will it contend that the South African government has not complied with its own statute (the argument that the investor would have raised), or that it breached customary international law by failing to provide the minimum standard of treatment to aliens? Arguments that it would have used if arguing a diplomatic protection case?[149] The Act does not

---

148 *Progress Office Machines CC v South African Revenue Services*, 2008 2 SA 13 (SCA) (establishing that parties can rely on the provisions of a treaty in a domestic court only if the treaty has been incorporated into South African law 17E–F).

149 *See also* Won Kidane, Contemporary international investment law trends and Africa's dilemmas in the draft Pan-African Investment Code, 50 *The George Washington International Law Review* 523 (2018) 566 et seq. He reads into the act that 'South Africa's new attempt now permits the private investor to grant *locus standi* to the home state presumably through a simple private contractual instrument (at 560). I do not see anything in the Act that remotely makes this an option.

provide clarity on the substantive law that will govern the arbitration other than the reference to a vague standard for fair administrative treatment.

If the question arises under the Act, it is doubtful that reliance on international law principles will succeed unless the parties agree that the dispute will be settled purely on that basis. The interplay between international law and South African law especially where it comes to the interpretation of statutes and in particular the application of customary law in South Africa is not settled, and disputes that may arise in terms of the Protection of Investment Act, especially in relation to the minimum standard of treatment, is fraught with uncertainty.[150]

The second question is whether the South African Constitution will, as a matter of domestic law, displace any relevant commitments under customary international law. While Section 3 of the Protection of Investment Act requires that the interpretation and application of the Act must be done consistently with international law,[151] the Act is subject to the South African Constitution, which provides that customary international law forms part of South African law "unless it is inconsistent with the Constitution or an Act of Parliament".[152] For investors, this hierarchy of authority could prove problematic because it is black-letter law in South Africa that the compensation to be paid after expropriation need not reflect market value, which is merely one of several factors that influence the amount of the award.[153] Moreover, the South African parliament has just approved a proposal to amend its constitution to permit expropriation without compensation.[154] The process to amend the Constitution will take a

150 See Erika de Wet, The Reception of International Law in the South African Legal Order: An Introduction in Erika de Wet, Holger Hestermeyer and Rüdiger Wolfrum (eds.), *The Implementation of International Law in Germany and South Africa* (Pretoria: Pretoria University Press, 2015) 23, 37 et seq.

151 "3 Interpretation of Act
This Act must be interpreted and applied in a manner that is consistent with –
(a) its purposes as contemplated by Section 4;
(b) the Constitution, including –
  (i) the interpretation of the Bill of Rights contemplated in Section 39 of the Constitution;
  (ii) customary international law contemplated in Section 232 of the Constitution; and
  (iii) international law contemplated in Section 233 of the Constitution; and
(c) any relevant convention or international agreement to which the Republic is or becomes a party."

152 Sections 232 and 233 of Constitution of the Republic of South Africa, 1996.

153 Section 25(3) of Constitution of the Republic of South Africa, 1996.

154 *See* "Review of Parliament" 2018 (*supra* note 14): "there was no unanimity on this and ultimately the majority view prevailed, *which recommended that Section 25 of the Constitution*

while but once the amendment is done and it becomes constitutionally possible to expropriate without compensating the owner, customary international law-based claims against expropriation will conflict with the Constitution more clearly than ever before, and will thus fail on account of the doctrine of constitutional supremacy.[155]

The possibility of constitutional displacement of customary international law is significant for several reasons. One is that absent the ability to rely on international law in South African courts, investors from states that lack a bilateral investment treaty with South Africa will have to rely on their home states to raise international law-based objections at the intergovernmental level or in future arbitral proceedings under the Protection of Investment Act.[156] The other reason is that constitutional displacement would likely generate disparate outcomes in similar disputes depending on the nationality of the investor. In international investment arbitration based on BITS, arbitrators are not bound to consider the constitutional law that influences and often dictates a government's actions. As a result, investors from states that still have a bilateral investment treaty with South Africa are unlikely to encounter the displacement problem. In contrast, investors from other states may have to present their disputes to municipal courts that must follow the South African Constitution. Until there is one uniform investor-state dispute settlement system in South Africa, the availability of different fora for different investors is likely to generate disparate outcomes in comparable disputes.

The final question is whether South Africa's new regime is consistent with international law. A state generally has the right to choose the policies by which it will govern within its own national borders. Still, all states are bound by international law, regardless of what municipal law might say. Absent bilateral investment treaties, the legality of South Africa's regulation of foreign

---

be amended to make it explicitly clear that expropriation of land without compensation by the state in the public interest should be one mechanism to address the injustices of the past" (emphasis added).

155 Before this may become a reality, the normal legislative process will need to take its course and as it stands, some of the political parties and interest groups have already indicated that they are going to challenge the process. See "Review of Parliament" (*supra* note 14).

156 Section 13(5): "The government *may consent to international arbitration* in respect of investments covered by this Act, subject to the exhaustion of domestic remedies. The consideration of a request for international arbitration will be subject to the administrative processes set out in Section 6. Such arbitration will be conducted between the Republic and the home state of the applicable investor" (emphasis added). As a result, there is no obligation on the South African government to agree to international arbitration with an investor's home state.

investment is likely to depend heavily on customary international law, but the contours of that law are often contested and indeterminate. In this sense, the consistency of South Africa's regulatory actions with international law may become harder to ascertain.

7 The Bases of Investor Protection in South Africa after the Termination of BITS

The bases for the protection of foreign investors and the resolution of investor-state disputes in South Africa are currently diverse, which is the direct result of the decision not to renegotiate existing BITS but to terminate some and to allow others to lapse and it may mean that potentially three legal regimes may govern the resolution of investor-state disputes. Investing in South Africa now means firstly, that an investor is protected by general South African law.[157] This law might incorporate principles of international law – especially on state responsibility and the treatment of aliens – that do not conflict with the South African Constitution. Secondly, an investor, depending on its nationality, might fall under the protection of a BIT either because the treaty has not lapsed or terminated, or because it contains a so-called survival or sunset clause that renders its provisions applicable to investments made while the treaty was in force for a particular period of time. To illustrate, the Russia-South Africa and China-South Africa BITS are currently in force, but even if they lapse, each contains a survival clause: foreign investors that enjoyed the benefit and protection of the BIT at the time of their investment will continue to do so for a specified number of years, which is ten for China and fifteen for Russia respectively.

Thirdly, another possible means of protection is provided by the Southern African Development Community Protocol on Finance and Investment. In terms of the unamended version, all foreign investors were granted protection of their investments in the SADC region. However, the definition of investor[158]

157 Amongst others the protection provided by the Bill of Rights in chapter 2 of the Constitution of the Republic of South Africa, 1996 and the Protection of Investment Act 22 of 2015.

158 Investor was initially defined as 'a person that has been admitted to make or has made an investment' (art. 1 Annex 1 of the SADC Protocol on Finance and Investment) and it has now been amended to read 'a natural or a juridical person *of a State Party* making an investment in another State Party, in accordance with the laws and regulations of the State Party in which the investment is made' (emphasis added – art. 1 of the Agreement amending Annex 1 (Co-operation on Investment) of the Protocol on Finance and Investment).

and investment have changed, and the scope of 'investors' is now limited to nationals of SADC countries.[159]

All foreign investors face these different regimes, including those investors from the other BRICS countries. Of the latter, only Russia and China have BITS with South Africa.[160] Thus, for the time being, three legal regimes may potentially apply to a foreign investor which contain material variations either in the duration or the type of protection.

8 Future Framework of Investor-State Dispute Settlement in Relation to South Africa

The adoption of the Washington Convention[161] and the resultant surge in the conclusion of BITS over the decades were perceived as resulting from the lack of trust in both legal systems and courts of capital-importing countries,[162] and the political will of home states to assist their citizens through diplomatic protection when the need arose. BITS presented the assumed ideal solution by introducing investor-state arbitration. It was no longer necessary to rely on the home state for intervention. The foreign investor was also free to choose (at least some of) the arbitrators – who were to be knowledgeable, independent, and impartial – and could thus be certain that its case would be properly resolved. It was also thought that the arbitration awards would be easy to enforce, and that the system as a whole would depoliticise disputes. However, the legitimacy of investor-state arbitration came under fire for various reasons, including that the claims instituted against a state can amount to more than the gross domestic product of a state[163] and that defendant states included not only those perceived to have questionable legal systems and perhaps

159 South Africa only recently ratified the amendment. The amended protocol came into force for the SADC on 24 August 2017.

160 After the publication of the contribution entitled "Dispute Settlement in Investment-Related Matters: South Africa and the BRICS" as part of the "Symposium on the BRICS Approach to the Investment Treaty System" in 112 *AJIL Unbound* 212 (2018) 212–216, confirmation was received from the South African Department of Trade and Industry that the treaties are still in force but that the contracting parties had been contacted to discuss termination (email correspondence on file with author).

161 Convention on the Settlement of Investment Disputes Between States and Nationals of Other States, 18 March 1965, 17 UST 1290, 575 UNTS 159.

162 *See* Rudolf Dolzer and Christoph Schreuer, *Principles of International Investment Law* (Oxford: Oxford University Press 2012) 349.

163 *See* Julie Maupin, Remarks by Julie Maupin, 109 *Proceedings of the ASIL Annual Meeting* 238 (2015) 238–244.

not-so-independent judiciaries but also developed states.[164] Arbitration tribunals also made findings concerning governments' internal policies and the validity of their legislation in instances where the domestic courts would often not have jurisdiction or would be compelled to take a country's constitutional obligations into consideration.

South Africa faced early disputes in this regard. The most well-known case concerned whether the mineral law amendments implemented as part of the socioeconomic reforms related to its black economic empowerment policies were compatible with its treaty commitments.[165] The government reacted to this case by deciding that it needed to rethink its BIT and investor-state arbitration policy so as to ensure, among other things, the primacy of its constitutional commitments. Accordingly, the investor-state dispute resolution mechanisms provided for in South Africa's BITs were not replicated in the new Act. For all practical purposes, dispute resolution is limited to litigation in the domestic courts and mediation. International arbitration is allowed (after exhaustion of domestic remedies) only if the government consents to it, and then '[s]uch arbitration will be conducted between the Republic and the home state of the applicable investor.'[166]

The Act thus effectively removes any possibility for the investor to take any investment-related dispute with the government to arbitration.[167] If the investor does not get satisfaction either through mediation or the South African courts, it must rely on its government to initiate arbitration on the matter with the South African government, provided that the South African government consents.

8.1 *Investor Protection in the Southern African Development Community – the Position of South Africa*

8.1.1 The Protocol on Finance and Investment

As a member of the Southern African Development Community (SADC), South Africa is obliged to comply with its international law obligations, which

164 *See for example* the *Vattenfall* case against Germany – *Vattenfall AB and others v Federal Republic of Germany*, ICSID Case No. ARB/12/12. The German decision to phase out nuclear power triggered this dispute pursuant to the Energy Charter Treaty.

165 *Foresti v Republic of South Africa*, ICSID No. ARB(AF)/07/1 (Aug. 4, 2010). See *also* Schlemmer, *supra* note 26); Peter Leon, Creeping Expropriation of Mining Investments: An African Perspective, 27 *Journal of Energy and Natural Resources Law* 597(2009).

166 Section 13(5) of Protection of Investment Act.

167 No such provision applies to other forms of international commercial arbitration. See Section 5 of International Arbitration Act of 2017.

arise from its membership of this regional economic community. The SADC Protocol on Finance and Investment recognises the need for cooperation to "enhance the attractiveness of the Region as an investment destination"[168] and it is concerned with the "low levels of investment into the SADC".[169] It thus seems as if the protocol is meant to address not only intra-SADC investment but also investment *into* the region. Before the amendment of the Annex, provisions protected both investors within the SADC region and investors from third parties. This protocol came into force in 2010[170] but was amended – in particular its Annex 1 – in 2016 after the South African Protection of Investment Act was passed but before it came into operation.[171] The timing of the amendment of the SADC protocol seems to coincide with the South African Protection of Investment Act which was not in line with the SADC Protocol on Finance and Investment or the SADC Model BIT[172] especially in relation to the dispute resolution mechanisms introduced and the removal of the possibility of investor-state arbitration. Thus, giving the impression that the Protocol was amended to ensure that South Africa's new policy did not cause it to be in breach of its international law obligations as a member of the Southern African Development Community.

8.1.2 The SADC Protocol on Finance and Investment and Investors from Outside the SADC Region

The amendments to Annex 1 (Co-operation on Investment) of the Protocol on Finance and Investment[173] are far-reaching but interestingly enough, when

168 Preamble of the SADC Protocol on Finance and Investment.

169 Preamble of Annex 1 of the SADC Protocol – dealing with co-operation on investment.

170 South Africa also ratified it, the instrument of ratification of the Protocol was signed on 19 June 2008 by the South African President.

171 The Department of Trade Industry states that "[c]hallenges with the Bilateral Investment Treaties (BITs) including investor to state disputes, reducing policy space/regulatory autonomy, necessitated SADC to review the Protocol". See the presentation by the Department of Trade and Industry to the Parliamentary Committee on Trade and International Relations 7 November 2018 'Ratification of the Agreement Amending Annex 1 (Co-operation on Investment) of the SADC Protocol on Finance and Investment (FIP)2017' 3, available at https://pmg.org.za/files/181107SADC-Amendment_to_Annex_1.ppt (visited November 20, 2018).

172 Both of which were finalised during the period where the South African government's review of its investment policy framework was taking place and with the active participation of South Africa.

173 The amended Annex came into force on 24 August 2017 – see Department of Trade and Industry, "Briefing and ratification of the Agreement amending Annex 1 (Co-operation on Investment) of the SADC Protocol on Finance and Investment (FIP)" – Meeting of the

the ratification of the Amendment Agreement was (only recently) put to the parliamentary committee – on 7 November 2018 – the presentation to the committee merely notes[174] the following amendments: changes to the definition of investment and investor (without giving any detail); the fact that the following phrase was deleted "the prohibition on modification of terms, conditions and benefits agreed to, on admission of investment"; that the compensation standard in relation to expropriation was changed from "prompt and effective" to "fair and adequate";[175] national treatment is replacing most favoured nation treatment; and that the amended protocol only allows for state-state dispute settlement before the SADC tribunal, thus that investor-state arbitration has been removed.

It is indeed alarming that these amendments that removed the protection initially granted to investors from any other state regardless of their nationality or incorporation, was not pointed out nor discussed in the parliamentary committee, yet the decision was made to support ratification of the amendment.

The implication for non-SADC investors and thus also BRIC investors in South Africa (and the SADC region) is that their standing before an international arbitration tribunal[176] to deal with disputes that may arise as a result of treaty breaches by the host state has been removed.[177] This was achieved by amending the definition of investor, which initially did not contain any indication of nationality or incorporation,[178] to limit the protection to investors who are SADC nationals.[179] Furthermore, the provision on fair and equitable

Committee on Trade and International Relations of the National Council of Provinces on 7 November 2018, available at https://pmg.org.za/committee-meeting/27469/ (visited November 18, 2018).

174 The impact of these amendments was not pointed out and neither was there any debate on the amendments or their implications.

175 And that details are given in article 5 in relation to the determination of what amounts to "fair and adequate" compensation. The issue of expropriation and the measure of compensation applied in terms of the protocol will not form part of the rest of the discussion albeit to note that the approach that the South African government is seemingly taking in that it has approved a report to amend the South African constitution to allow for expropriation without compensation is not in line with its international law obligations also in terms of these provisions of the SADC Protocol on Finance and Investment.

176 After exhaustion of local remedies.

177 Art. 28 Annex 1, SADC Protocol on Finance and Investment.

178 Thus, allowing the protection to also cover investors from other states than the States Party to the Protocol.

179 "Investor" means "a natural or a juridical person of a State Party making an investment in another State Party, in accordance with the laws and regulations of the State Party in which the investment is made". Art. 1 Annex 1, SADC Protocol on Finance and Investment.

treatment was replaced by national treatment standards thereby curtailing the protections for foreign investors even more.[180]

The removal of the protection for foreign (non-SADC) investors is particularly problematic especially in the light of the fair and equitable treatment standard that was part of the Annex and, if generally applied, requires host states to provide to international investments treatment that does not affect the basic expectations that were taken into account by the foreign investors to make the investment.[181] The protection guaranteed in Annex 1 of the Protocol on Finance and Investment which included investor-state arbitration as dispute settlement mechanism could have influenced non-SADC investors to invest in the SADC and thus have created an expectation that this position would continue.[182] With this amendment and the absence of a survival clause, the SADC member states have effectively removed the international law protection – including investor-state arbitration – of foreign investors in SADC with the stroke of a pen which, in my view, not only breaches the fair and equitable standard of treatment and but also potentially amounts to a denial of justice through removing the access to investor-state arbitration which gave the parties an additional avenue for the resolution of their dispute with the state outside of the domain of domestic courts and other tribunals.[183]

180 In the unamended version of Annex 1, Art. 6 provided that 'investments and investors shall enjoy fair and equitable treatment in the territory of any State Party. 2. Treatment referred to in paragraph 1 shall be no less favourable than that granted to investors of the third State'.

181 *See* the finding by the tribunal in *Tecnicas Medioambientales Tecmed SA v The United Mexican States* (ICSID CASE No. ARB (AF)/00/2), Award of 29 May 2003 para. 154. *See also* Benedict Kingsbury and Stephan Schill, Investor-State Arbitration as Governance: Fair and Equitable Treatment, Proportionality and the Emerging Global Administrative Law New York University School of Law, Public Law & Legal Theory Research Working Paper No. 09–46 (2009) 10.

182 *See generally* Tomaso Ferrando, BITing land abroad: the anti-redistributive impact of bilateral investment treaties, *African Yearbook of International Law* 249 (2015) 251 et seq.

183 It is telling that the South African Constitutional Court recently held in *Law Society of South Africa v President of the Republic of South Africa* (CCT67/18) [2018] ZACC 51 (11 December 2018) that South Africa's President's "participation in the decision-making process and his own decision to suspend the operations of the Southern African Development Community Tribunal is unconstitutional, unlawful and irrational and that his signature has to be withdrawn" (para. 97). It was found that South Africa was "party to denying citizens of South Africa and other SADC countries access to justice at a regional level in relation to their disputes including those relating to human rights, democracy and the rule of law" (para. 15) by the decision to emasculate the Tribunal. This was also found in relation to the act when the SADC leaders "sign[ed] the Protocol whose mission it is to deprive individuals of pre-existing access to the Tribunal" (para. 18). The court held that

The position of SADC nationals is also precarious, but at least they are guaranteed access to the domestic courts and tribunals of SADC member states.[184] The fact that the international law-based dispute settlement mechanism has been removed without providing anything similar, may amount to a breach of the right of access to justice.[185]

---

the right which is threatened is the right of access to justice as enshrined in the Bill of Rights and the SADC Treaty "and the threat extends to the rule of law" (para. 29).

The Court further held that "[t]he President may therefore not approve anything that undermines our Bill of Rights and international law obligations. We are about access to justice and *access to all appropriate justice-dispensing platforms*. He thus lacked the authority to sign any international agreement that seeks to frustrate the pre-existing right of South Africans to access justice, that was secured for them by our supreme law-making body." (paras. 77 my emphasis.) That this decision may have implications for non-SADC investors who invested in South Africa after the coming into operation of the SADC Protocol on Finance and Investment is something to be investigated further.

184 In terms of the Annex, the state parties are to "ensure that investors have the right of access to the courts, judicial and administrative tribunals, and other authorities competent under the laws of the Host State for redress of their grievances in relation to any matter concerning their investment including *but not limited to the right for* judicial review of measures relating to expropriation or nationalization and determination of compensation in the event of expropriation or nationalisation." Art. 25 of the amended Annex (2016) – the emphasised words indicates additions to the article.

185 For a more detailed discussion, see the judgment in *Law Society of South Africa v President of the Republic of South Africa*. Also note that the South African courts have held per justice Van Heerden in *Dawood, Shalabi and Thomas v Minister of Home Affairs* 2000 1 SA 997 (C) that "[i]t is a well-established principle of international law that, as a consequence of its territorial sovereignty, a state has the right to control the entry of aliens into its territory. However, once an alien has entered its territory, the State concerned is obliged under international law to 'respect basic human rights norms in its treatment of such alien'. Moreover, under the South African Constitution an alien who is inside this country is entitled to all of the fundamental rights entrenched in the Bill of Rights, except those expressly limited to South African citizens" (1043I–1044E). The decision was confirmed by the Constitutional Court (2000 3 SA 936 (CC)); see also *Kiliko v Minister of Home Affairs* 2006 4 SA 114 (C). *See also* Max du Preez: '[I]t is an accepted principle of international law that once a foreigner has been permitted to enter the territory of a state, obligations on that state are engaged vis-à-vis the foreign national. More particularly, the authorities are obliged to execute deportations in a humanitarian manner and in strict compliance with the law. Consistent with this understanding of international law is the position under South Africa's Constitution: once a foreigner has entered South Africa the Bill of Rights applies to him or her. Section 7(1) of the Constitution expressly provides that the Bill of Rights enshrines the rights of "all people in our country". Bearing in mind this provision, the Constitutional Court has accepted that, in the absence of any indication that a particular right is to be restricted to citizens, the right should be interpreted as applying to everyone in the country and therefore includes non-citizens.' (footnotes omitted) – "Removals, terrorism and human rights – reflections on *Rashid*", 2009 *SAJHR* 353(2009) 356.

Whether Article 26 of the SADC Protocol will or can include disputes in relation to investments made by nationals of the state parties, is not clear. The article heading is "Settlement of Investment Disputes", while the contents do not seem to be pointing in the direction of a state taking up the case of its complaining national but rather that it is remnant of the previous version of the Annex which has not been properly edited.

Article 25 is the only article which refers to some or other dispute resolution facility for the investors which is now (like the position in South Africa) limited to the domestic courts and tribunals with no access whatsoever to arbitration with the host state. It is also noteworthy that this Protocol (or its Annex 1) does not provide for a survival clause to deal with those investments that were entitled to the protection of the protocol since 2010 when it came into operation. Moreover, the protection provided for investors from third states have abruptly been taken away in its totality without any notice – they are no longer protected in terms of the amended Annex, and it is particularly at this level where one would have expected a transition or survival clause due to the far-reaching consequences of these amendments. The unamended Annex 1 did not contain any explicit protections extending to the time after its termination or amendment, and neither does the new amended Annex refer to investments made prior to its coming into effect or to investments from investors from third states.[186]

One could argue that investors from a third state (which could be one of the investors from the BRICS countries) have been severely prejudiced as a result of the amendment and the question that remains is whether South Africa (as the host state),[187] should have acted in the way it did by agreeing to the amendment of the protocol, taking its membership of the BRICS into account and also its relations with other countries with whom no bilateral or other investment treaties have been concluded. The removal of an investor's "right" without any compensation is tantamount to expropriation – and the fact that for these investors their standing for purposes of investor-state arbitration in relation to international treaty breaches has been removed, might amount to a denial justice especially since there are no longer any possibility to rely on the protections that were accorded to them and their investments

186 Prior to the amendment, investors were given the option of international arbitration in relation to investor-state disputes. This has now been taken away with the stroke of a pen and unlike in the case of bilateral investment treaties, there is no survival clause which provides for a fixed period after a treaty or provision has lapsed during which period the investor can still rely on the same protection as that which was applicable during the duration of the treaty.

187 The potential liability of SADC may also arise.

in terms of the SADC Protocol which will include their access to investor-state arbitration.[188]

9 Concluding Remarks

There is currently a fairly uncertain and fluid situation regarding the treatment of new investments by new investors in South Africa. A few investment treaties are still in force, as indicated, but the others that were terminated are not providing any protection to new investors and investments. The existing foreign investors and their investments who were entitled to protection under the now terminated investment agreements will continue to have the protection of those treaties until the sunset term expires.[189]

There is thus currently more than one system of protection in place. The BITs that are still operational will continue to provide protection and so will the provisions of the terminated BITs albeit for a limited period of time; those investments that had been made by investors from countries whose governments have not concluded any treaties or whose treaties have not come into operation, are governed by the normal South African law which contains no express provisions relating only to foreign investors and specifically regarding expropriation issues, the position regarding compensation is not final and certain. With the Protection of Investment Act, a new dispensation has arisen – new investors will potentially have fewer rights than their country men who already have investments in South Africa.

In relation to South Africa's membership of BRICS: the position concerning the protection of investors and investments in South Africa and the related investor-state dispute settlement possibilities are far from clear and harmonised. The diversity of approaches is not only found within South Africa but can also be seen when looking at the practice in BRICS as a whole. There is no one-size-fits-all when it comes to the protection of investment or the investor-state dispute settlement in existence. New investors from China and Russia may in future also have to forebear the protection of the BITs since the termination of these BITs are being discussed.

188 The application of this Protocol in South Africa has not been considered in detail and there are a number of unanswered questions in relation it which calls for closer scrutiny.

189 Which ranges anything between 10 and 15 years, all depending on the provisions of the relevant treaties.

South Africa is also not the only BRICS member that has had problems with investor-state arbitration. The *Yukos* case garnered extensive publicity,[190] and it seems that governments are plainly reluctant to accept awards and even more so to comply with them, notwithstanding their initial consent to international investment arbitration. From a political standpoint, this attitude may be understandable, especially in the light of the magnitude of the damages awarded in some instances and the lack of a system of appeal, however, awards follow only after a determination of illegality. From a legal perspective, non-compliance is not defensible.

Whether the above deficiencies should cause governments to shy away from proper ways of resolving disputes and complying with awards and enforcing them is questionable and are issues that the future negotiators in the BRICS will have to consider. If the goal is to treat all investors within the BRICS equally, the diverse approaches to investor protection and dispute resolution now followed by the different members should preferably be replaced by a uniform or harmonised approach. Moreover, the members should undertake to recognise, enforce, and comply with one another's arbitral awards and domestic judgments.

For BRICS, the most advisable route may be to reach an agreement on general principles of protection for investors based on the principle of reciprocity, as well as on the role of constitutional imperatives in this scenario. Clear guidelines about the types of protection that should be accorded to investors and investments and different modes of dispute resolution need to be considered. It is doubtful at this stage whether a uniform approach to dispute resolution can be achieved, but a way needs to be found for all investors to be treated equally and fairly through the application of the same legal principles to the extent possible. More wisdom than that of Solomon will be required.

In the meantime, investors should carefully consider their activities in a potential host state. The nature of their activity may be considered an investment in one state whereas it may not qualify as an investment in another and when one looks at South Africa as a host state, there may be different regimes applicable to a particular act all depending on whether it qualifies as an investment. It may thus be wise to consider whether it is indeed beneficial to be considered an investor in South Africa or whether the potential use of international commercial arbitration as a means of dispute settlement may not be more beneficial thus causing the potential "investor" rather to structure its business activities in such a way that it does not qualify as an investment.

190 *Yukos Universal Ltd (Isle of Man) v Russian Federation*, PCA Case No. AA 227 (UNCITRAL 18 July 2014).

CHAPTER 7

Recalibrating Policy Space in Bilateral Investment Treaties: Is There a Common B(R)ICS Approach?

Andreas Buser

1 Introduction

International investment law is currently in a time of contestation and transition.[1] To be sure, this is not the first time. The international investment regime has long been subject to various contestations. Many newly independent (developing) countries early opposed the ideas of capital-exporting States of an international minimum standard of investment protection, as such, a minimum standard was meant to protect imperial and colonial "investments" of state-owned companies and citizens of the former colonizers and imperialists from redistribution.[2] In the 1970s, a broad coalition of developing States promoted the permanent sovereignty over natural resources and, more generally, a New International Economic Order (NIEO) which highlighted States sovereignty and regulatory powers rejected standards of compensation for expropriation brought forward by capital exporting States.[3] Yet, those efforts were not to succeed. Instead, in the late 1980s and 1990s, capital-exporting countries of the Global North and international organizations largely under their control successfully promoted economic neo-liberalism and strong investment

1 *See e.g.*, Steffen Hindelang and Markus Krajewski, Towards a More Comprehensive Approach in International Investment Law, in Steffen Hindelang and Markus Krajewski (eds), *Shifting Paradigms in International Investment Law: More Balanced, Less Isolated, Increasingly Diversified* (Oxford: Oxford University Press, 2016) 1–18.

2 For example the promotion of the Calvo Doctrine by several Southern American States, *see in detail* M. Sornarajah, *The International Law on Foreign Investment*, 3rd ed. (Cambridge: Cambridge University Press, 2010) 21 et seqq.; 71 et seqq.; Sundhya Pahuja, *Decolonising International Law: Development, Economic Growth and the Politics of Universality* (Cambridge: Cambridge University Press, 2011) 95 et seqq.

3 Permanent Sovereignty over Natural Resources, General Assembly resolution 1803 (XVII), New York, 14 December 1962, para. 4 (promoting "appropriate compensation" instead of the Hull Criteria); Declaration on the Establishment of a New International Economic Order, General Assembly Resolution 3201 (S-VI), New York, 1 May 1974, particularly para. 4 e) and g).

 | DOI:10.1163/9789004376991_008

protection through Bilateral Investment Treaties (BITs).[4] Nowadays up to 3000 of those treaties span all over the globe.

Today the need for international investment protection and arbitration has again become severely contested. Critical scholars have highlighted the colonial heritage and continuing power imbalances that characterize the regime.[5] Investment protection's economic justification that prohibiting (or limiting) state interference is necessary to attract investments to foster development, particularly in impoverished Nations has seriously been called into question.[6] Human rights lawyers have further highlighted possible conflicts between human rights law (most important economic, social and cultural rights) and BIT obligations and stressed the need for States to create an international enabling environment through investment cooperation.[7]

At the heart of much criticism against international investment law's basic orientation seems to be the balance, or lack thereof, between the interests of transnational business entities (or individual freedom as some might say) and public interests (or government's interests).[8] There appears to be a broadly

4 On the assumed failure of the NIEO, *see* Margot E. Salomon, From NIEO to Now And the Unfinishable Story of Economic Justice, 62 *International and Comparative Law Quarterly* 31 (2013). On the reasons why developing countries signed BITs, see Andrew T. Guzman, Why LDCs Sign Treaties That Hurt Them: Explaining the Popularity of Bilateral Investment Treaties, 38 *Virginia Journal of International Law* 639 (1998).

5 *See* Sundhya Pahuja, *supra* note 2; Kate Miles, *The Origins of International Investment Law: Empire, Environment and the Safeguarding of Capital* (Cambridge: Cambridge University Press, 2013) and generally accounts by TWAIL scholars, for introductions *see*, B.S. Chimni, Third World Approaches to International Law: A Manifesto, 8 *International Community Law Review* 3 (2006); James Thuo Gathii, TWAIL: A Brief History of its Origins, its Decentralized Network, and a Tentative Bibliography, 3 *Trade, Law and Development* 26 (2011).

6 For useful overviews of arguments and empirical studies, *see* M. Sornarajah, *supra* note 2, at 11 et seqq.; Robert Howse, International Investment Law and Arbitration: A Conceptual Framework, 1 IILJ Working Paper (MegaReg Series) (2017) 11 et seqq.

7 *See e.g.* Diane A. Desierto, *Public Policy in International Economic Law: The ICESCR in Trade, Finance, and Investment* (Oxford: Oxford University Press, 2015) 17 and 29. On possible conflicts between international investment protection law and human rights, see Howard Mann, International Investment Agreements, Business and Human Rights: Key Issues and Opportunities (Report prepared for Prof. John Ruggie, UN Special Representative to the Secretary General for Business and Human Rights (International Institute for Sustainable Development, February 2008)), 2008, available at: http://www.iisd.org/pdf/2008/iia_business_human_rights.pdf (visited April 6, 2018); Javier Perez, Myriam Gistelinck and Dima Karbala, Sleeping Lions: International Investment Treaties, State-Investor Disputes and Access to Food, Land and Water, Oxfam Discussion Papers 1, available at https://policy-practice.oxfam.org.uk/publications/sleeping-lions-international-investment-treaties-state-investor-disputes-and-ac-132350 2011 (visited April 6, 2018).

8 *See e.g.*, S.A. Spears, The Quest for Policy Space in a New Generation of International Investment Agreements, 13 *Journal of International Economic Law* 1037 (2010); Hindelang and

shared concern that the balance between private investor interests and public interests, between protection from state interference and a state's right to regulate, needs recalibration.[9] Importantly, the UN Guiding Principles on Business and Human Rights stressed that "States should maintain domestic policy space to meet their human rights obligations when pursuing business-related policy objectives with other States or business enterprises, for instance through investment treaties or contracts".[10]

A "backlash" against international investment law is also evident in state practice and civil societies. Several Southern American states, such as Bolivia, Ecuador and Venezuela have denounced the ICSID Convention and terminated some of their BITs.[11] Other states of the Global South, such as South Africa and Indonesia, have also become wary of investor-state dispute settlement (ISDS) and consequently terminated a considerable number of their BITs.[12] Increasingly states and societies of the Global North also question the need for international investment protection and "special rights" for huge

---

Krajewski, *supra* note 1, at 5; see for a recent document stressing the right to regulate and the need to reform investment treaties with a focus on promoting sustainable development: African Society of International Law, 2016 AFSIL Principles on International Investment for Sustainable Development in Africa, Ghana, 28–29 October 2016, available at https://www.cdiph.ulaval.ca/sites/cdiph.ulaval.ca/files/2016_afsil_principles_on_international_investment_for_sustainable_development_in_africa.pdf (visited April 6, 2018).

9 This is not to say that investment tribunals have not taken up public concerns, but finding the right balance remains an issue. The arbitrational tribunal that first explicitly acknowledged "legitimate regulatory interests" was the tribunal in *Saluka Investments B. V. v. Czech Republic*, UNCITRAL, Partial Award of 17 March 2006, para. 306.

10 See Principle 9 of the "Guiding Principles on Business and Human Rights: Implementing the United Nations 'Protect, Respect and Remedy' Framework", Report of the Special Representative of the Secretary-General on the issue of human rights and transnational corporations and other business enterprises, John Ruggie, Human Rights Council, Seventeenth session, A/HRC/17/31, 21 March 2011, Annex.

11 Bolivia has terminated 10 BITs (with Argentina, Austria, BLEU, France, Germany, Netherlands, Spain, Sweden and United States) out of a total of 23 BITs; Venezuela has terminated its BIT with the Netherlands but 29 of its BITs are still in force; Ecuador has terminated 11 of its BITs (with Cuba, Dominican Republic, El Salvador, Finland, Germany, Guatemala, Honduras, Nicaragua, Paraguay, Romania, and Uruguay) out of a total of 29 BITs; Indonesia has terminated 26 BITs (with Argentina, Bulgaria, Cambodia, China, Egypt, Finland, France, Germany, Hungary, India, Italy, Lao PDR, Malaysia, Netherlands, Norway, Pakistan, Romania, Singapore, Slovakia, Spain, Switzerland, Turkey, Viet Nam) out of a total of 71 BITs. All information on the status of BITs is taken from UNCTAD's Investment Policy Hub, available at: www.investmentpolicyhub.unctad.org.

12 South Africa has terminated 9 BITs (Austria, BLEU, Denmark, France, Germany, the Netherlands, Spain, Switzerland and the United Kingdom) out of a total of 49 BITs; Indonesia terminated 27 BITs (Argentina, Belgium, Bulgaria, Cambodia, China, Denmark, Egypt, Finland, France, Germany, Hungary, India, Italy, Lao People's Democratic Republic,

companies. Just think of the anti-TTIP protests in the EU, President Trump's opposition to TPP and efforts to renegotiate NAFTA (all of which include investment chapters), or the criticism the Vattenfall arbitration[13] sparked in Germany. Consequently, Northern States have also been keen on highlighting public interest considerations and recalibrate treaty language in that regard.[14] Powerful Western States like the US, Canada and the States united in the EU also support changes to the ISDS system, including ideas like an appellate mechanism or even a world investment court system in case of the EU.[15] Countries around the world, including both developed and developing countries, have engaged in restructuring International Investment Agreements (IIAs) towards framing them more development-friendly and allowing for policy space for public purposes.[16] Connectedly, even much-loathed arbitral tribunals have begun to take public concerns more seriously (even under older international investment agreements).[17]

In the context of this ongoing reform, this chapter wants to shed light on approaches of five important actors, the BRICS. These States' approaches are of particular interest for a variety of reasons. First, most of those States have become important destinations for investments and some even prominent capital exporters,[18] meaning that their treaty practice will affect a vast number

---

Malaysia, the Netherlands, Norway, Pakistan, Romania, Singapore, Slovakia, Spain, Switzerland, Turkey, Viet Nam) out of its total of 71 BITs.

13 *Vattenfall AB and others v Federal Republic of Germany*, ICSID Case No ARB/12/12.

14 Examples include Article 12 (Environment), Article 13 (Labour rights) and Article 14 (Opt-out clause for non-conforming measures) of the US Model BIT 2012; Article 8.9 (Investment and regulatory measures) in the investment chapter of the European Union-Canada Comprehensive Economic and Trade Agreement (CETA), 2016. The texts of all cited BITs are available online on UNCTAD's Investment Policy Hub, available at: www.investmentpolicyhub.unctad.org.

15 For the proposal to establish a multilateral investment dispute settlement mechanism, including an appeal mechanism, *see* European Commission and Government of Canada, the case for creating a multilateral investment dispute settlement mechanism, discussion paper prepared for an informal ministerial meeting, World Economic Forum Davos, 20 January 2017, available at http://trade.ec.europa.eu/doclib/docs/2017/january/tradoc_155264.pdf (visited April 6, 2018).

16 For an overview of these reform efforts, *see* UNCTAD, Taking Stock of IIA Reform, March 2016, available at http://unctad.org/en/PublicationsLibrary/webdiaepcb2016d3_en.pdf (visited April 6, 2018).

17 *See* Paul Barker, Legitimate Regulatory Interests: Case Law and Developments in IIA Practice, in Andreas Kulick (ed), *Reassertion of Control Over the Investment Treaty Regime* (Cambridge: Cambridge University Press, 2017) 230–258.

18 A 2013 UNCTAD report entitled "the Rise of BRICS FDI and Africa" showed that BRICS countries' share of inward FDI as well as their outward FDI flows had risen dramatically in the period between 2000–2012. Their overall share of world FDI flows reached 20% in

of investors and investments. Given this substantial economic relevance, it is also assumed that legal practice by those States factually will have a more significant impact than others'.[19] Secondly, given their status as emerging powers and their efforts to join forces in BRICS the field of investment law provides an important case study on whether newly powerful (former) developing countries (except Russia) will challenge existing international law which historically was primarily influenced by developed States' interests. Given that emerging powers have often been associated with a preference for strong sovereignty and non-interference, due to historical and other reasons,[20] it will be asked whether this focus translates into shielding the right to regulate in international investment law.

2 B(R)ICS as Loyalists, Reformers or Revolutionaries?

In the context just described, the study will ask whether B(R)ICS are loyalists/ traditionalist, reformers or revolutionaries when it comes to the balance between private rights and public interests in BITs.[21] While broadly framed, those terms

2012, up from 6% in 2000. The overall share of outward FDI flows increased from only 1% to 9%. Foreign investments from BRICS mainly flow to developing countries with 42% of BRICS outward foreign investments going to developing countries. *See* UNCTAD, The Rise of BRICS FDI and Africa. Global Investment Trends Monitor (25 March 2013). UNCTAD's more recent World Investment Report based on data up until 2015 shows that South Africa and Brazil suffered some decline in FDI inflows, but numbers are still much higher than in 2000. Intra-BRICS FDI flows remain low as total FDI flows to the group remained below 1 per cent between 2014–2015. China compared to other B(R)ICS clearly is distinctive as both investment inflows as well as outflows clearly succeed those of the other States. *See* UNCTAD, *2016 World Investment Report* (New York/Geneva: United Nations, 2016).

19 As for power and its relevance for international law making, *see* Richard H. Steinberg and Jonathan M. Zasloff, Power and International Law, 100 *American Journal of International Law* 64 (2006); Krisch, International Law in Times of Hegemony, 16 *European Journal of International Law* 369 (2005). As to great powers and international law, *see e.g.*, Hermann Mosler, *Die Grossmachtstellung im Völkerrecht* (Heidelberg: Lambert Schneider, 1949); Wilhelm Georg Grewe, *The Epochs of International Law* (*transl. by Michael Byers*) (Berlin: Walter de Gruyter, 2000); Michael Byers and Georg Nolte (eds.), *United States Hegemony and the Foundations of International Law* (Cambridge: Cambridge University Press, 2003); Congyan Cai, *New Great Powers and International Law in the 21st Century*, 24 *European Journal of International Law* 755 (2013).

20 One example is their approach on the responsibility to protect, *see* Oliver Stuenkel, *The BRICS and the Future of Global Order* (New York: Lexington Books, 2016) 125 et seqq.

21 I borrow some of those terms from Anthea Roberts, who used them to describe States approaches on Investor-State Arbitration, *see* Anthea Roberts, The Shifting Landscape of Investor-State Arbitration: Loyalists, Reformists, Revolutionaries and Undecideds,

will help to systematize States' approaches. The chapter defines those terms as follows.

Loyalists are States that continue to embrace strong classical investment protection provisions. As it is assumed that States continually evolve treaty practice to be qualified as a loyalist does not exclude the possibility of incremental reform, but the general direction is to keep strong protections for investors accompanied by ISDS provisions.

Reformists, on the other hand, seek more pronounced reform. Examples could be distinctly narrowed definitions of protected investments, the inclusion of (general) exception clauses to protect regulatory policy space or the installation of an ISDS appellate mechanism. It is also considered to be reformist if a State promotes creative but not radical new provisions in IIAs, such as non-binding corporate social responsibility (CSR).

Revolutionaries also seek reform but are much more radical than reformists. They might seek to terminate BITs all together, or they might limit the scope of and or investor's rights in BITs to such an extent that they are effectively meaningless. New creative provisions could be termed revolutionary if they bring substantial legal changes, with meaningful obligations for investors (or their home countries) being a long-discussed example.

For further systematization, we can distinguish between different levels, namely the international and the national level. A State might, for example, apply a revolutionary approach in that it terminates all its BITs, but may instead enact domestic laws that guarantee for strong investment protection. Such a State should be considered a revolutionary at the international level, but a loyalist at the national level.

Still, to qualify States according to these terms remains to some extent simplistic. A State might loyally embrace some existing provisions but completely reject others or include revolutionary new obligations in addition to traditional ones. Therefore, these categories will be applied on a provision-by-provision basis, only revealing some overall "trend" for any individual State. Lastly, provision by provision patterns, if not fully conclusive, may reveal that a State so far belongs to the clear majority of States that remains "undecided" or ambiguous as to the future course of the international legal investment regime.[22] However, before analyzing individual States' approaches, we will briefly evaluate whether BRICS have taken a common approach to the future of investment law.

June 15, 2017, available at https://www.ejiltalk.org/the-shifting-landscape-of-investor-state-arbitration-loyalists-reformists-revolutionaries-and-undecideds/ (visited August 8, 2017).

22 See on the category of undecided States also *id.*

2.1 *A Common BRICS Approach?*

The BRICS grouping is important for international law in many ways. The group, in its short time of existence, has managed to create the New Development Bank and the BRICS Contingent Reserve Arrangement.[23] In BRICS joint statements, issued at annual meetings of heads of States, they have addressed a variety of topics relevant for international law, ranging from the prohibition of the use of force to trade law.[24] Increased cooperation on investment has been addressed so far mostly as an economic and political matter but not as a legal one.[25] Besides embracing non-legal strategies to increase direct investment flows between group members, there are no known intentions to produce something like a BRICS plurilateral investment treaty or a "mega-regional" free trade agreement with an investment chapter. Correspondingly, there only exists a limited number of BITs between BRICS members, mostly between Russia and other Members.[26]

However, the grouping has managed to produce a short joint statement on the "BRICS Perspective on International Investment Agreements", which sets out some voluntary shared legal preferences.[27] It is necessary to quote the document in full:

1. Foreign direct investment (FDI) can make a positive contribution to sustainable development when integrated into national development strategies. These benefits of FDI may include, amongst others, technology transfer, skills development, enhanced research at the national level,

23 *See* Agreement on the New Development Bank, Fortaleza, July 2015, available at http://www.ndb.int/wp-content/themes/ndb/pdf/Agreement-on-the-New-Development-Bank.pdf (visited April 6, 2018); and Treaty for the Establishment of a BRICS Contingent Reserve Arrangement, Fortaleza, July 2015, available at http://brics.itamaraty.gov.br/press-releases/220-treaty-for-the-establishment-of-a-brics-contingent-reserve-arrangement-fortaleza-july-15 (visited April 6, 2018).

24 *See e.g.*, "Ninth Summit: BRICS Leaders Xiamen Declaration", Xiamen, 4 September 2017; "BRICS in Africa: Collaboration for Inclusive Growth and Shared Prosperity in the 4th Industrial Revolution", 10th BRICS Summit Johannesburg Declaration, 26 July 2018 (all BRICS statements are available at http://www.brics.utoronto.ca/ (visited April 6, 2018)).

25 *See e.g.*, BRICS, Outlines for BRICS Investment Facilitation, Annex II to the 7th Meeting of BRICS Trade Ministers Statement, 31 August 2017.

26 China-India BIT (2007); China-Russia BIT (2009); India-Russia BIT (1996); Russia-South Africa BIT (2000).

27 The document has been mentioned in The 4th Meeting of the BRICS Trade Ministers: Joint Communiqué, Fortaleza, Brazil, 14 July 2014 ("The Ministers reaffirmed the importance of a continued dialogue on international investment agreements. They noted the principles outlined in the document 'A BRICS Perspective on International Investment Agreements' as a voluntary reference for countries to advance a more balanced approach to investment treaties") the full document is available at http://brics.itamaraty.gov.br/category-english/21-documents/227-brics-perspective-on-international-investment-agreements (visited April 6, 2018).

and the establishment of stronger supply chains between domestic and foreign firms.

2. BRICS Member States note that International Investment Agreements may, depending on their formulation, promote investment liberalization and protect the rights of investors. *Investment agreements should strike a balance between the protection of investors and the Government's sovereign right to regulate in the public interest.* In this regard, a robust national legal framework is conducive to the effective protection to both domestic and foreign investments.
3. *BRICS Members States call for further improvements of International Investment Agreements*, including in their dispute settlement mechanisms.
4. It is also important International Investment Agreements *serve the purpose of sustainable development*, which is defined and outlined in the United Nations Conference on Sustainable Development. To this end, *International Investment Agreements should encourage foreign investors to support national development strategies, inter alia through responsible business practices and offer greater attention to investment promotion and facilitation.*
5. BRICS Member States are encouraged to build common approaches in various multilateral dialogues on international investment policy.[28]

While held rather vaguely the document nevertheless provides some insights into which concerns about international investment law individual BRICS member States share. The statement only reluctantly embraces investment protection and requires it to serve national development objectives. Investment agreements are required to balance rights of investors and a State's sovereign right to regulate (para. 2). The third and fourth paragraph call for changes in investment agreements including a stronger focus on sustainable development and reforming dispute settlement (albeit with no indication what this could mean more precisely).

This perspective might further evolve in precision, as indicated in the last paragraph of the statement. A joint communique of 2015 further states that there is an inter BRICS dialogue on "investment policies and international investment rules".[29] However, so far, BRICS were only able to reiterate their preference for the right to regulate in public statements without providing further details.[30] A recent document entitled "Outlines for BRICS Investment

28 *Id.* (Highlighting added).

29 The Fifth Meeting of the BRICS Trade Ministers: Joint Communiqué, Moscow, Russia, 7 July 2015, para. 17.

30 In 2017 BRICS Trade Ministers reiterated that they "fully preserve the right to regulate, national policy space, policy making and approaches to investment in […] bilateral,

Facilitation" seems to take up the Brazilian Model investment agreements focus on investment facilitation (to be explained in more depth below) but makes no reference to international investment law as such.[31]

The cited statements suggest that BRICS are reformists as in the above-defined sense regarding policy space in international investment law. They argue for some decisive changes but remain loyal to the system as such. However, the vagueness of the statement also suggests that BRICS States either were unable, unwilling or merely undecided on how to balance investor rights with a State's right to regulate and sustainable development objectives more concretely. Therefore, we need to look at case studies from three BRICS countries to provide some insights on whether and in how far individual approaches align and could form a more precise BRICS approach on international investment law.

Before analyzing individual treaty practice and Model investment agreements in more depth, the next section will look at historical approaches of four BRICS countries, namely Brazil, China, India and South Africa. Russia is excluded, as it is no former developing country. As for reasons that will become obvious throughout the historical part, South Africa will not be considered in the comparative part.

2.2 *B(R)ICS' Investment Agreements in Historical Perspective*

B(R)ICS States' policies towards international investment protection from a historical perspective are quite diverse.[32] Generally speaking, all developing country BRICS members, while initially being sceptical of foreign investment protection, have turned towards signing BITs as part of their liberalization projects in the wake of the world's general trend towards liberalized markets in the 1980s and 1990s.[33] Brazil, however, while signing 14 BITs in the 1990s has never ratified any of those treaties. According to Brazilian State representatives,

---

plurilateral and multilateral frameworks and processes", *see* 7th Meeting of the BRICS Trade Ministers Statement, Shanghai, 2. August 2017, para. 6.

31 *See* Outlines for BRICS Investment Facilitation, Annex II to the 7th Meeting of the BRICS Trade Ministers Statement, 31 August, 2017.

32 For a comparative historical perspective, *see* Mihaela Papa, BRICS and the Politics of Reforming Global Governance: The Case of Investment Arbitration, in Gráinne de Búrca, Claire Kilpatrick and Joanne Scott eds., *Critical Legal Perspectives on Global Governance. Liber Amicorum David M. Trubek* (London: Bloomsbury Publishing, 2014) 405–423, 415 et seqq.

33 Brazil signed its first BIT with Portugal in 1994, which was followed by 13 signed BITs in the years until 1999. China signed its first BIT in 1982 with Sweden and subsequently concluded numerous BITs with mostly developed but increasingly also with developing countries. Until now China has signed 129 BITs of which 110 are in force. India signed its first BIT with the United Kingdom in 1994 and until now has concluded another 68 BITs.

provisions on indirect expropriation and Investor State Dispute Settlement contained in those initial BITs "were considered as non-compliant with the Brazilian Constitution" and were "considered to impose restrictions on the adoption of public policies critical to the country's development".[34] Despite this variance, Brazil, like all other B(R)ICS, has experienced high inflows of capital during the late 1990s and 2000s.[35]

Times have changed, however. Some B(R)ICS have experienced slow-downs of investment inflows, and some have fundamentally changed their approach to BITs. Brazil, South Africa and India have recently reviewed their agreements and have reformed their policy of investment protection. Both India and South Africa had initially concluded traditional-style BITs that were providing broad protection for investors and allowing for ISDS.[36] The review process in both States was triggered by (first) investment cases brought against them.

South Africa faced a case brought by several Italian nationals and a Luxembourg-based cooperation engaged in the mining business against South African legislation that was part of its black economic empowerment policies.[37] Although the case was ultimately settled, and the claimants were granted the demanded mining rights without having to fully satisfy the requirement that 26 per cent of the ownership stake of the enterprise be held by black South Africans (which was the main obstacle), the case highly raised public and governmental awareness that investors may challenge black economic

---

South Africa concluded its first BIT with the United Kingdom and until 2009 concluded another 39 BITs.

34 Daniel Godinho, Secretary of Foreign Trade, Ministry of Development, Industry and Foreign Trade, Brazil, Speech delivered at the UNCTAD World Investment Forum 2014: Investing in Sustainable Development, 16 October 2014, available at http://unctad-worldinvestmentforum.org/wp-content/uploads/2014/10/Godinho.pdf (visited April 6, 2018).

35 This assessment is based on World Bank data, available at: https://data.worldbank.org/indicator/BX.KLT.DINV.CD.WD (visited April 6, 2018).

36 For overviews of the respective States' treaty practice, *see* Prabhash Ranjan, India's International Investment Agreements and India's Regulatory Power as a Host Nation, PhD Thesis, King's College London, 2012, available at https://papers.ssrn.com/sol3/cf_dev/AbsByAuth.cfm?per_id=446970 (visited April 6, 2018); Anniruddha Rajput, Shifting Treaty Practice of India: From 2003 Model BIT to 2015 Model BIT, 7 *Jindal Global Law Review* 201 (2016); Sean Woolfrey, The Emergence of a New Approach to Investment Protection in South Africa, in Steffen Hindelang and Markus Krajewski eds., *Shifting Paradigms in International Investment Law. More Balanced, Less Isolated, Increasingly Diversified* (Oxford: Oxford University Press, 2016) 266–290, 267 et seqq.

37 *See Piero Foresti, Laura de Carli and others v Republic of South Africa*, ICSID Case No. ARB(AF)/07/1, Award of 4th August 2010. For an overview of the legal questions involved, see *id.* 270 et seqq.

empowerment policies and other South African policies before international arbitral tribunals.[38]

In 2011, India even lost its first investment arbitration case against the Australian investor *White Industries*[39] of which Indian government circles and scholars appeared utterly surprised and irritated.[40] Subsequently, India faced several claims by investors against other regulatory measures, including new retroactive tax laws.[41]

These experiences have sparked resistance against international investment protection and ISDS within government circles of both countries. South Africa consequently has terminated several of its BITs mostly with the European States and replaced them with national legislation through the Protection of Investment Act.[42] Further, South Africa did not ratify a number of already signed other BITs and so far has not concluded any new investment treaties since 2010.[43] Government officials have indicated that South Africa may develop a new model BIT and based on that model may negotiate new treaties in the future.[44] So far, no new model BIT has been published while reports indicate that South Africa might sign a new investment treaty with Brazil.[45]

---

38 *Id.* 272.

39 *White Industries Australia Limited v. Republic of India*, UNCITRAL, Final Award of 30 November 2011.

40 This assessment is based on personal interviews undertaken as a research visitor at NLUD Delhi in March 2017. A particular point of criticism from the Indian side was the fact that *White Industries* had relied on a clause of the India Kuwait BIT which was 'imported' into the Australia-India BIT via an MFN clause.

41 *See e.g.*, *Vodafone v. India*, UNCTIRAL, Notice of Arbitration (not public), 17 April 2014; *Cairn Energy PLC and Cairn UK Holdings Limited (CUHL) v. India*, PCA Case No. 2016–7; *Deutsche Telekom v. India*, ICSID Additional Facility, Notice of Arbitration (not public), 2. September 2013; *CC/Devas (Mauritius) Ltd., Devas Employees Mauritius Private Limited, and Telecom Devas Mauritius Limited v. India*, PCA Case No. 2013–09 (pending).

42 Protection of Investment Act, Act No. 22 of 2015, Republic of South Africa, Government Gazette, Vol. 606, 15 December 2015, No. 39514.

43 See for an overview of South Africa's investment treaties and their status, South Africa's country page at UNCTAD's investment policy hub, available at http://investmentpolicyhub.unctad.org/IIA/CountryBits/195 (visited April 11, 2018).

44 Xavier Carim, 'South African Input by the South African Permanent Representative to the WTO', Trade and Development Board, Sixty-Second Session Item 7: Investment for Development – Reforming the International Investment Regime (16 September 2015) available at http://investmentpolicyhub.unctad.org/Upload/Documents/Ambassador%20Xavier%20Carim_Speaking%20Points.pdf (visited April 11, 2018).

45 Nathalie Bernasconi-Osterwalder & Martin Dietrich Brauch, Comparative Commentary to Brazil's Cooperation and Investment Facilitation Agreements (CIFAs) with Mozambique, Angola, Mexico, and Malawi, 2015, available at http://www.IISD.org (visited April 11, 2018).

India on the other hand has reviewed its BIT program beginning in 2012 and came up with a new Model BIT in 2015 (Indian Model BIT)[46] which, according to government officials, is "aimed at providing appropriate protection to foreign investors in India and Indian investors in the foreign country, in the light of relevant international precedents and practices, while maintaining a balance between the investor's rights and the Government Obligations [sic]".[47] Consequently, the Indian government is in the process of terminating 58 treaties out of its total of 83 signed treaties, intends to replace them with BITs based on its new Model BIT and bases its ongoing BIT negotiations with the US on the new Model BIT.[48] Moreover, India appears to have invited several treaty partners to sign joint interpretative statements, which are based on provisions found in India's new Model BIT.[49]

Brazil, in contrast, while initially rejecting ratification of signed BITs, has recently adopted a new approach.[50] As part of a new investment policy, it had developed a new type of international investment treaty named Cooperation and Facilitation Investment Agreement (CFIA).[51] The new CFIA has been described by Brazilian State representatives as follows:

---

46 Indian Model BIT (2015) is available at http://investmentpolicyhub.unctad.org/Download/TreatyFile/3560; Earlier the Indian government had published a much more radical Draft of its Model BIT. For critical analysis of this first draft, *see* Law Commission of India, Analysis of the 2015 Draft Model Indian Bilateral Investment Treaty, Report No. 260 (August 2015).

47 *See* Government of India, Ministry of Commerce & Industry, Department of Industrial Policy & Promotion, Lok Sabha, Unstarred Question No. 1290, to be answered on Monday, the 25th July 2016, available at http://dipp.nic.in/sites/default/files/lu1290.pdf (visited April 11, 2018).

48 This intention has been stated by Shrimati Nirmala Sitharaman (the Minister of State of the Ministry of Commerce & Industry) as a response to questions raised in the Lok Sabha, *see*: Government of India, Ministry of Commerce & Industry, Department of Industrial Policy & Promotion, Lok Sabha, Unstarred Question No. 1290, to be answered on Monday, the 25th July 2016, available at http://dipp.nic.in/sites/default/files/lu1290.pdf (visited April 11, 2018).

49 *See* Government of India Ministry of Finance Department of Economic Affairs (Investment Division), Issuing Joint Interpretative Statements for Indian Bilateral Investment Treaties: F. No. 26/07/2013-IC, 8 February 2016, available at http://indiainbusiness.nic.in/newdesign/upload/Consolidated_Interpretive-Statement.pdf (visited April 11, 2018).

50 For an overview of Brazil's approach to IIAs and a first in detail analysis of newly concluded treaties, *see* Michelle Ratton Sanchez Badin and Fabio Morosini, Navigating between Resistance and Conformity with the International Investment Regime: The Brazilian Agreements on Cooperation an Facilitation of Investments (ACFIs), in Fabio Morosini and Michelle Ratton Sanchez (eds.), *Reconceptualizing International Investment Law From the Global South* (New York: Cambridge University Press, 2018) 218–250.

51 The Model CFIA is available at http://investmentpolicyhub.unctad.org/IIA/CountryIris/27#iiaInnerMenu (visited April 11, 2018).

> CFIA consists in an innovative alternative to traditional IIAs. It recognizes the role of governments in fostering a positive environment for investment, takes into full consideration the interests of private investors, retain [sic] policy space for pursuing the development needs of the parties, and adopts a constructive and proactive view aimed at bridging potential differences between investors and the host country.[52]

Several CFIAs have been concluded with other developing countries either from Southern America or Africa (with a focus on lusophone countries). Contracting States include Angola, Chile, Colombia, Malawi, Mexico and Mozambique.[53] There are further reports of negotiations with Algeria, Morocco, Peru, South Africa and Tunisia.[54] This time Brazil appears willing and able to ratify signed agreements, as the agreement with Angola has already been ratified and entered into force,[55] and the Brazilian Senate reportedly has approved the agreements with Mexico and Peru.[56]

China, in the context of its opening-up policy in the late 1970, was the first B(R)ICS country to make use of BITs. However, China only gradually embraced the BIT regime and ISDS. Initial BITs already contained fairly typical BIT clauses on fair and equitable treatment (FET), most-favored-nation (MFN), expropriation and free transfer of funds.[57] However, other clauses and recourse to arbitration were textually limited.[58] National treatment (NT) clauses, for

52 Daniel Godinho, Secretary of Foreign Trade, Ministry of Development, Industry and Foreign Trade, Brazil, Speech delivered at the UNCTAD World Investment Forum 2014: Investing in Sustainable Development, 16 October 2014, available at http://unctad-worldinvestmentforum.org/wp-content/uploads/2014/10/Godinho.pdf (visited April 11, 2018).

53 Angola-Brazil ICFA (2015) (official language Portuguese); Brazil-Chile ICFA (2015) (official languages Spanish and Portuguese); Brazil-Malawi ICFA (2015) (official languages English and Portuguese); Brazil-Mexico ICFA (2015) (official languages Spanish and Portuguese); Brazil-Mozambique ICFA (2015) (official language Portuguese).

54 Bernasconi-Osterwalder and Dietrich Brauch, *supra* note 45, at 1.

55 Presidência da República (Brazil), Decree 9167/2017, 13 October 2017.

56 *See* José Henrique Vieira Martins, Brazil's Cooperation and Facilitation Investment Agreements (CFIA) and Recent Developments, 12 June 2017, available at https://www.iisd.org/itn/2017/06/12/brazils-cooperation-facilitation-investment-agreements-cfia-recent-developments-jose-henrique-vieira-martins/#_edn11 (visited October 6, 2017); the ratification status of Brazil's CFIAs can be assessed at Brazil's Investment Policy Hub Country Page but apparently the provided assessment lacks behind, available at http://investmentpolicyhub.unctad.org/IIA/CountryBits/27 (visited October 6, 2017).

57 *See* Chester Brown ed., *Commentaries on Selected Model Investment Treaties* (Oxford: Oxford University Press, 2013) 131–181, 140.

58 *See* Karl P. Sauvant and Michael D. Nolan, China's Outward Foreign Direct Investment and International Investment Law, *Journal of International Economic Law* 893 (2015) 914.

example, included exceptions for State-owned enterprises and arbitration was textually limited to the amount of compensation for expropriation.[59] In later years China has concluded more ambitious BITs incorporating traditional style investor protection and ISDS. While China's early focus was on attracting foreign investment, it increasingly has encouraged its own (state-owned) companies to invest abroad and has become one of the most important foreign investors worldwide.[60]

This shift has not gone unnoticed by other countries. Especially traditional capital exporters have become wary of Chinese investors who compete with their local businesses and are accused of pursuing strategical political objectives rather than solely business.[61] Similarly, some developing countries have become wary of growing Chinese economic influence in the developing world and the danger of a new "scramble for Africa".[62] NGOs and other civil society actors from those countries have accused Chinese investors of disregarding labour and environmental standards.[63] Consequently, China is expected to seek stronger investment protects for Chinese investors abroad against host-States interference.[64]

China currently uses the third version of its original Model BIT, which was drafted and used in the 1980s.[65] The current 1997 Model BIT (Chinese Model BIT) is already quite old, and there have been some speculations that China

59 *See e.g.*, Shan and Gallagher, "China", in Chester Brown ed., *supra* note 57, at 132.

60 As to China's "going abroad" strategy and the regulatory framework to support outward FDI, *see* Sauvant and Nolan, *supra* note 58, at 896.

61 Recently President Donald Trump blocked the sale of a US semiconductor maker to a consortium backed by a Chinese State-owned company on national security concerns. *See* Anna Swanson, Trump Blocks China-Backed Bid to Buy U.S. Chip Maker, The New York Times (online), 13. September 2017, available at https://www.nytimes.com/2017/09/13/business/trump-lattice-semiconductor-china.html (visited April 6, 2018). An earlier example is the veto of President Barack Obama in 2012 against a Chinese windmill project near a military base in Oregon citing national security, which was the first such veto in 22 years and only the second one in the history of the Committee on Foreign Investment in the USA, *see* Obama blocks Chinese firm's purchase of four US wind farms, The Guardian, 28. September 2012, available at https://www.theguardian.com/environment/2012/sep/28/obama-blocks-chinese-firm-wind-farm (visited April 11, 2018).

62 Joseph M. Isanga, The United States, the European Union, and China: The Triadic Contest for Africa and its Implications for International Human Rights and Democracy, 3 *Northwestern Interdisciplinary Law Review* 175 (2010).

63 For a compilation and empirical study on the many concerns among different actors (governments, media, business community and trade unions) in several important host countries, *see* Sauvant and Nolan, *supra* note 58, at 901–913.

64 *See also id.*, at 898.

65 The Model BIT can be found in Shan and Gallagher, *supra* note 57, Appendix IV Chinese Model BIT Version III (Current).

will adopt a new Model BIT. There are no official confirmations of such speculations. Although it has been argued that Chinese BIT practice has largely resembled the content of the respective Model BIT "in force" at the time of negotiations,[66] we will see below that Chinese BIT practice over the years has departed from its 1997 Model BIT.

2.3 *Comparative Analysis of Model Investment Agreements and Treaty Practice: Brazil, China and India*

Difficulties in describing a State's approach to international investment protection law stem from the fact that the law is mainly codified in BITs. These bilateral treaties are not necessarily evidence of a State's legal preferences, as they are shaped by differing interests and complex power relations of negotiating States. A weak State's BITs may be evidence of the preferences of its stronger partners, but not necessarily it is own. Therefore, the following comparison will largely rely on so-called Model BITs.[67] Such Model BITs are not legally binding but serve as templates for future negotiations and provide a clear picture of a State's legal preferences. In the past, Model BITs developed by powerful capital-exporting States were presented to weaker developing countries largely in a "take it or leave it" manner. It remains to be seen whether emerging powers will be able to translate their models into actual agreements. In any case, their approaches have the potential to shape the debate surrounding the future of the investment regime as their model agreements are closely followed by practitioners and scholars.[68]

Unfortunately, only two of the four States under scrutiny here have up to date model investment treaties, namely India (2015) and Brazil (2015). China's Model BIT (1997), given its age, may not necessarily reflect today's Chinese BIT preferences. Therefore, I will combine the analysis of the Chinese Model BIT with an evaluation of recent Chinese BIT practice to be able to present an up to date picture of the Chinese approach. As South Africa has not published a new model BIT and appears reluctant, if not opposed, to concluding new

---

66 *Id.*, at 142.

67 For an overview of different Model BITs and a commentary, *see* Chester Brown ed., *Commentaries on Selected Model Investment Treaties* (Oxford: Oxford University. Press, 1st edition, 2013).

68 *See e.g.*, the numerous articles and commentaries that analyse the new Brazilian and Indian Model investment agreements: Martins, *supra* note 56; Prabhash Ranjan and Pushkar Anand, The 2016 Indian Model Bilateral Investment Treaty: A Critical Deconstruction, 38, 1 *Northwestern Journal of International Law and Business* 1 (2018); David M. Trubek and Sonia E. Rolland, Legal Innovation in Investment Law: Rhetoric and Practice in the South, University of Wisconsin, School of Law, Legal Studies Research Paper Series Paper No. 1406 1.

international agreements, it will not be subject to the further analysis of this chapter.[69]

As this study focuses on the protection of regulatory powers of host States not all provisions of (Model) BITs are considered relevant, even though if understood every part of a BIT is able to limit States' policy space. However, for considerations of space, we will focus on most crucial parts, including the preamble (a reference to the right to regulate or the like), standards of treatment (NT, MFN and FET), (indirect) expropriation clauses and exception and safeguard clauses. As States may factually increase their discretion by simply avoiding or limiting ISDS, provisions on ISDS are generally of relevance for States' policy space. However, as other contributions to this edited volume focus on ISDS reform, we will not consider such an alternative path to 'factually' extending States' policy space in this chapter. Still, table 7.1 provides a quick overview also covering ISDS provisions and other provisions connected to States' policy space such as investor obligations.

Table 7.1 below provides a quick overview of relevant provisions in individual Model IIAs and treaty practice. These provisions will be qualitatively analyzed and quantitatively compared to the majority of investment agreements in the following section. To this end, the study relies on UNCTAD's International Investment Agreements Mapping Project, which has analyzed 2575 investment treaties from countries all over the world and mapped their individual treaty provisions to allow for quantitative assessments.[70]

2.3.1 Preamble and Objective

Both the Brazilian Model CFIA and the Indian Model BIT prominently highlight regulatory policy space in their preambles. The Model CFIA's preamble as most preambles to investment agreements highlights the spirit of cooperation, the importance of investments for development and mutual benefits. Unlike traditional BITs, it also highlights State Parties' regulatory powers and policy space. The preamble generally embraces the "essential role of investment in promoting sustainable development" and the need to facilitate investments and cooperate on the matter but also reassures State Parties

69 For an analysis of South Africa's new investment protection act, *see* Malebakeng Agnes Forere, The New South African protection of investment act: striking a balance between attraction of FDI and redressing the Apartheid Legacies The New South African Protection of Investment Act: Striking a Balance Between Attraction of FDI and Redressing the Apartheid Legacies, in Fabio Morosini and Michelle Ratton Sanchez eds., *Reconceptualizing International Investment Law From the Global South* (New York: Cambridge University Press, 2018) 218–250.

70 The project is available at http://investmentpolicyhub.unctad.org/IIA (visited April 11, 2018).

TABLE 7.1 Overview of treaty provisions

Treaty provision	Brazil	China	India
Preamble (Reference to right to regulate or policy space)	Included	Avoided in older BITS but included in newer BITS	Included
National treatment	More detailed provision; "legitimate public interest objectives" relevant for the determination of 'like circumstances'	Limited in older BITS; Enlarged in newer BITS but still grandfather and standstill clauses limit NT The trend towards market access coverage	More detailed; "legitimate regulatory objectives" relevant for the determination of 'like circumstances'
MFN	Limited and more detailed	Exclusion of ISDS in newer BITS	Not included
FET	Not explicitly included but some aspects are covered (for example, due process)	Increasingly "limited" by reference to customary international law	Connects reference to customary international law with an exclusive list of protections
Indirect expropriations	Explicitly excluded	Covered but more detailed language	Covered but more detailed language and broad exceptions
Exception clauses	The self-judging general exception clause Security clause (not subject to dispute settlement)	Flexible approach towards the inclusion of general exceptions Security clauses (some self-judging)	The broad general exception clause Self-judging security clause
Investor obligations	Non-binding Corporate Social Responsibility (CSR)	Not included	Non-binding CSR; potentially a binding reference to domestic obligations
ISDS	Not included	Broad ISDS jurisdiction	Severely limited (exhaustion of domestic remedies + immunity of domestic court decisions)

"regulatory autonomy and policy space". Such a reference is not unknown to traditional BITs but is a rather rare phenomenon only found in more recently concluded BITs.[71] India's approach is rather similar. The Indian preamble includes references to economic cooperation, but also prominently reaffirms "the right of Parties to regulate investments in their territory in accordance with their law and policy objectives". Both preambles further include references to sustainable development.

The preamble of the Chinese Model BIT, in contrast, is kept traditional. It promotes three fairly standard principles, "namely to (i) facilitate and attract investment; (ii) contribute to the prosperity of both Contracting States; and (iii) cooperate on the basis of equality and mutual benefits."[72] No reference is made to the right to regulate, regulatory autonomy or policy space.

However, Chinese BITs have increasingly incorporated more balanced formulations since the late 1990s.[73] The BITs with Trinidad and Tobago (2002) and Guyana (2003) and the tripartite investment agreement between China, Japan and the Republic of Korea (2012) acknowledge in their preambles that the promotion and protection of investment can be achieved without "relaxing health, safety and environmental measures of general application".[74] The recent Australia-China FTA – which also includes an investment chapter – upholds "the rights of their governments to regulate in order to meet national policy objectives, and to preserve their flexibility to safeguard public welfare".[75] Still, other recent treaties avoid such a reference[76] or only provide for a rather vague reference to "economic sovereignty".[77] Therefore, it appears that there is a tendency that Chinese investment treaties acknowledge the right to regulate in investment treaties but no clear Chinese approach on the subject matter.

---

71 The IIA Mapping Project lists 43 out of 2575 mapped treaties that include a reference to the right to regulate (e.g. regulatory autonomy, policy space, flexibility to introduce new regulations) of these 43 treaties 34 have been concluded since the turn of the century. The reference to 'sustainable development' can be found in 75 out of the 2575 mapped treaties, only three of which have been concluded before the year 2000.

72 China's Model BIT (1997), Preamble. The first ever concluded BIT contained those principles, *see* Germany-Pakistan BIT, 25 November 1959, 1963 UNTS 6575.

73 For an analysis, *see* Shan and Gallagher, *supra* note 59, at 146.

74 China-Trinidad and Tobago BIT (2002), Preamble, China-Guyana BIT (2003), Preamble, China-Japan-Republic of Korea Trilateral Investment Agreement (2012), Preamble.

75 Free Trade Agreement between the Government of Australia and the Government of the People's Republic of China (2015), Preamble.

76 Canada-China BIT (2012), Preamble.

77 China-Tanzania BIT (2013), Preamble ("respecting the economic sovereignty of both States").

2.3.2 Standards of Treatment

Traditional BITs identify several different standards of treatment, which usually include at least NT, MFN and FET.[78] For our purposes here it suffices to take a closer look at these classical provisions.

2.3.2.1 *National Treatment*

National treatment is probably the least contested provision of international investment protection law.[79] Consequently, it is no wonder that national treatment clauses can be found in all three States' Model agreements. Still, those provisions differ markedly in detail.

Brazil and India pursue rather similar reformist approaches on NT. Both have included more specific treaty language in their NT provisions and have highlighted public interests that could be considered when determining 'like circumstances'. The provision on NT in the Brazilian Model CFIA specifies that to determine whether treatment is accorded in 'like circumstances' depends on "whether the relevant treatment distinguishes between investors or investments on the basis of legitimate public interest objectives".[80] Moreover, contracting States are exempted from compensating "any inherent competitive disadvantages which result from the foreign character of the investor or investments."[81] Similarly, the Indian Model BIT states that the assessment of "like circumstances" depends on "the totality of the circumstances, including whether the relevant treatment distinguishes between investors or investments on the basis of legitimate regulatory objectives. These circumstances include, but are not limited to, (a) the goods or services consumed or produced by the investment; (b) the actual and potential impact of the investment on third persons, the local community, or the environment, (c) whether the investment is public, private, or state-owned or controlled, and (d) the practical challenges of regulating the investment".[82] Thereby both States bring in public concerns through the "backdoor" of the assessment of "like circumstances". Following these propositions, discrimination is considered to be necessary in some cases to shield public concerns. This is a potentially far-reaching implication, which substantially increases States' (developmental) policy space, for example, to

---

78 *See e.g.*, Sornarajah, *supra* note 2, at 201.

79 Notably even the Calvo Doctrine embraced national treatment. For an introduction, *see e.g.*, Patrick Juillard, Calvo Doctrine/Calvo Clause, in Rüdiger Wolfrum ed., *The Max Planck Encyclopedia of Public International Law* (Oxford: Oxford University Press).

80 Brazilian Model CFIA (2015), art. 5(3).

81 Brazilian Model CFIA (2015), art. 5(4).

82 Indian Model BIT (2015), art. 4, footnote 2.

enact so-called buy-local policies or other discriminatory regulation and policies aimed at supporting local businesses and investors.

The non-discriminatory treatment provision of the Chinese Model BIT is tailored rather narrowly, as it subjects the guarantee of reasonable and non-discriminatory treatment to the host States' laws and regulations.[83] This approach is consequently also used for national treatment.[84] The provision only prohibits discriminatory means other than laws and regulations.[85] This thin NT provision still is an improvement for investors, as China's initial Model BIT contained no NT provision at all and the second version only contained a 'best endeavours' provision.[86] This approach is likely to be connected to China's planned economy legacy and the Chinese government's unwillingness to put its nascent economy under global competitive pressure.[87]

Such subjections of NT to domestic laws and regulations can still be found in some newer Chinese BITs (albeit not as narrowly framed).[88] Some other recent BITs contain broader NT clauses which contain no general "subject to domestic laws and regulations" formulation but still grant exceptions, e.g. exclude certain sectors, which are subject to a prior approval process.[89] Some more recent treaties also contain so-called "freezing clauses" or "grandfather clauses" in their protocols, allowing China to maintain discriminatory measures and amend them as long as the level of inconsistency does not increase.[90] While China thereby commits not to increase discriminatory practices, it still was able to shield existing discriminatory measures substantially.

Some years ago, there have been rumours that China might be willing to accept a comprehensive NT standard which could even cover the pre-establishment phase in negotiations with the US over a prospective China-US BIT.[91] While negotiations became stalled under the Obama administration, the Trump administration reportedly plans on reviving negotiations and

83 China's Model BIT (1997), art. 2(3).

84 China's Model BIT (1997), art. 3(2).

85 Shan and Gallagher, *supra* note 59, at 157.

86 For an historic overview, *id.*, at 160.

87 *Id.*, at 160.

88 *See* China-Tanzania BIT (2013), art. 3 (1) ("Without prejudice to its applicable laws and regulations, with respect to the operation, management, maintenance, use, enjoyment, sale or disposition of the investments in its territory, each Contracting Party shall accord [...]"). *See also* China-Uzbekistan BIT (2011), art. 3.

89 *See* Canada-China BIT (2012), art. 6(3).

90 *See e.g.*, China-Bosnia and Herzegovina BIT (2002), Protocol, Ad art. 3(1); Germany-China BIT (2003), Protocol, Ad arts. 2 and 3; Finland China BIT (2004) Protocol, Ad art. 2(3) and art. 3(2)–(3); China-New Zealand FTA, art. 138.

91 Sauvant and Nolan, *supra* note 58, at 923 with further references.

seeks an investment treaty that grants broader access for U.S. investors to the Chinese market.[92] Analysts suggest that given changing Chinese interests and increased FDI exports, it is like to increasingly promote high standards of investment protection that could also include market access commitments.[93] Still, it remains to be seen whether China will really accept market access commitments to its market, which appears as a necessity for achieving market access commitments from other States.

In essence, China is still reluctant to embrace the national treatment of investment and consequently shields its existing policy space. In contrast, both Brazil and India accept national treatment more broadly but claim that in some cases foreign investors may not be in like circumstances than national ones, which allows them to regain some policy space. All three States deny investors and their investments to be treated absolutely similar to domestic investors and their investments.

2.3.2.2 *Most-Favored-Nation Treatment*

MFN provisions are commonly included in traditional BITs and allow investors to profit from favourable treatment (including other BITs) that may be granted to investors of third States. Such provisions generally have not experienced much opposition, with one single exception: The 'importation' of favourable provisions from BITs between third States (not the home State of the investor) and the host State. Some tribunals have even interpreted MFN clauses to include investor State dispute settlement provisions.[94] This practice has inter alia allowed investors to borrow favourable ISDS provisions from secondary BITs even though the BIT between their home country and the host

---

92 U.S. Treasury Secretary Mnuchin, China Bilateral Investment Treaty "On Our Agenda", *The Wall Street Journal (online)*, 6 June 2017, available at https://www.wsj.com/articles/u-s-treasury-secretary-mnuchin-china-bilateral-investment-treaty-on-our-agenda-1496774628 (visited April 6, 2018).

93 *See* Sauvant and Nolan, *supra* note 58, at 898; Vivienne Bath, The South and Alternative Models of Trade and Investment Regulation: Chinese Investment and Approaches to International Investment Agreements, in Fabio Morosini and Michelle Ratton Sanchez (eds.), *Reconceptualizing International Investment Law From the Global South* (New York: Cambridge University Press, 2018) 47–94 48, 83.

94 The first known award that allowed an investor to use an MFN provision in that way is *Maffezini v. Spain*, ICSID Case No. ARB/97/7, Award of 13 November 2000, English translation available in 16 (1) ICSID Review 248 (2001). For deeper analysis, *see e.g., Dana H. Freyer and David Herlihy, Most-Favored-Nation Treatment and Dispute Settlement in Investment Arbitration: Just How "Favored" is "Most-Favored"?, 20 ICSID Review* 58 (2005); Stephen Fietta, Favoured Nation Treatment and Dispute Resolution under Bilateral Investment Treaties: A Turning Point?, 8 *International Arbitration Law Review* 131 (2005).

State did not provide for this mode of dispute settlement (but for an unrestricted MFN clause). All three countries examined have responded to those developments and continuing uncertainties.

Brazilian Model CFIA (2015) contains a classic MFN provision but expressly excludes from MFN treatment "(i) provisions relating to investment dispute settlement contained in an investment agreement or an investment chapter of a commercial agreement; or (ii) any agreement for regional economic integration, free trade area, customs union or common market, of which a Party is a member."[95] For investors of partner countries, this provision is, of course, superfluous, because Brazil has not concluded any investment treaty that covers ISDS. Yet, the provision is not utterly meaningless as it prevents Brazilian investors from relying on ISDS provisions which might be included in BITs of host States with third States.

Another important part of the CFIA's MFN clause is that it again highlights a State's policy space through the determination of whether treatment is accorded in like circumstance. As the provision on NT, the MFN provision clarifies that "whether treatment is accorded in 'like circumstances' depends on the totality of the circumstances, including whether the relevant treatment distinguishes between investors or investments based on legitimate public welfare objectives".[96]

China, in recent treaty practice, has also excluded ISDS clauses from the scope of MFN.[97] Historically, China started with only very limited MFN clauses but subsequently embraced rather broad ones.[98] The question of whether those MFN clauses would allow Chinese investors to use ISDS provisions in treaties of host States with third States has become of high relevance. This is because early Chinese ISDS provisions were textually limited to the amount of compensation for expropriation. If Chinese investors could have relied on host States treaties with third countries that covered broader ISDS clauses through MFN clauses in Chinese BITs, they could have circumvented the narrow clause in Chinese BITs. This has become of relevance in the ICSID case of *Señor Tza Yap Shum v. The Republic of Peru*.[99] However, the tribunal found a different

95 Brazilian Model CFIA (2015), art. 6.

96 Brazilian Model CFIA (2015), art. 6(4).

97 *See e.g.*, China-New Zealand FTA (2008), art. 139(2); China-Colombia BIT (2008), art. 3(3); China ASEAN-China Investment Agreement (2009), art. 5(4); China-Uzbekistan BIT (2011), art. 3(3); China-Japan-Korea Trilateral Investment Agreement (2012), art. 4(3); Australia-China FTA (2015), art. 9.4(2).

98 Shan and Gallagher, *supra* note 59, at 160 et seq.All of the 122 mapped Chinese investment treaties by the IIA mapping project contain MFN clauses.

99 *Señor Tza Yap Shum v. The Republic of Peru*, ICSID Case No. ARB/07/6.

solution. While denying the enlargement of the subject matter scope of the tribunal's jurisdiction by relying on the MFN clause (as brought forward by the investor), it argued that the wording "involving the amount of compensation for expropriation" in the ISDS clause necessitated an assessment of whether the expropriation was lawful in the first place.[100] Relying on this finding the textual limitations in MFN clauses of recent Chinese BITs are not even of reformatory but only of confirmatory character. Still, they are important for clearly resolving the disputed issue.

India, in contrast, has taken a more radical approach. The MFN treatment is completely absent in the new Indian Model BIT. This absence is a response to the *White Industries v. India* award.[101] The Australian investor White Industries had relied on the MFN provision of the India-Australia BIT to import a favorable substantive provision from the India-Kuwait BIT.[102] The Indian government had argued that such an importation would "fundamentally subvert the carefully negotiated balance of the [India-Australia] BIT,"[103] but to no avail. Subsequently, the Indian government decided not to include an MFN provision in its Model BIT.[104] This exclusion of MFN will also prevent investors from relying on older unterminated Indian BITs with broader protections.

However, the radical exclusion of MFN has been heavily criticized by Indian scholars.[105] Ranjan and Anand essentially argued that India should have kept the MFN provision but may have limited the provision by excluding the possibility of investors to rely on treaty clauses with third countries. By excluding MFN altogether, so they argue, India exposes investors to discriminatory treatment by domestic measures. While this indeed tilts the Model BIT's balance in favour of host States' regulatory power,[106] this seems to be precisely the outcome the Indian government has sought.

100 *Señor Tza Yap Shum v. The Republic of Peru*, ICSID Case No. ARB/07/6, Decision on Jurisdiction and Competence of 19 June 2009 (only available in Spanish). For an overview, *see* Andrew Newcombe, Another misapplication of MFN? *Tza Yap Shum v. The Republic of Peru*, Kluwer Arbitration Blog, 21 October 2009, available at http://kluwerarbitrationblog.com/2009/10/21/another-misapplication-of-mfn-tza-yap-shum-v-the-republic-of-peru/ (visited April 6, 2018).

101 *White Industries Australia Limited v. Republic of India*, UNCITRAL, Final Award of 30 November 2011.

102 *White Industries Australia Limited v. Republic of India*, UNCITRAL, Final Award of 30 November 2011, para. 11.1.1–11.1.5.

103 *Id.* para. 11.1.1–11.1.5.

104 Ranjan and Anand, *supra* note 68, at 19 with further references.

105 *Id.*, at 20.

106 *Id.*, at 21.

2.3.2.3 *Fair and Equitable Treatment*

Fair and Equitable Treatment is a rather vague and allegedly broad provision open to different interpretations.[107] Nevertheless, or possibly because of its alleged broadness, it has become one of the most important and most invoked clauses in international investment arbitration.[108] FET has often been regarded as "fall-back clause", or even "catch-all clause", that allows arbitrators to do justice to investors who suffer unfair or arbitrary treatment, which is not covered by other treaty provisions.[109] However, others have argued that FET "only" reaffirms the customary international minimum standard (IMS) and adds nothing new, meaning that it mainly comprises access to justice and due process.[110] Consequently, the precise relation between FET and IMS remains subject to scholarly controversy. Some recent arbitration instead suggests that the distinction is essentially meaningless.[111] Arbitral tribunals have argued that IMS has substantially evolved towards greater protection for investors,[112] suggesting that IMS today "provides for the fair and equitable treatment of investors within the confines of reasonableness".[113]

The following obligations for host-States are commonly regarded to form part of FET: to act according to due process, transparently, non-arbitrarily

---

107 *See e.g.*, Sornarajah, *supra* note 2, at 349 et seqq.

108 On the importance of FET and an analysis of arbitration cases, *see e.g.*, Rudolf Dolzer, Fair and Equitable Treatment: Today's Contours, 12 *Santa Clara Journal of International Law* 7 (2014); Rudolf Dolzer, Fair and Equitable Treatment: A Key Standard in Investment Treaties, 39, 1 *The International Lawyer* 87 (2005); Ioana Tudor, *The Fair and Equitable Treatment Standard in the International Law of Foreign Investment* (Oxford: Oxford University Press, 2009).

109 *See e.g.*, Rudolf Dolzer and Christoph Schreuer, *Principles of international investment law*, 2nd ed. (Oxford: Oxford University Press, 2012) 122; Dolzer, *supra* note 108, at 12; among numerous arbitral awards providing for this extensive interpretation see: *PSEG Global Inc. v. Republic of Turkey*, ICSID Case No. ARB/02/5, Award (19 January 2007), para. 238–240.

110 *See e.g.*, Sornarajah, *supra* note 2, at 349 et seqq. with reference to NAFTA Free Trade Commission, Notes of Interpretation of Certain Chapter 11 Provisions, 31 July 2001, B. 2; and OECD, Council Resolution on the Draft Convention for the Protection of Foreign Property, 7 ILM 117 (1967).

111 For an analysis, *see* Roland Kläger, *"Fair and Equitable Treatment" in International Investment Law* (Cambridge: Cambridge University Press, 2013) 439.

112 *See William Ralph Clayton, William Richard Clayton, Douglas Clayton, Daniel Clayton and Bilcon of Delaware, Inc. v. Government of Canada*, UNCITRAL, PCA Case No. 2009–04, Award on Jurisdiction and Liability of 17 March 2015, para. 435 et seqq.

113 *Merrill & Ring Forestry L.P. v. Government of Canada*, UNCITRAL, ICSID Administered Case, Award of 31 March 2010, para. 213. In stark contrast, scholars like Patrick Dumberry argue that FET has not become a rule of customary international law, see Patrick Dumberry, Has the Fair and Equitable Treatment Standard Become a Rule of Customary International Law?, 8 *Journal of International Dispute Settlement* 155 (2017).

and non-discriminatory, refrain from coercion and harassment, to act predictably, a general duty of due diligence and maybe most controversially to refrain "from frustrating the investor's reasonable expectations with respect to the legal framework affecting the investment".[114,115] Those reasonable expectations must stem from objective conduct of State which might involve assurances through contract or verbal communications but might also be based on the stability and predictability of existing laws and policies.[116] Such an interpretation puts considerable pressure on a State's ability to change policies and regulation as those changes might negatively affect investors' profits, even if changes are required to address changing and sometimes urgent public needs, such as the increasing need to tackle climate change, the need to contain economic crises, or an increasing awareness of the dangers of nuclear energy.

Wary of such broad interpretations States have begun to narrow FET clauses or intend to so,[117] inter alia through tying FET to IMS[118] or international customary law more broadly[119] and by providing more specific FET clauses (e.g. a

---

114 *Bayindir Insaat Turizm Ticaret Ve Sanayi AS v. Islamic Republic of Pakistan*, ICSID Case No. ARB/03/29, Award of 27 August 2009, para. 178. A huge number of awards have relied on notions of "legitimate expectations", *see Metalclad v. Mexico* (2000) 5 ICSID Reports 209; (2001); *Tecmed v. Mexico* (2006) 10 ICSID Reports 54; *MTD v. Chile* (2007) 12 ICSID Reports 6; *Occidental v. Ecuador, London Court of International Arbitration* (Award, 1 July 2004); *CMS Gas Transmission Co v. Argentina* (2003) 30 ILM 788; (2005) 44 ILM 1205; *Waste Management v. Mexico* (2001) 40 ILM 56; *International Thunderbird Gaming Corporation v. Mexico*, UNCITRAL (NAFTA) Arbitration Proceedings, Award of 26 January 2006; *Saluka Investments B. V. v. Czech Republic*, UNCITRAL, Partial Award of 17 March 2006; *LG&E Energy Corporation v. Argentina* (2007) 46 ILM 36; *Enron Corporation v. Argentina*, ICSID Case No. ARB/01/03 (Award, 22 May 2007); *Sempra Energy International v. Argentina*, ICSID Case No. ARB/02/16, Award of 28 September 2007; *Parkerings-Compagniet AS v. Lithuania*, ICSID Case No. ARB/05/8, Award of 11 September 2007; *Suez v. Argentine Republic*, ICSID Case No. ARB/03/19, Decision on Liability of 30 July 2010, 226; *Electrabel S.A. v. Hungary*, ICSID Case No. ARB/07/19, Decision on Jurisdiction, Applicable Law and Liability of 30 November 2012.

115 For a critical discussion, *see, e.g.*, Eric de Brabendere, States' Reassertion of Control over International Investment Law: (Re)Defining 'Fair and Equitable Treatment' and 'Indirect Expropriation', in Andreas Kulick (ed.), *Reassertion of Control Over the Investment Treaty Regime* (Cambridge: Cambridge University Press, 2017) 285–308, 287 et seq. For scholarly overviews and analyses, *see e.g.*, Tudor, *supra* note 108, at 157, 186.

116 *See e.g.*, Dolzer, *supra* note 108, at 17 et seq., 20, with further analysis of arbitral decisions.

117 *See e.g.*, European Commission, Investment in TTIP and Beyond – The Path for Reform: Enhancing the Right to Regulate and Moving from Current Ad Hoc Arbitration towards an Investment Court, 12 May 2015, available at http://trade.ec.europa.eu/doclib/docs/2015/may/tradoc_153408.PDF (visited April 4, 2018) 2, 6.

118 US Model BIT (2012), art. 5(1)–(2).

119 *See, e.g.*, Croatia-Oman BIT Article 3 para. 2.

reference to the denial of justice, due process and non-discrimination).[120] It remains to be seen how arbitrators will interpret those clauses and whether the reference to customary law standards will be able to narrow FET and allow States to change existing laws for public purposes without compensation. Given that some tribunals, as mentioned above, have simply considered FET to be the new customary minimum standard of treatment, this remains doubtful.[121] However, detailed lists provide more clarity and notions of legitimate expectations can be limited to those expectations stemming from "specific representation to an investor to induce a covered investment".[122]

However, how have States under supervision here responded to controversies over extensive interpretations of FET? Both Brazil and India have responded to extensive interpretations prevalent in arbitral decisions by omitting FET clauses in their model treaties,[123] leading some scholars to assume that FET is completely absent.[124] Yet, a closer look reveals that there are some provisions in both models that cover important aspects of FET's contents.

While an explicit FET clause is absent in the Brazilian CFIA, Article 4 Model CFIA entitled "Admission and treatment" grants investors and investments "treatment according to the due process of law" and requires Parties to "ensure that all measures that affect investments are administered in a reasonable, objective and impartial manner, in accordance with their respective laws and regulations" (para. 3). These provisions at least cover some aspects of FET like due process, protection against arbitrariness, protection against targeted discrimination and protection against abusive treatment. As the CFIA incorporates some aspects of FET and omits others, it can be argued that the later was intentionally left outside the treaty. Yet, arbitrators (or others) may bring in notions of 'legitimate expectations' of investors by interpreting Article 4 para. 3 ("administered in a reasonable, objective and impartial manner") widely. The Brazilian CFIA could be clearer by either not providing any provision on

---

120 *See* US Model BIT (2012), art. 5(2); ASEAN Comprehensive Investment Agreement, art. 11; CETA (2016), art. 8.10 (1) and (2).

121 *See also* Brabendere, *supra* note 115, at 298.

122 *See e.g.*, CETA (2016), art. 8.10 (4).

123 In a statement for an UNCTAD IIA conference, state representatives of India in their official capacity argued that FET was "susceptible to wide interpretations" and therefore must be subject to "careful analysis" in future treaties. *See* Arvind Mayaram, Paper presented at the IIA Conference (16 October 2014), World Investment Forum 2014: Investing in Sustainable Development, available at http://unctad-worldinvestmentforum.org/wp-content/uploads/2014/10/Mayaram.pdf (visited April 4, 2018).

124 With regard to the Brazilian Model CFIA, *see* Catharine Titi, *International Investment Law and the Protection of Foreign Investment in Brazil*, 2 *Transnational Dispute Management* 1 (2016) 11.

"treatment" at all or by explicitly excluding (or including) the frustration of 'legitimate expectations' as a basis for any claim in the new "Admission and treatment" provision.

Several aspects of FET are also included in Article 3 of the Indian Model BIT ("Treatment of Investments"). The Article protects investors against treatment that violates customary international law "through" "denial of justice in any judicial or administrative proceedings", "fundamental breach of due process", "targeted discrimination on manifestly unjustified grounds, such as gender, race or religious belief" and "manifestly abusive treatment, such as coercion, duress and harassment". This list and also the reference to customary law can be seen as an attempt to narrow treatment of investors avoiding the vagueness of FET.[125] Notably, the notion of "legitimate expectations" has not been explicitly covered, leading scholars to assume that India distanced itself from arbitral case law that interpreted that notion expansively.[126] In my opinion, the reference to customary law rather complicates the matter and may provide a backdoor for arbitrators to bring in broad interpretations.[127] On the other hand, the "violation of customary law" is directly connected to listed examples with the wording "through", suggesting that the list is exclusive. Moreover, as the four examples on the list are relatively narrow, it can reasonably be assumed that the clause does not cover legitimate expectations based simply on the status quo of legislation.

However, has the clause now tilted towards allowing a State too much discretion to maltreat investors? Some Indian scholars have argued in that direction, criticizing the clause for omitting any reference to arbitrariness to cover cases when host States act in bad faith or a manifestly unreasonable manner.[128] On the other hand, it is acknowledged that such a standard may find its way into the agreement through the reference to customary law.[129] One might add that several aspects of protection against manifestly arbitrary treatment are included in the listed cases (e.g. fundamental breach of due process, targeted discrimination on manifestly unjustified grounds and manifestly

125 Cf. Ranjan and Anand, *supra* note 68, at 23.

126 Cf. *Id.* at 24 who also criticise the provision for not protecting legitimate expectations even in cases where those expectations were clearly induced by a State's assurances to attract the investment.

127 I consider this likely despite the fact that in depth studies show that the FET standard has not become a rule of customary law because treaty practice while being general, widespread and representative is not uniform and consistent when it comes to the concrete content of FET, *see* Dumberry, *supra* note 113.

128 Ranjan and Anand, *supra* note 68, 29 et seq.

129 *Id.* 30.

abusive treatment) all of which appear to be worded broad enough to include most cases of arbitrary treatment.

China's approach to the FET is more ambiguous than others. Generally, FET clauses can be found in nearly all Chinese BITs.[130] China's Model BIT (1997) contains a traditional unrestricted FET clause.[131] Initial BITs avoided any reference to customary international law because of a historic wariness about the contents of the international minimum standard or limited applicable customary standards to those that had been accepted by both Contracting Parties.[132] Later BITs however increasingly brought in references to "international law", "customary international law" or "principles of international law".[133] The underlying purpose seems to be the idea that broad FET standards can be limited by stating that FET does not require anything "in addition to or beyond that which is required by the international law minimum standard of treatment of aliens".[134] These provisions indicate China's increased willingness to accept customary legal standards and at the same time, the intent of China and its treaty partners to narrow FET clauses. Whether this approach will be successful remains to be seen, as customary law with all its uncertainties and inaccuracy might be interpreted extensively by arbitrators. Additionally, some of the more recent Chinese BITs and FTA investment chapters provide for qualified FET clauses that provide a list of indicative elements of FET.[135] However, the listed cases are only given as examples, and the provisions do not explicitly exclude other elements of FET, such as the protection of legitimate expectations of investors.

In conclusion, all three states have reformed their FET clauses, but none of the analyzed approaches explicitly excludes notions of 'legitimate expectations'. However, both the Brazilian as well as the Indian Model leave little room for extensive interpretations, while the unlimited reference in Chinese BITs to customary law may provide more space for such extensive interpretation. It

130 The IIA Mapping project lists only 4 out of 112 mapped Chinese investment treaties that do not explicitly contain FET clauses. See also: Sauvant and Nolan, *supra* note 58, 921.

131 Article 3, Chinese Model BIT (1997).

132 Shan and Gallagher, *supra* note 57, 159, with reference to China-Belgium-Luxembourg BIT 1984, Article 7 of the Protocol.

133 *See e.g*, China-Cyprus BIT (2001), art. 9(7); China-Czech Republic BIT (2005), art. 9(5); China-Mexico BIT (2008), art. 5(2); China-Colombia BIT (2008), art. 2(3)–(4); China-Japan-Republic of Korea Trilateral Investment Agreement (2012), art. 2(3)–(4).

134 China-Mexico BIT (2008), art. 5(2); China-Japan-Korea Trilateral Investment Agreement (2012), art. 3(2); China-Colombia BIT(2008), art. 2(3)–(4); China-Canada BIT (2012), art. 4; China-Republic of Korea FTA (2015) chapter 12 (investment), art. 12.5 (2).

135 *See* China-Colombia BIT(2008), art. 2(4)(c) ("'Fair and Equitable Treatment' includes the prohibition against denial of justice in criminal, civil, or administrative proceedings in accordance with the general accepted principles of customary law.")

would be in the interest of legal certainty if States provided clearer answers to those crucial questions.

2.3.3 Expropriation and Compensation

Clauses on nationalisation and expropriation of property can be found in all but eight of all IIAs mapped by UNCTAD. Those provisions subject nationalizations and expropriations to certain procedural criteria and require the host State to pay compensation. On the requirements for compensation, the so-called Hull Formula has largely prevailed (albeit variations exist in treaty practice) against earlier efforts of developing countries to establish more flexible standards.[136] According to the Hull Formula compensation must be prompt (without undue delay), adequate (equivalent to fair market value) and effective (Be completely payable and transferable).[137]

While direct nationalisations are mainly a phenomenon of the past, increasingly the concept of indirect expropriations has played a more critical role.[138] However, the concept of indirect expropriation is much more challenging to define and determine,[139] and it poses inherent threats to legal regulations. In the past, arbitral tribunals have looked primarily at the effects of a measure on the investment and required them to be comparable to the effects of a formal expropriation.[140] This 'sole effects doctrine' has increasingly been criticized for neglecting a State's intention behind the measure.[141] Newer arbitral decisions

136 The standard of "appropriate" compensation e.g. would have provided (Developing) States more flexibility to take into account factors such as the profits made by the investor and the period during which they were made in assessing the amount of compensation due, *see*, Sornarajah, *supra* note 2, 209 et seq.

137 *See e.g.*, Jeswald W. Salacuse, *The Law of International Investment Treaties* (Oxford: Oxford University Press, 2010) 324 et seqq.

138 *See e.g.*, Rudolf Dolzer and Christoph Schreuer, *Principles of International Investment Law* (Oxford: Oxford University Press, 2nd edition, 2014) 101, 286.

139 Some BITs further include concepts of "measures tantamount to expropriation", yet it is unclear whether this forms a separate category. It appears that the terms indirect expropriation and "measures tantamount to expropriation" are largely used as synonyms.

140 This practice goes back to the Chorzow Factory case (*Case Concerning Certain German Interests in Polish Upper Silesia* (*FRG v. Poland*), 1926, PCIJ Series A, No. 7, 44) and the jurisprudence of the Iran-US claims tribunal (e.g. *Tippets et al. vs. TAMSEFTA* (1984) 6 Iran-USCTR 219. More recently NAFTA cases like *Metalclad v. Mexico* (2000) 5 ICSID Reports 209; (2001) para. 111 have emphasized the effects and neglected the intentions; another good example is *Compañía del Desarrollo de Santa Elena S.A. v. Republic of Costa* Rica, ICSID Case No. ARB/96/1, Award of 17 February 2000, para. 71 et seqq. For a further analysis, *see* Salacuse, *supra* note 137, at 316 et seq.

141 For a critical appraisal, see *id.*, at 318; Barker, *supra* note 17, at 245 et seqq. For supporters of the sole effects doctrine, *see e.g.*, August Reinisch, Expropriation, in Peter Muchlinski, Federico Ortino and Christoph Schreuer (eds.), *The Oxford Handbook of International Investment Law* (Oxford: Oxford University Press, 2008) 405.

point to a number of relevant criteria including the degree of interference with investor property rights (severity and duration of impact), the frustration of investor's legitimate expectations, lack of proportionality, non-transparency, arbitrariness and discrimination and the purpose of the measure (most importantly their relevance for a public interests).[142] Increasingly, arbitral tribunals have also acknowledged the concept of legitimate regulatory interests through adjusting their standard of review to provide for greater regulatory flexibility when legitimate regulatory interests are concerned.[143]

Nevertheless, cases concerning indirect expropriations have raised and still raise the fear that legitimate legislation (like adopting environmental standards or health legislation) or related administrative measures might get challenged and require compensation. Consequently, States might be deterred from such measures leading to a regulatory chill. Problematic cases included inter alia expropriation cases against Argentina for measures aimed at resolving an economic crisis,[144] against Tanzania for measures concerning the supply of drinking water,[145] against Mexico for environment-related measures,[146] against South Africa for affirmative action policies,[147] against Australia and Uruguay for tobacco plain-packaging legislation[148] and claims against Germany for phasing out nuclear energy for security and ecological reasons.[149]

142 Barker, *supra* note 17, at 307 et seqq.

143 *See e.g., Occidental Petroleum Corporation and Occidental Exploration and Production Company v. Republic of Ecuador*, ICSID Case No. ARB/06/11, Award of 5 October 2012, para. 302–409; *Philip Morris Brands Sarl, Philip Morris Products S.A. and Abal Hermanos S.A. v. Oriental Republic of Uruguay*, ICSID Case No. ARB/10/7, Award of 8 July 2016, para. 398 et seq. *See also* C. Henckels, Balancing Investment Protection and the Public Interest: The Role of the Standard of Review and the Importance of Deference in Investor-State Arbitration, 4 *Journal of International Dispute Settlement* 197 (2013).

144 For an intensive analysis, *see* Jose Alvarez and Kathryn Khamsi, The Argentine Crisis and Foreign Investors: A Glimpse into the Heart of the Investment Regime, in Karl P. Sauvant ed., *The Yearbook on International Investment Law and Policy 2008/2009* (New York: Oxford University Press, 2009) 379–478.

145 *Biwater Gauf (Tanzania) LTD. v. United Republic of Tanzania*, ICSID Case No. ARB/05/22, Award of 19 January 2007.

146 *Metalclad v. Mexico* (2000), 5 ICSID Reports 209 (2001).

147 *Piero Foresti, Laura de Carli and others v Republic of South Africa*, ICSID Case No. ARB(AF)/07/1, Award of 4 August 2010.

148 *Philip Morris Brands Sarl, Philip Morris Products S.A. and Abal Hermanos S.A. v. Oriental Republic of Uruguay*, ICSID Case No. ARB/10/7, Award of 8 July 2016; *Philip Morris Asia Limited (Hong Kong) v. Commonwealth of Australia*, UNCTAD, PCA Case No. 2012–12, Award on Jurisdiction and Admissibility of 17 December 2015. Both cases however were dismissed, the later on jurisdictional grounds, the former mainly on the finding that the measures were a reasonable exercise of police powers for the protection of public health, para. 307, 420.

149 *Vattenfall v. Germany*, ICSID Case No. ARB/12/12, Notice of Arbitration of 31 May 2012 (not public).

However, it is now relatively clear in arbitrational practice that international investment law recognises the State's right to regulate in principle.[150] Consequently, States are not liable to pay compensation when "in the normal exercise of their regulatory powers, they adopt in a non-discriminatory manner bona fide regulations that are aimed at the general welfare".[151] Still, other tribunals have taken narrower approaches,[152] and much depends on the concrete BIT in question and how it balances the protection of private investors and the public interests of host States, in particular as expropriation provisions tend to become more detailed.[153]

As no clear and uniformly applied criteria exist to distinguish between indirect expropriation and non-compensable legitimate regulation,[154] the challenge remains to find such criteria to balance between investors' property rights and the host governments' right to regulate investments in the interest of the public good. The following paragraphs provide a more in-depth analysis of how Brazil, India and China have positioned themselves on this issue.

2.3.3.1 *Brazil*

At first sight, the expropriation clause in Brazilian Model CFIA (2015) is rather standard and resembles traditional BIT expropriation clauses.[155] It prohibits Parties to nationalize or expropriate investments except for a public purpose, in a non-discriminatory manner, on payment of effective compensation and under due process of law.[156] It also essentially includes the Hull-criteria on compensation.

However, it contains a very decisive limitation, namely the exclusion of indirect expropriations from its scope.[157] This is in line with earlier Brazilian

150 *Saluka Investments B.V. v. Czech Republic*, UNCITRAL, Partial Award of 17 March 2006, para. 255; *Philip Morris Brands Sarl, Philip Morris Products S.A. and Abal Hermanos S.A. v. Oriental Republic of Uruguay*, ICSID Case No. ARB/10/7, Award of 8 July 2016, 307, 420. *See also* Barker, *supra* note 17, at 234 et seqq.

151 *Saluka Investments B.V. v. Czech Republic*, UNCITRAL, Partial Award of 17 March 2006, para. 255.

152 *See e.g., Daimler Financial Services AG v. Argentine Republic*, ICSID Case No. AR/05/1, Award of 22 October 2012, para. 100.

153 *Cf.* Barker, *supra* note 17, at 235.

154 There have of course been numerous accounts of how to strike that balance, such as to exempt 'police powers', to require proportionality between the effect on the investment and the public interest behind the regulatory measures, or to decrease the standard of review, but it appears that none of them has yet achieved the status of the new prevailing opinion.

155 Brazilian Model CFIA (2015), art. 7. *See also* Bernasconi-Osterwalder and Dietrich Brauch, *supra* note 45, at 8.

156 Brazilian Model CFIA (2015), art. 7(1)(a)–(d).

157 Brazilian Model CFIA (2015), art. 7(5) ("For greater certainty, this article only provides for direct expropriation, where an investment is nationalized or otherwise directly

concerns against expropriation clauses in BITs that played a role in the non-ratification of BITs in the 1990s. Thereby, the provision proposes a rather radical solution to extensive interpretations of notions of indirect expropriations. The policy space of a State is fully restored, while regulatory takings are not subject to limitations (except those provided by other provisions of the CFIA, such as NT) and do not require compensation.

2.3.3.2 *India*

The Indian model BIT includes an expropriation clause that contains the usual protections but is very precise and contains several exceptions.[158] Two of the three typical Hull criteria for compensation (adequate and effective) are addressed (if not explicitly),[159] while the third criteria 'prompt' is missing. In contrast to the Brazilian provision, direct as well as indirect expropriations are covered.[160] However, the Indian clause contains a very detailed definition of what is to be considered an indirect expropriation is limiting the provision's scope. According to that definition an "indirect expropriation occurs if a measure or series of measures of a Party has an effect equivalent to direct expropriation, in that it substantially or permanently deprives the investor of the fundamental attributes of property in its investment, including the right to use, enjoy and dispose of its investment, without formal transfer or title or outright seizure."[161] The determination of whether a measure is equivalent to expropriation must then be assessed on "a case-by-case, fact based inquiry" that takes the following criteria into consideration: the economic impact, the duration of the measure, the character of the measure (including the object, context and intent) and "whether a measure by a Party breaches the Party's prior binding written commitment to the investor whether by contract, license or other legal document".[162]

While the provision primarily still focuses on an effects test, it prominently brings in other considerations such as the "object, context and intent" of a

---

expropriated through formal transfer of title or ownership rights."). Note that concluded CFIAs do not contain an explicit exclusion of indirect expropriations. However, as they include the qualification "directly" before "nationalize" they should be interpreted to exclude indirect expropriations as well, *see, e.g.*, Brazil-Malawi BIT (2015), art. 8(2).

158 Indian Model BIT (2015), art. 5.

159 Indian Model BIT (2015), art. 5(2).

160 Indian Model BIT (2015), art. 5(1) ("Neither Party may nationalize or expropriate an investment of an investor [...] either directly or through measures having an effect equivalent to expropriation.")

161 Indian Model BIT (2015), art. 5(3)(a).

162 Indian Model BIT (2015), art. 5(3) (b) (i)–(iv).

measure. This allows assessing whether the measure supports public interests, such as protection of the environment or human rights considerations.

Even more importantly, the provision completely exempts "non-discriminatory regulatory measures or awards by judicial bodies of a Party that are designed and applied to protect legitimate public interest or public purpose objectives such as public health, safety and the environment" completely from being able to be considered as an expropriation.[163] Thereby the provision sharply limits the scope of the expropriation clause altogether and allows for a considerable reclaim of policy space of host States.

This broad-based exception has been criticized for leaving "a major gap in protection of foreign investment"[164] and possibly facilitating misuse by States. The non-discrimination requirement and the need to justify such regulatory measures with a public interest are comparatively soft requirements for the Host-State. Other States in comparison while also having turned to promote exception clauses have included exceptions from the exception, such as the formulation "except in rare circumstances" and further require the measure to be adopted in good faith, following due process and not being manifestly excessive.[165]

All in all, the provision marks a substantial departure from the traditional "sole effects doctrine". By bringing in other aspects of a measure such as its objective and context, it allows arbitrators to consider public concerns. The broadly framed exception, on the other hand, while surely protecting a State's policy space, might be considered as overly restrictive when compared to other States' newer treaty practice.[166]

2.3.3.3 *China*

Expropriation has been described as "the most controversial part of the Chinese attitude towards foreign investment".[167] However, expropriation clauses in Chinese Model BITs and BIT practice have been rather classical (with some

163 Indian Model BIT (2015), art. 5(5).

164 Ranjan and Anand, *supra* note 68, at 36.

165 *Id.* at 35 et seqq. with reference to Annex 8-A (3) of the EU-Canada CETA (2016). See also the discussion of the Chinese expropriation clause below.

166 According to the IIA Mapping Project 150 out of 2575 mapped treaties contain a definition of indirect expropriation and 97 treaties contain a carve-out for general regulatory measures, of which the majority has been concluded after 2000. However, even treaties that contain such carve outs tend to require further qualifications to the exempted measures.

167 Qingjiang Kong, Bilateral Investment Treaties: The Chinese Approach and Practice, in B.S. Chimni, Ko Swan Sik, Miyoshi Masahiro, M.C.W. Pinto and S.P. Subedi eds., *Asian Yearbook of International Law, Volume 9 (1998–1999)* (Leiden: Brill Academic Publishers, 2003) 105–136, 125.

exceptions) while recent treaties take a more nuanced approach in line with recent trends.[168]

On first sight, one Chinese exceptionality is the Chinese Model BIT's reference to "local legal procedure" instead of "due process of law", which is a more common reference in other States' BITs.[169] Yet, BIT practice in that regard is not uniform. China's earlier Model BIT versions used formulations like 'under appropriate legal procedure' (Version II),[170] and several more recent BITs mix domestic legal procedure requirements with international due process requirements.[171] Therefore, it appears that Chinese more modern BIT practice safeguards due process appropriately.

While neither the Chinese Model BIT nor Chinese BITs directly use the Hull Formula, their formulations provide for comparable criteria.[172] The Chinese Model BIT requires compensation to be "equivalent to the value of the expropriated investments", that the "value shall be determined in accordance with generally recognized principles of valuation", the inclusion of interest, that compensation "shall be made without delay" and "be effectively realizable and freely transferable".[173] Actual BIT practice saw differing wordings, such as "fair and equitable compensation,"[174] "fair, effective and non-discriminatory compensation"[175] and "fair and reasonable compensation,"[176] yet those standards as well as the Model BIT standard do not differ decisively in practical terms from general BIT practice and the Hull Formula.[177]

Nearly all Chinese investment treaties contain a direct reference to indirect expropriations ("similar measures").[178] Interestingly, however, some of China's more recent BITs contain definitions of indirect expropriations either

---

168 China's Model BIT (1997), art. 4. For an overview of Chinese BIT practice, *see* Shan and Gallagher, *supra* note 59, at 163.

169 *Id.* at 163.

170 China's Model BIT (1997), art. 4(1)(b).

171 *See e.g.*, China-Japan-Korea Trilateral Investment Agreement (2012), art. 11 (1)(c) ("in accordance with its laws and international standard of due process of law"); China-Colombia BIT (2013), art. 4 (1)(b) ("under domestic legal procedure and respecting due process"); China-Tanzania BIT (2014), art. 6(1)(b) ("in accordance with domestic legal procedure and relevant due process").

172 *Id.* 164.

173 China's Model BIT (1997), art. 4(2).

174 *See, e.g.*, China-India BIT (2006), art. 5 (1).

175 *See, e.g.*, China-United Arab Emirates BIT (1993), art. 6(1).

176 *See, e.g.*, China-Kuwait BIT (1985), art. 5(1).

177 Norah Gallagher and Wenhua Shan, *Chinese Investment Treaties: Policies and Practice* (Oxfordk: Oxford University Press, 2009) 165 and more generally chapter 7.

178 According to the IIA Mapping Project 110 out of 112 mapped Chinese treaties cover indirect expropriations.

directly in the expropriation clause or a separate protocol.[179] These provisions generally require indirect expropriations to effect equivalent to direct expropriation without formal transfer of title or outright seizure. However, they do not solely rely on a 'sole effects test' but require a case-by-case inquiry that takes into account the economic impact, reasonable expectations arising out of investments, whether measures are discriminatory, the character and intent of the measure and proportionality. Moreover, regulatory measures that are non-discriminatory and pursue public interests are considered to amount to indirect expropriations only in "rare circumstances"[180] specified in most recent BITs as "when an action or a series of actions by a Contracting Party is extremely severe or disproportionate in light of its purpose" or similar formulations.[181] Thereby China's BITs take a similar approach as taken in the US model BIT (2004).[182]

In contrast to more narrow definitions, China seeks – or at least allows for – the protection of reasonable expectations of investors. However, the exclusion of regulation pursuing public purposes "except in rare circumstances" clearly seeks to protect host State's right to regulate and policy space. As formulations are quite similar in several of China's newer BITs, it can be assumed that China favours its inclusion based on some form of a template.

2.3.3.4 *Interim Conclusion*

All three countries examined here have changed their approach to expropriation clauses in recent years. While Brazil has taken a more radical approach, omitting indirect expropriations altogether, both India and China have kept the provision but provided more precise treaty language to narrow the scope of indirect expropriation and depart from the sole effects doctrine to allow for public interests to be considered more appropriately.

---

179 China-India BIT (2006), Protocol, III. Ad art. 5; China-Colombia BIT (2008), art. 4 (2); China-Uzbekistan BIT (2011), art. 6(1)–(2); China-Japan-Republic of Korea Trilateral Investment Agreement (2012), Protocol, para. 2; China-Tanzania BIT (2012), art. 6 (2); China-Canada BIT (2012), Annex B.10; China-Republic of Korea BIT (2015), Protocol.

180 *See e.g.*, China-India BIT (2006), Protocol.

181 China-Japan-Republic of Korea Trilateral Investment Agreement (2012), Protocol. *See also* China-Republic of Korea BIT (2015), Protocol; China-Colombia BIT (2008), art. 4 (2); China-Tanzania BIT (2012), art. 6(3); China-Canada BIT (2012), Annex B.10, para. 2.

182 *See* 2004 US Model BIT, Annex B (Expropriation) ("Except in rare circumstances, non-discriminatory regulatory actions by a Party that are designed and applied to protect legitimate public welfare objectives, such as public health, safety and the environment, do not constitute indirect expropriations.")

2.3.4 Exception Clauses

Broad safeguards and exceptions clauses have never featured prominently in traditional BITs. This markedly changed with the newest generation of BITs.[183] The new trend to include broader framed exceptions and safeguards is at least partly the result of increasing environmental and human rights concerns against unrestricted investment protection.[184] Such safeguards and exceptions are intended to preserve a State's policy space by allowing parties to justify measures even if they violate other clauses of the relevant BIT.[185] Usually such exception clauses contain at least three elements: First, the permissible objectives (e.g. security or environment); second, the nexus requirement between the measure and the permissible objective (e.g. necessary, or related to) and third some (procedural) requirements (e.g. obligations to notify the other party, to follow due process and transparency clauses). To further increase a State's latitude, some of the exception provisions are self-judging. While this increases a State's discretion substantially, it has been convincingly argued that States are nevertheless required to invoke self-judging exception clauses in "good faith" which is not completely beyond the jurisdiction of an investor-state tribunal or of another judicial body.[186]

2.3.4.1 *Brazil*

One of the most striking features concerning safeguarding a State's policy space in Brazilian Model CFIA (2015) is its exception clauses.[187] The most interesting provision for the concerns of this chapter is contained in Article 16 Model CFIA which points out that the Agreement shall not prevent a Party from adopting, maintaining or enforcing any measure that "it deems appropriate to ensure that investment activity in its territory is undertaken in a manner according to labour, environmental and health legislations of that Party" provided that it is not an "arbitrary or unjustifiable discrimination or a disguised restriction". Importantly the provision contains self-judging language ("it deems appropri-

183 According to the IIA mapping project 234 out of 2575 mapped treaties include a General public policy exception for public health and the environment. While some of those treaties were concluded in the late 90s most of them were concluded in the 2000s and a high concentration is prevalent in most recently concluded treaties.

184 Sornarajah, *supra* note 2, at 223.

185 Some scholars have criticized such safeguards for being less effective than provisions attached to the definition of investment itself (e.g. requiring the investment to conform to the regulatory regime of the host State). *See id.*, at 223.

186 Salacuse, *supra* note 137, at 345, 370; Stephan Schill and R. Briese, "If the State Considers": Self-Judging Clauses in International Dispute Settlement, 13 *Max Planck Yearbook of United Nations Law* 61 (2009).

187 Brazilian Model CFIA (2015), arts. 11–13, 15 (2) and art. 16.

ate") as a nexus requirement and thereby allows State parties a wide margin of appreciation when considering what is necessary and proportionate to protect, e.g. the environment. Conditions, on the other hand, are reasonably strong, protecting against arbitrary treatment, unjustifiable discrimination and disguised restrictions.

Brazilian Model CFIA (2015) further includes a security exception, which is not self-judging but is not subject to dispute settlement under the agreement.[188] This clause allows State Parties to shield measures taken in times of war or other emergencies, which might impact on investments. Other exceptions inter alia shield the imposition or collection of taxes from legal challenge under the CFIA (subject to some conditions), the adoption or maintenance of prudential measures (protection of financial market participants, maintenance of safety and integrity of financial institutions etc.) and exclude certain investments involving illegal acts from protection of the treaty.[189]

Additionally, Article 16 para. 2 contains an interesting provision that aims at discouraging the lowering of standards of labour or environmental legislation or measures of health to attract investment. To avoid a race to the bottom, the clause prohibits State Parties to offer investors to repeal or amend such legislation to attract investors. At first sight, such a clause further limits a State's policy space, which may, in the long run, preserve a State's policy space because the international community avoids a race to the bottom which forces States' to lower regulatory standards to attract investments. However, the clause is not subject to dispute settlement[190] and may only be enforced through consultations between Parties. While such a provision is an interesting development per se, it is not a creative invention of Brazil but has been used in a number of 21st century investment agreements.[191]

2.3.4.2 *India*

The Indian Model BIT (2015) also contains two broadly framed exception clauses, one general exception clause and one security exception clause.[192] These clauses are quite similar to the exception clause in GATT 1994, namely Articles XX and XXI. These provisions allow for some leeway for a State to take

188 Brazilian Model CFIA (2015), art. 13(2).

189 Brazilian Model CFIA (2015), arts. 11, 12, 13 and 15.

190 Brazilian Model CFIA (2015), art. 24(3).

191 The IIA Mapping project counts 70 out of 2575 mapped treaties that include such a clause, of which nearly all were concluded in the 21st century.

192 Indian Model BIT (2015), arts. 32, 33.

measures for certain legitimate purposes which otherwise would be deemed in violation of the treaty.[193]

The general exception clause contains a long list of permissible objectives, including the protection of public morals and order, protection of human, animal or plant life or health, to ensure compliance with domestic laws that are consistent with the treaty, the protection of the environment and the protection of national treasures such as cultural and historic objects.[194] As a nexus requirement, the provision contains the relatively strong "necessary" which according to Footnote 6 of the Model CFIA requires Parties to assess whether there are less restrictive alternative measures reasonably available. Conditions are relatively weak only requiring "general applicability" and application "on a non-discriminatory basis". In particular, there is no chapeau such as in Article XX of GATT 1994, which could ensure that there is no misuse of the provision (e.g. prohibiting disguised restrictions).[195] It can reasonably be assumed that if there is a manifest misuse by a host State, then arbitrators might find that the State has violated the treaty by not applying it in good faith.

Apart from this general exception clause, the Indian Model BIT incorporates a self-judging security exception. Security exceptions have a long tradition in States' treaty practice but only in more modern treaties have self-judging clauses become more frequent.[196] The Indian Model BIT not only covers times of war or other emergencies but also extends to traffic in arms, actions related to fissionable materials and the protection of public infrastructure.[197]

2.3.4.3 *China*

The Chinese Model BIT does not contain any explicit exceptions clauses. Still, a rather limited number of both older and newer Chinese BITs do contain general public policy exceptions for public health, the environment, public order, cultural heritage or other public interests.[198] Several of the newer BITs also include security exception clauses of which only a limited number is self-judging.[199]

---

193 *Cf.* Salacuse, *supra* note 137, at 340.

194 Indian Model BIT (2015), art. 32.

195 Ranjan and Anand, *supra* note 68, at 37.

196 The IIA Mapping Project maps 143 out of 2575 mapped treaties which contain such a clause, all of which have been concluded after 2000.

197 Indian Model BIT (2015), art. 33 (1)(ii).

198 According to the IIA Mapping Project 9 out of 112 mapped Chinese investment agreements contain one or more of those exceptions.

199 According to the IIA Mapping Project 12 out of 112 mapped Chinese investment agreements contain security exceptions, of which four contain self-judging security clauses, including

The Canada-China BIT (2012) for example contains a general exception clause and also a self-judging security exception.[200] Accordingly, "nothing in this Agreement shall be construed to prevent a Contracting Party from adopting or maintaining measures, including environmental measures" that are necessary to ensure compliance with laws and regulations not inconsistent with the Agreement, necessary to protect human, animal or plant life of health, or relate to conservation of natural resources if they are applied in a non-arbitrary and justifiable manner and do not constitute disguised restrictions.[201] The general exceptions clause further covers non-discriminatory monetary, credit and exchange rate policies.[202] As the clause strongly resembles the general exception clause in the Canadian Model BIT,[203] China here seems to have accepted the Canadian template.

Among South-South BITs, the China-Tanzania BIT also contains a clause on "Health, Safety and Environmental Measures" that exempts non-arbitrary measures which do not constitute a disguised restriction "necessary to protect human, animal or plant life or health."[204] However, other recent treaties with economically weaker States do not contain such exception clauses.[205] Overall, China appears not to follow a clear policy here but rather is flexible on whether to incorporate general exceptions or not.

3 Concluding Remarks

Historically B(R)ICS have taken diverse approaches on international investment treaties. While Brazil has remained outside the system altogether, India, South Africa and more reluctantly China have signed and ratified traditional style BITs up until the early 21st century. However, approaches by several of these States have changed remarkably. South Africa has taken a radical approach in deciding to withdraw from international investment law and arbitration and instead promote more flexible domestic investment protection. Still, as government officials have stated that a new model IIA is in the drafting process and reports indicate that early treaty negotiations have been

the Australia-China FTA (2015); China-Colombia BIT (2008); China-Japan-Republic of Korea Trilateral Investment Agreement (2012) and China-Republic of Korea FTA (2015).

200 *See* China-Canada BIT (2012), art. 33.

201 China-Canada BIT (2012), art. 33 (3).

202 *Id.*, art. 33 (4).

203 *See* Canadian Model BIT (2004), art. 10 ("General Exceptions").

204 China-Tanzania BIT (2014), art. 10(2).

205 China-Malta BIT (2009); China-Uzbekistan BIT (2011); China-Congo BIT (2015).

conducted with Brazil, South Africa remains open to conclude new agreements in the future and therefore might not be called a revolutionary. Brazil, India and China so far remain in, or in the case of Brazil have just entered, the legal regime of international investment treaties, but all have reformed their approaches.

Through their joint statements, BRICS has called for further improvements of international investment law and highlighted States' right to regulate and policy space. This aim is also clearly visible in Brazil's and India's reformed investment agreement models. Both States reformed many provisions including NT, MFN, FET, indirect expropriations, investor obligations and ISDS towards increasing States' policy space. On several but differing provisions, Brazil and India have taken even more radical positions. Brazil has excluded indirect expropriations from its expropriation clause, has included a self-judging general exception clause and has omitted ISDS and instead focused on institutional dispute prevention and amicable resolution. India has omitted an MFN clause, and radically limited the availability of ISDS. However, overall, both States have taken a reformist rather than a revolutionary position carefully recalibrating States' policy space vis-à-vis the protection of foreign investors and investments.

China, in contrast, largely remains a loyalist, albeit recent treaty practice saw some incremental reforms towards more policy space (FET, MFN and indirect expropriation). In other areas, China's BIT practice so far remains ambiguous without a clear trend (Preamble, exceptions and safeguards). Despite some recalibration, the newest generation of Chinese BITs is far more investor-friendly than older generations.[206] This seems to correlate with China's increasing capital exports. Increased embracement of traditional style strong protection can be seen in more comprehensive NT- and unrestricted ISDS provisions. However, as the assessment of China's approach is based on treaty practice which is often a compromise between negotiating States, it has proven challenging to distil a transparent Chinese approach on policy space in international investment law. On many provisions, China appears rather flexible or undecided, apparently following recent trends and preferences of partner countries.

All in all, there appears to be no clear common BRICS approach on policy space in international investment law. While all States rhetorically embrace the recalibration of investment treaties towards more regulatory policy space, actual approaches are quite diverse. However, the approaches taken by Brazil and India are quite similar. Now, much depends on the future course of China's

206 Sauvant and Nolan, *supra* note 58, at 933.

investment treaties. If China resists the temptation to strengthen investment protection and instead further recalibrates its BITs not only a common BRICS approach is possible, but China may also calm host States wary of increased Chinese influence and competition.

Today emerging powers are in a special position. While they are still recipients of investments, they have substantially increased both their South-North as well as South-South capital exports. This intermediary position requires them to negotiate and lobby for BITs which seek a compromise between investment protection and legitimate interests of recipient States. As traditional powers increasingly are in quite a comparable situation as emerging powers, with still important capital outflows but increased capital inflows from Southern Countries, rebalancing efforts should provide win-win situations, if populist movements afraid of anything "foreign" and "different" are not to prevail.[207] The author of this article hopes that the rise of certain Southern powers will strengthen recent trends that international investment law will become "more balanced, less isolated, and in terms of regulatory approaches increasingly diversified."[208]

---

207 Rebalancing should of course not become "an ill-camouflaged attempt to get rid of the bonds of the international rule of law and accountability by maximizing regulatory arbitrariness", see Hindelang and Krajewski, *supra* note 1, 9.

208 *Ibid.* 5.

CHAPTER 8

Investment Barriers, Investment Facilitation and the BRICS Countries' Investment Treaty Policies and Practice

Xiuyan Fei

1 Introduction

International investment governance has been witnessing a profound transformation since the 1990s, which was especially characterized by the gradual de-regulation of investment regimes at the national level and by the rapid increase of investment treaties of high treatment and protection at the international level. Indeed, since the second ten years of the twenty first century, there has been a perceivable trend that states tend to affirm their regulatory power in investment affairs both at the national level and at the international level. For instance, many states, including those who have long advocated liberal investment treaty regime (especially the US), have begun to reform their investment treaty policies and practice, giving more respect to the regulatory power of host states. Nevertheless, the basic trend to liberalize investment regimes appears not to have reversed. States still welcome foreign investment by enhancing market access and reducing investment barriers.

To a large degree, the investment treaty policy and practice of a State depends on its domestic investment regime. In other words, the approach to, and the evolution of, the investment treaties of Brazil, Russia, India, China and South Africa (BRICS) has been fundamentally influenced by their changing investment regimes. In a new context where the trend of de-regulating investment regimes, generally speaking, continues and investment treaty regimes have been substantially transforming, how the BRICS countries deal with investment barriers obviously has important bearing on the future investment treaty policies and practice of the BRICS countries, their role in the process of reforming investment treaty regime, and, specifically, cooperation among BRICS countries.

Noticeably, at the ninth annual BRICS Summit in 2017 the BRICS issued the Outlines for BRICS Investment Facilitation (BRICS Outlines), which is expected to enhance BRICS countries to eliminate investment barriers and

 | DOI:10.1163/9789004376991_009

thereby share their comparative advantages in terms of value, economics, political structure and geography.[1] However, the Outlines is not a legally binding document and how the BRICS Outlines will be implemented remains unclear. After two years have passed, there is no convincing evidence that the BRICS countries, within the framework of the Outlines, have taken further concrete measures to eliminate intra-BRICS investment barriers.

Therefore, the handling of investment barriers is an important perspective through which to examine and evaluate the investment treaty policies and practice of the BRICS countries. By examining those investment barriers in existence and analyzing relevant measures adopted by the BRICS, along with considering the scenarios that foreign direct investment (FDI) inflows into BRICS countries have faced in recent years, it can be determined whether the BRICS countries effectively cooperate with each other to improve the investment environment. The FDI flows among BRICS countries are influenced by a variety of factors, such as a country's domestic regulation on foreign investment, natural resources, language and cultural barriers. Therefore, it is difficult if not impossible to isolate the effect of BRICS cooperation in promoting investment from other factors. In other words, any empirical evaluation on the relationship between BRICS's efforts on investment cooperation and the change of intra-BRICS FDI flows is not reliable. Be that as it may, a qualitative, legal examination is still helpful. Obviously, there is no dispute that any foreign investor prefers a host state with less investment barriers. Thus, this chapter aims to identify investment barriers in BRICS countries and further provides policy suggestions on how to strengthen the BRICS cooperation in investment promotion.

The chapter is divided into five sections including an Introduction and Concluding Remarks. Section 2 provides an overview of BRICS FDI inflows in recent years, which serve as points of reference to analyze the effect of BRICS cooperation in investment promotion and facilitation. Section 3 examines the investment barriers in BRICS countries and the efforts of BRICS to reduce investment barriers at the domestic level. Section 4 reviews the new approach and practice of BRICS countries to investment treaties from the perspective of investment facilitation.

1 Tarequl Islam Khan, Ujjal Barua and Md. Iftekharul Islam Bhuiya, BRICS Economy: An Appealing Investment Opportunity on the International Stage, 3(1) *Journal for Worldwide Sustainable Development* 15 (2015) 38.

TABLE 8.1 Amount of FDI that flowed to individual BRICS countries[a] (millions of dollars)

Region/economy	2013	2014	2015	2016	2017	2018
Brazil	59089	63846	49514	52751	67583	61223
Russia	53397	29152	11858	37176	25954	13332
India	28199	34582	44064	44481	39904	42286
China	123911	128500	135610	133710	134063	139043
South Africa	8300	5771	1729	2235	2007	5334

a The data come from UNCTAD, Annex Table 1 of *2019 World Investment Report*, at 212–14.

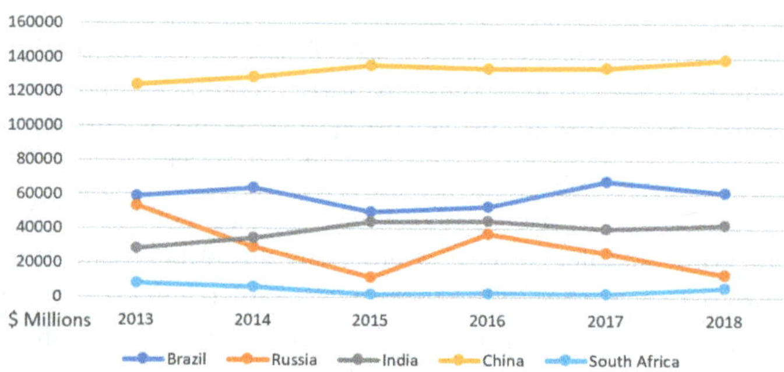

FIGURE 8.1 Trend of FDI inflows to individual BRICS countries (compiled by the author on the basis of Table 8.1)

2 An Overview of the BRICS FDI Inflows

FDI inflows to a country to a large degree depend on the health of the country's investment climate. In general, the better the investment climate of a host state is, the more FDI that country will attract.[2] Therefore, an examination of FDI inflows is helpful to analyze the investment climate of the BRICS and find out, albeit not conclusively, what investment barriers exist in the BRICS.

2.1 *FDI Inflows to BRICS Countries*

Table 8.1 and Figure 8.1 present the state of FDI inflows to BRICS countries from 2013 to 2018. Table 8.1 shows the amount of FDI that flowed to individual BRICS countries and Figure 8.1 demonstrates the trend of FDI inflows to individual BRICS countries. As to Brazil and Russia, they attracted similar

2 Nihal Bayraktar, Importance of Investment Climate for Inflows of Foreign Direct Investment in Developing Countries, 5(1) *Business and Economic Research* 24 (2015) 27.

TABLE 8.2 Total amounts of FDI inflows to BRICS countries[a] (millions of dollars)

Region/economy	2013	2014	2015	2016	2017	2018
BRICS	272896	261851	242775	270353	269511	261218
World	1431164	1357239	2033802	1918679	1497371	1297153
BRICS/World (%)	19.07%	19.29%	11.94%	14.09%	18.00%	20.14%

a The data of BRICS FDI inflows were calculated by the author according to Figure 8.1; the data of world FDI inflows come from UNCTAD, Annex 1 of *2019 World Investment Report*, at 212.

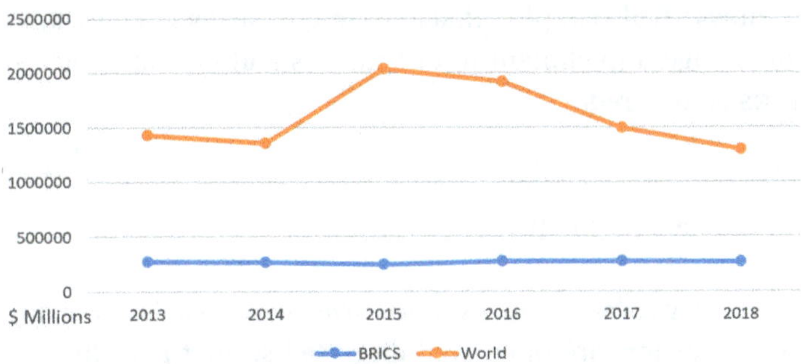

FIGURE 8.2 Trend of global FDI inflows (compiled by the author according to Table 8.2)

amounts of foreign investment in 2013 and also experienced sharp downs in 2015; nevertheless, Brazil has performed much better than Russia since 2016. In contrast, China, India and South Africa have been relatively stable in attracting foreign investment.

2.2 *BRICS and Global FDI Inflows*

A comparison between the BRICS and global FDI inflows can indicate the performance of the BRICS as a whole in attracting FDI inflows. It is seen in Table 8.2 and Figure 8.2 that the total amounts of FDI inflows to BRICS countries during this period were stable, which did not reflect the ups and downs of global FDI inflows. The share of the BRICS FDI inflows among the world reached the lowest level in 2015 for the period of 2013–2018, which was mainly due to the decline of FDI inflows to Brazil and Russia.

2.3 *Intra-BRICS FDI Inflows*

According to the World Investment Report (2017), while the amount of intra-BRICS investment remains small, it has been increasing, growing from 3 per cent in 2010 to 10 per cent of the outward FDI stock of BRICS countries in 2015.[3] This trend is especially noticeable in terms of intra-BRICS mergers and acquisitions (M&As). In 2014 and 2015, only two and three M&As respectively occurred within the BRICS countries. In contrast, the number sharply increased to 22 in 2016.[4] There is a trend that investors from a BRICS country are displaying growing interest in investing in other BRICS countries, which reflects that the economic connectivity within BRICS countries has been growing. Nevertheless, given the fact that the Gross Domestic Product (GDP) of the BRICS countries accounted for 22 per cent of global GDP and they only received 11 per cent of global inward FDI stock in 2016,[5] it is suggested that there is still huge potential to expand FDI inflows to BRICS countries, including intra-BRICS FDI flows.[6] It also implies that investment barriers in the BRICS countries constitute a huge impediment to FDI inflows and further cooperation among the BRICS is required.

3 Investment Barriers in the BRICS

It seems that there is no legal definition given to "investment barrier". Equally important, investment barriers are often well disguised so that it is difficult to identify them.[7] Numerous factors, such as political stability, market size, expectation for economic growth, availability of infrastructure, market access, investment facilitation, and labour, may affect foreign investors' decisions as to whether, when, how and where to invest.[8] Here the Chapter focuses on three factors, namely, market access for foreign investment, investment facilitation, and labour, which are highly relevant to investment barriers from the legal perspective.

3 UNCTAD, *2017 World Investment Report*, at 19.

4 UNCTAD, *2017 World Investment Report*, at 17.

5 UNCTAD, *2017 World Investment Report*, at 18.

6 Xinhua, "Much Potential to Tap in Intra-BRICS Cooperation – Indian Expert", *China Daily* 7 August 2017, available at http://usa.chinadaily.com.cn/business/2017-08/07/content_30359702.htm (visited September 1, 2019).

7 Christian Gormsen, The Declining Barriers to Foreign Direct Investments and How to See Them, Documents de Travail du Centre d'Economie de la Sorbonne 2012.15 – ISSN: 1955-611X.2012, at 23.

8 KusiHornberger, Joseph Battat& Peter Kusek, Attracting FDI: How Much Does Investment Climate Matter?, Viewpoint: Public Policy for the Private Sector (2011), World Bank Note No. 327, at 2.

3.1 *Market Access*

The restrictions on foreign investment are directly concerned with foreign investment access. Understandably, a country may restrict foreign investment in some areas due to considerations such as infant industry protection and national security concerns. Nevertheless, the restrictions should be deemed to be investment barriers if they are designed for the protection of domestic industry or interest groups. The five BRICS countries' restrictions on market access are as follows.

3.1.1 Brazil

Brazil is a major host state of foreign investment. In 2017 Brazil was ranked the world's sixth largest FDI destination.[9] It has adopted a "negative" approach to the market access of foreign investment.[10] Foreign investors receive the same legal treatment as local investors in most economic sectors. Foreign ownership of local companies is normally permitted except in sectors that are considered to be of strategic importance. Those sectors mainly include the healthcare, mass media, telecommunications, aerospace, maritime, and air transport sectors, but the automobile, renewable energy, life sciences, oil and gas, and transportation infrastructure sectors all have been encouraged as targets for foreign investment. An approval is required before a foreign investor starts operating certain types of businesses, such as banks and financial institutions, mining companies, oil refineries, maritime companies, road and air transport companies, and companies involved in health products and health care. Except for the restricted sectors, 100% foreign ownership of local enterprises and joint ventures is generally permitted.

3.1.2 Russia

Russia was ranked the fourteenth largest investment destination in 2017 around the world.[11] The legal framework governing foreign investment in Russia[12] arguably attempts to guarantee equal rights for foreign and local investors in Russia. However, exemptions are permitted when Russia's government finds it

9 UNCTAD, *2019 World Investment Report*, at 4.

10 Trade Policy Review Body, Trade Policy Review: Brazil, WT/TPR/S/358 (2017), at 38.

11 UNCTAD, *2019 World Investment Report*, at 4.

12 It includes *On Foreign Investment in the Russian Federation* (Law 160-FZ of 9 July 1999), *On Investment Activity in the Russian Federation in the Form of Capital Investment* (Law No. 39-FZ of 25 February 1999), *Order of Investing by Foreign Persons in Companies Having Strategic Importance for Ensuring the Defense of the Country and Security of the States* (Law No. 57-FZ of 29 April 2008), and *On Investment Activity in the Russian Soviet Federative Socialist Republic* (Law of the RSFS No. 1488–1 of 26 June 1991).

necessary to protect the Russian constitution, morality, health, human rights, and national security or defense. According to Russia's Strategic Sectors Law, a list of 45 "strategic" sectors has been provided in which the establishment of companies, investments, and transactions or purchases of controlling interests by foreign investors must be pre-approved by the Commission on Control of Foreign Investment of Russia.[13] As regards foreigners' ownership of land, there are two restrictions: one is that the land located in border areas or other specifically assigned sensitive territories is restricted from foreign ownership, and the other one is that foreign citizens and foreign legal entities cannot own more than 50 per cent of a plot of agricultural land. In addition, foreign ownership of any Russian media company is restricted to 20 per cent under the law "On Mass Media".[14]

3.1.3 India

The Indian government has taken steps to relax restrictions on foreign investors in sectors including insurance, defense, railways, construction, and medical devices, but restrictions on some other sectors, for instance, multi-brand retail, remain. Furthermore, the Indian government has the authority to allow FDI share up to 100% without Parliamentary approval, except in businesses involving pensions, insurance, and defense. In order to increase FDI inflows into India *inter alia* by liberalizing investment access in various sectors and streamlining the approval process, a new consolidated FDI policy document was adopted on August 28, 2017 by the Indian government which consolidates the changes previously introduced in 2016 while also introducing some new elements.[15] The Foreign Investment Policy Board (FIPB) of India was abolished, and thereby relevant governmental ministries were given authority to approve foreign investment in eleven sectors which previously required the approval from the FIPB.[16] Nevertheless, many sectors still require a multi-step process for approval by central and state government authorities. Moreover, equity limits for foreign capital are required in many sectors, which may deter foreign investment.

13 *See* Clifford Chance, A Legal Overview of Foreign Investment in Russia's Strategic Sectors, May 2014, at 2.

14 Vera Zakem, Paul Saunders, Umida Hashimova & P. Kathleen Hammerberg, Mapping Russian Media Network, *CNA Analysis & Solutions* 2018, at 14.

15 *See* Department of Industrial Policy and Promotion Ministry of Commerce and Industry Government of India, *Consolidated FDI Policy*, D/o IPP F. No. 5(1)/2017-FC-1 Dated the August 28, 2017, at 4.

16 Bradley Dunseith, India Abolishes FIPB. What Does it Mean for Foreign Investors?, *India Briefing* June 20, 2017.

3.1.4 China

China was the second largest FDI recipient in the world in 2017 and 2018.[17] The Catalogue for the Guidance of Foreign Investment in Industries (Catalogue) provided a market access guide for foreign investors, specifying that there were three categories of "encouraged", "restricted" or "prohibited" investment. In June 2017, the National Development and Reform Commission (NDRC) and the Ministry of Commerce (MOC) adopted an updated Catalogue.[18] A salient feature of the Catalogue (2017) was that it consolidated the two categories of "restricted" and "prohibited" into a "negative list". Foreign investors intending to invest in those industries not on the negative list will no longer be required to get pre-approval from the MOC, but rather need only register their investment with the MOC. Another important change to the Catalogue (2016) is that the number of restrictive measures in the Catalogue (2017) was reduced from 93 to 63, and the number of sectors that completely ban foreign investment from 36 to 28. The industries that fall under the "prohibited" category on the negative list include (1) aerial photography mapping, editing and publishing of books, (2) newspapers and periodicals, (3) editing, publishing, and production of audio-visual products and electronic publications, (4) radio, television video-on-demand business, and satellite television broadcasters receiving facility installation services, (5) internet public information services, and (6) research institutes of humanities and social sciences.

3.1.5 South Africa

FDI inflows into South Africa recovered in 2018, more than doubling from 2,007 million dollars in 2017 to 5,334 million dollars, and the increased FDI was primarily concentrated on natural resources sectors.[19] Most sectors in South Africa are open to foreign investment,[20] although certain sectors require governmental approval for foreign participation, including energy, mining, banking, insurance, and defense. Except for those sectors, no governmental approval is required, and only a few restrictions on the form or share of foreign investment still exist.[21] Importantly, and in the opposite vein, President Zuma

---

17 UNCTAD, *2019 World Investment Report*, at 4.

18 No. 4 Order of the NDRC and the MOC, available at http://www.ndrc.gov.cn/zcfb/zcfbl/201706/t20170628_852857.html (visited August 1, 2019).

19 UNCTAD, 2019 *World Investment Report*, at 213, 37.

20 See PwC, Investment Decisions: Why South Africa, and Why Now? (2018), available at https://www.pwc.co.za/en/assets/pdf/investment-decision-why-sa.pdf (visited January 1, 2019).

21 U.S. Department of State, 2018 Investment Climate Statements: South Africa, available at https://www.state.gov/reports/2018-investment-climate-statements/south-africa/ (visited August 2, 2019).

announced that he would launch a land reform bill that would restrict foreign ownership and convert foreign-owned land to long-term leases.

3.2 *Investment Facilitation*

Investment facilitation refers to a set of policies and actions aimed at making it easier for foreign investors to establish or expand their investment, as well as to conduct their day-to-day business in host countries.[22] Investment facilitation helps a host State to establish a transparent, predictable, stable, and efficient investment environment for foreign investors. Given that the nature of investment activity is forward-looking,[23] a robust legal system, which offers transparency, certainty and predictability, is a crucial factor for any foreign investor in making decisions as to investment.[24] In particular, a judicial system which is efficient, effective, impartial and independent is significant for all investors.[25] International organizations do not rank states in terms of investment facilitation, but the World Bank provides worldwide rankings of the states' ease of doing business.[26] A high ranking of a state's ease of doing business indicates its high development of investment facilitation.

3.2.1 Brazil

The World Bank ranked Brazil 109th out of 190 economies in 'ease of doing business' in 2018.[27] Due to complex bureaucratic procedures,[28] it takes around 101.5 days to start a business in San Paulo, compared to an average of 31.7 days in Latin America & Caribbean countries and 8.5 days in the Organization for Economic Cooperation and Development (OECD) countries.[29] Closing a business is also cumbersome, bureaucratic and costly.[30] In addition, it takes an average of 1,958 hours per year for a medium-sized company to comply with Brazilian tax codes in Sao Paulo in 2016, compared to 332.1 hours in Latin America & Caribbean countries and 160.7 hours in OECD high economic economies.[31] These circumstances, such as the difficulty starting a business and paying taxes, significantly damage investment environment in Brazil.[32]

---

27 The World Bank, *Rankings & Distance to Frontier*, available at http://www.doingbusiness.org/en/rankings (visited August 1, 2019).

28 Kajsa Mattsson, Analysis of Foreign Direct Investment Climate in Brazil, Bachelor Thesis (2017), at 37.

29 The World Bank, *Doing Business 2018 Indicators: Economy Profile of Brazil*, at 6.

30 Trade Policy Review Body, *Trade Policy Review: Brazil*, WT/TPR/S/358 (2017), at 38.

31 Trade Policy Review Body, *Trade Policy Review: Brazil*, WT/TPR/S/358 (2017), at 67.

32 International Monetary Fund, *Brail: Selected Issues*, IMF Country Report No. 17/216, at 19.

As for the investment treatment, foreign investors usually can receive the same treatment as domestic investors under the same circumstances.[33] However, it is widely acknowledged that the Brazilian legal system is notoriously inefficient and cumbersome.[34] While the judicial system in Brazil is generally independent, the workload of courts is terribly large and thereby it often takes several years for judges to make a final decision.

However, in recent years Brazil has made efforts to improve legal transparency and accessibility. For instance, in 2012, the Federal Government established a unified platform for registering online access to information required for registration, and thus foreign investors may make use of this platform to obtain necessary information on registration requirements.[35] Besides, foreign investors may use a single database in the Brazilian Legal and Legislative Information Portal,[36] attaining information concerning legislation, judiciary and executive activities. In 2014, the Ministry of Industry, Foreign Trade and Services, and the Ministry of Foreign Affairs worked together to establish an online information dissemination platform,[37] providing guidelines to conduct trade and investment in English, Spanish and Portuguese. Importantly, in order to promote investment facilitation, in 2015 Brazil adopted a new model of investment agreements, the Cooperation and Facilitation Investment Agreement (CFIA), which places the priority on the investment facilitation, institutional cooperation and investment protection.

3.2.2 Russia

In recent years Russia has significantly reduced the regulatory burden on business. Thus, the World Bank ranked Russia the 31st in ease of doing business in 2018.[38] According to the World Bank, starting a business in Moscow in 2018 takes around 11 days, compared to 8.5 days in OECD countries.[39] Getting electricity, registering property and enforcing contracts are efficiently regulated in Russia, which were respectively ranked by the World Bank as the 10th, 12th and

33 Kajsa Mattsson, *Analysis of Foreign Direct Investment Climate in Brazil*, Bachelor Thesis (2017), at 37.

34 PwC, *Doing Business and Investing in Brazil* (2013 edn.), at 13.

35 The platform website is http://www.informacao.gov.br.

36 Its website is http://projeto.lexml.gov.br/documentacao/resumo-em-ingles.

37 Its website is http://www.investexportbrasil.gov.br/?l=en.

38 The World Bank, Rankings & Distance to Frontier, available at: http://www.doingbusiness.org/en/rankings (visited 1 August 2019).

39 The World Bank, Doing Business 2018 Indicators: Economy Profile of Russian Federation, at 6.

18th easiest out of 190 economies in 2017.[40] In order to improve its investment environment, the Russian government worked with foreign investors, creating the Foreign Investment Advisory Council (FIAC) in 1994.[41] Currently, the FIAC is chaired by the Russian Prime Minister and includes 53 international companies and banks helping tackle various problems that foreign investors face, as well as export experts who help the Russian government to improve its regulatory and legal frameworks.[42] In 2011, Russia established the Agency for Strategic Initiatives (ASI)[43] which aimed, among others, to enhance regulatory innovation and to reduce bureaucracy. There is also a "National Regional Investment Climate Ranking" that is sponsored by the ASI to encourage competition among local governments for attracting investment.

The Russian governmental authorities at all levels have taken various measures to improve the regulatory system, but more efforts need to be taken. Drafts of laws and regulations are open to the public for comments in accordance with the Government Resolution 851 of 2012. Important regulatory actions are announced on a centralized web site (https://www.pravo.gov.ru). However, amendments of law are frequent and explanations for those amendments are not sufficient, which reduces the stability of regulatory environment.[44] Furthermore, the actual implementation of policies and laws is often selective and incoherent. It is suggested that the bureaucracy remains a major concern for foreign investors.[45] In particular, the judicial system in Russia has long been criticized for its lack of independence and allegations that the courts often fail to effectively enforce laws.[46]

---

40 The World Bank, Rankings & Distance to Frontier, available at http://www.doingbusiness.org/en/rankings (visited October 1, 2018).

41 Its website is https://www.fiac.ru/.

42 Trade Policy Review Body, Trade Policy Review: Russian Federation, WT/TPR/S/345, at 35.

43 Its website is https://asi.ru/eng/.

44 EY, Investment Climate in Russia: Foreign Investor Perception, at 2, 6, available at https://www.ey.com/Publication/vwLUAssets/EY_report_-_Investment_climate_in_Russia_2015/$FILE/EY-Investment-climate-in-Russia_eng%20EY%202015.pdf (visited October 1, 2018).

45 EY, Investment Climate in Russia: Foreign Investor Perception, at 7, available at https://www.ey.com/Publication/vwLUAssets/EY_report_-_Investment_climate_in_Russia_2015/$FILE/EY-Investment-climate-in-Russia_eng%20EY%202015.pdf (visited October 1, 2018).

46 *See* Conor Gilligan, Fake Crime and Real Punishment: How a Weak Judiciary Has Held Back Development in Russia (2017), available at https://chicagounbound.uchicago.edu/cgi/viewcontent.cgi?article=1044&context=international_immersion_program_papers (visited October 1, 2018).

3.2.3 India

India, according to the World Bank, improved its rankings in ease of doing business from 142nd in 2015 to 77th in 2018.[47] Although the Indian investment environment has been ameliorated, starting a business, registering property and enforcing contracts were respectively ranked 137th, 166th and 163rd in 2018.[48] It should be noted that India is a notoriously decentralized federal country. As a result, states possess extensive regulatory powers, and thus laws among different states often conflict with each other. Any investment in India must comply with laws and regulations enacted by central government and governments at the state level. Foreign investors are often frustrated by Indian bureaucracy and the multi-hub regulatory system in India. As a response, in 2015 the Modi administration established a multi-purpose and multi-model platform for Pro-Active Governance and Timely Implementation (PAGTI) with an aim to address a broad range of economic problems, monitor and review important programs and projects of the Government of India.[49] Prime Minister Modi, within the framework of the PAGTI, chairs the interaction between government authorities and relevant stakeholders and reviews investment-related issues. The Indian judicial system is believed to be independent and impartial, but the courts are understaffed and lack the technology necessary to resolve an enormous backlog of pending cases.[50]

3.2.4 China

China was ranked 46th out of 190 economies in ease of doing business by the World Bank in 2018.[51] The procedures for starting a business have been significantly streamlined, the ranking of which increased from 93rd in 2017 to 28th in 2018.[52] However, getting an approval for construction ranks 121st, which is China's lowest ranked category. In Shanghai, an investor has to take 279 days

47 The World Bank, Rankings & Distance to Frontier, available at http://www.doingbusiness.org/en/rankings (visited August 1, 2019).

48 The World Bank, Rankings & Distance to Frontier, available at http://www.doingbusiness.org/en/rankings (visited August 1, 2019).

49 Press Information Bureau of the Government of India, PM launches PRAGATI: a multi-purpose, multi-modal platform for Pro-Active Governance and Timely Implementation, available at http://pib.nic.in/newsite/PrintRelease.aspx?relid=117685 (visited October 1, 2018).

50 See Raj Kumar Bhardwaj, The Indian Judicial System: Transition from Print to Digital, 13 *Legal Information Management* 203 (2013), 204.

51 The World Bank, Rankings & Distance to Frontier, available at http://www.doingbusiness.org/en/rankings (visited October 1, 2018).

52 *Id.*

on average to handle construction permits, compared with 138.2 days in East Asia & Pacific countries.[53]

China publishes all foreign trade and investment-related laws in accordance with the WTO commitments that China has made. In accordance with the Legislation Law, drafts of "Law" (enacted by the National People's Congress (NPC) and its Standing Committee, the supreme legislature in China) and "Administrative Regulation" (enacted by the State Council),[54] are open to the public for comments.[55] Local governments at the provincial level are authorized to enact "Local Regulation", but they must conform with "Law" and "Administrative Regulation".[56] In particular, "Ministerial Rule" (enacted by ministries affiliated to the State Council), which might represent the largest part of Chinese legal system, "without the legal basis deriving from Laws, or Administrative Regulation, Decisions or Orders by the State Council", shall not "include provisions which derogate the rights of, or impose more obligations on, individuals, judicial persons and other entities, or expand the authorities or reduce the mandates of the relevant ministries."[57] Legally, this effectively prevents additional requirements from being imposed on foreign investors beyond the scope or extent that has been established by the NPC and its Standing Committee and the State Council. It is admitted that, in addition to laws that are enacted in accordance with the Legislation Law,[58] there exist many "soft" instruments, for instance, policy guidelines, which have bearings on foreign investment. According to some foreign investors, it is these "soft" instruments without legally binding force that impose a variety of investment barriers.[59] Furthermore, foreign investors are often frustrated by the arguably discriminatory and incoherent state of law enforcement.[60]

It should be noted that since 2013 China has established twelve free trade zones (FTZS) in order to explore new types of administration for trade and investment. To reduce investment barriers and facilitate foreign investment is

---

53 The World Bank, Doing Business 2018 Indicators: Economy Profile of China, at 7.

54 China's Legislation Law (2000, as amended in 2015), arts. 6, 65.

55 China's Legislation Law (2000, as amended in 2015), arts. 37, 67.

56 China's Legislation Law (2000, as amended in 2015), art. 74.

57 China's Legislation Law (2000, as amended in 2015), art. 80(2).

58 China's Legislation Law (2000, as amended in 2015), chapters, 2, 3 and 4.

59 For example, the US Trade Representative considered the policy tools used by China to achieve the goals of Made in China 2025 were restricting, taking advantage of, discriminating against or otherwise creating disadvantages for foreign enterprises. *See* US Trade Representative, *2019 National Trade Estimate Report on Foreign Trade Barriers*, at 99.

60 The U.S. Department of State, 2018 Investment Climate Statement – China, available at https://www.state.gov/e/eb/ifd/2008/103668.htm (visited October 1, 2018).

one of main working tasks for authorities in free trade zones. In March 2019, China's NPC approved the Foreign Investment Law. The new law aims to enhance high-level investment facilitation, build a stable, transparent, and foreseeable investment environment, improve foreign investment service in respect of laws and regulations, policies and measures, and investment project information, and enhance international exchange and cooperation in investment affairs.[61] The new law is expected to significantly reduce investment barriers.[62]

3.2.5 South Africa

Noticeably, South Africa's ranking in ease of doing business declined from 74th in 2017 to 82nd in 2018.[63] South African authorities fail to effectively coordinate with each other in handling investment affairs, which substantially increases the burden on foreign investors. The complexity of regulatory procedures and the high costs incurred to complete regulatory processes are also major investment barriers that South Africa needs to address.[64] South Africa has begun to make efforts to improve its regulatory regime. For instance, the InvestSA, a division of the South African Department of Trade and Industry ("DTI"), started to provide One Stop Shop ("OSS") services in 2017 in order to help remove bottlenecks for investors in establishing and running the business.[65] Nevertheless, there is huge room for South Africa to improve its regulatory regime.

Arguably South Africa has a good record of legal transparency. Drafts of legislation are generally open for public comments. However, the Protection of Investment Act (2015), which represents the trend of localization instead of internationalization of investment regime in South Africa,[66] arguably sent an unfavorable signal to foreign investors. National treatment enjoyed by foreign investors is subject to a broad range of exceptions, such as exclusion of the benefit, preference or privilege resulting from taxation arrangements, government procurement, public subsidies or grants, any law or other measure that aims to promote the achievement of equality in South Africa or is designed to protect or advance persons, or categories of persons, historically

---

61 *See* China's Foreign Investment Law, arts. 3, 11 and 12.

62 *See* China's Foreign Investment Law, art. 1.

63 The World Bank, Rankings & Distance to Frontier, available at http://www.doingbusiness.org/en/rankings (visited September 1, 2019).

64 The World Bank, Doing Business in South Africa 2018, at 2, 6.

65 See the InvestSA website, http://www.investsa.gov.za/about-investsa/ (visited October 1, 2018).

66 See Chapter of South Africa of this book.

disadvantaged by unfair discrimination on the basis of race, gender or disability in South Africa.[67] In addition, international arbitration is not available to foreign investors, but only available to home states of foreign investors under the conditions that foreign investors have exhausted domestic remedies and their request for international arbitration is approved pursuant to South African administrative process.[68]

3.3 *Labour*

Low cost of labour is appealing to labour-intensive industries, but it is only one consideration for foreign investors to make investment decisions. Production requires both skilled labour and unskilled labour.[69] Developed countries with skilled labour are more attractive for skilled-labour-intensive industries, while developing countries with unskilled labour may only attract unskilled-labour-intensive industries. In addition, a state's regulation on labour may also impact foreign investment. If such regulation over protects local labour, foreign investors may consider it costly to follow the law and thus see the regulation as an investment barrier.

3.3.1 Brazil

Brazil is abundant with unskilled and semi-skilled labour, but highly skilled labour is in short supply.[70] International companies may offer in-house training and education for employees to reach the skills that meet their requirements. Employers are often encouraged to pay an additional month's salary each year as a compulsory (Christmas) bonus, as well as contributing to various federal social security and welfare institutions.[71] Brazilian factory wages had more than doubled from 2004 to 2014, but total productivity improved only 1 per cent per year during that period.[72] Brazil is now one of the highest-cost countries

67 *See* Protection of Investment Act (2015), art. 8(3).

68 *See* Protection of Investment Act (2015), art. 13(5).

69 Qing Liu & Larry D. Qiu, Labor Training and Foreign Direct Investment, 22(1) *Review of International Economics* (2014) 151, 151.

70 Kajsa Mattsson, Analysis of Foreign Direct Investment Climate in Brazil, Bachelor Thesis (2017), at 35.

71 PWC, Doing Business and Investing in Brazil (2013), available at https://www.pwc.de/de/internationale-maerkte/assets/doing-business-and-investing-in-brazil.pdf (visited January 2, 2019), at 81.

72 Harold L. Sirkin, Michael Zinser & Justin R. Rose, The Shifting Economics of Global Manufacturing, available at http://iknow.stpi.narl.org.tw/Post/Files/The_Shifting_Economics_of_Global_Manufacturing_Aug_2014_BCG.pdf (visited January 1, 2019), at 10.

for manufacturing.[73] The unemployment rate in Brazil is high, and is nearing 12%.[74] In order to protect working opportunities for local workers, Brail does not encourage enterprises to employ foreign workers. It is required that foreign employees and their income in a Brazilian enterprise take up no more than 1/3 of the total employees and total salaries.[75] Brazilian labour legislation is notoriously favourable to local workers,[76] which is a barrier especially for FDI involved in manufacturing industries.

3.3.2 Russia

The shortage of qualified skilled labour is a serious problem in Russia, and Russian employers complain that the lack of a skilled workforce is an obstacle for business operation.[77] It is not only a problem of quality confronting the Russian workforce but also the quantity. Due to the ageing of the Russian population and falling birth rates, the number of young people entering the workforce is not adequate. In addition, some Russians, many of whom are researchers, entrepreneurs and people with IT skills, immigrate to the countries with more attractive economic opportunities.[78] One advantage of Russian labour is that the cost is not high. Compared to labour costs in Central and Eastern European countries, the cost of Russian labour is attractive to foreign investors, although it is not a low-cost destination in global terms.[79] The unemployment rate in Russia is around 5% in 2018.[80] Russian enterprises must obtain authorization from the state to hire foreign employees who need a visa to work in Russia. In order to protect the domestic labour market, the quota system is applied to restrict the number of foreign employees and an

---

73 Harold L. Sirkin, Michael Zinser & Justin R. Rose, The Shifting Economics of Global Manufacturing, available at http://iknow.stpi.narl.org.tw/Post/Files/The_Shifting_Economics_of_Global_Manufacturing_Aug_2014_BCG.pdf (visited January 1, 2019), at 3.

74 Trading Economics, Brazil Real Average Monthly Income, available at https://tradingeconomics.com/brazil/wages (visited January 1, 2019).

75 Chinese Academy of International Trade and Economic Cooperation, Economic and Commercial Counsellor's Office of the Embassy of the People's Republic of China in Brazil & Ministry of Commerce of the People's Republic of China Department of Outward Investment and Economic Cooperation, Guide on Foreign Investment and Cooperation: Brazil (2018), at 96.

76 PWC, Doing Business and Investing in Brazil (2013), at 81.

77 Martin Russell, Seven Economic Challenges for Russia, PE625.138-July 2018, at 11.

78 Martin Russell, Seven Economic Challenges for Russia, PE625.138-July 2018, at 8–9.

79 EY, Russia's Investment Attractiveness: Conditions for Foreign Capital, available at https://www.ey.com/ru/en/newsroom/pr-activities/articles/article-world-finance-review-sept-2012 (visited January 1, 2019).

80 Trading Economics, Russia Employment Rate, available at https://tradingeconomics.com/russia/employment-rate (visited on January 1, 2019).

annual work permit quota for foreign employees is set by the Russian cabinet each year.[81]

3.3.3 India

India has a vast labour market since almost half of its population of 1.2 billion is of working age, and the labour cost is low. Therefore, India has comparative advantages with low wages and access to a vast labour market. Nevertheless, highly skilled labour only amounts to 10% of the total labour force[82] and the Indian government acknowledges a shortage of skilled labour in high-growth sectors of the economy.[83] The unemployment rate in India was around 6.1% in 2018.[84] Employment laws in India are complicated and restrictive, with over 50 national and 150 state-level laws governing subjects ranging from conditions of employment to social security, health, safety, welfare, trade unions, industrial and labour disputes, etc.[85] Without prior permission from the government, enterprises employing 100 or more workers are not permitted to lay off or retrench employees. There are no clear rules based on which permission mentioned above would be given.[86] Downsizing or closure of loss-making businesses is difficult. Due to the overprotection of employees, entrepreneurs are reluctant to expose themselves to the risk of indefinite liability, which hinders FDI inflows into India. As for ordinary foreign engineers and ordinary skilled workers, they have difficulty obtaining work permits, and the application for such permits may take a long time.[87]

---

81 For the past four years, the total numbers of work permit for skilled foreign workers were 178,454 in 2018, 177,043 in 2017, 213,929 in 2016, and 275,856 in 2015. Sergei Blagov, Russia: Government Ups Foreign Workforce Quotas, available at https://www.bna.com/russia-government-ups-n73014481360/ (visited January 1, 2019).

82 India Briefing, The Labor Market in India: Structure and Costs, available at https://www.india-briefing.com/news/labor-market-india-structure-costs-18264.html/ (visited January 1, 2019).

83 Bureau of Economic and Business Affairs of the US Department of the State, 2018 Investment Climate Statements Report: India, available at https://www.state.gov/e/eb/rls/othr/ics/2018/sca/281700.htm (visited 1 January 2019).

84 Trading Economics, India Unemployment Rate, available at https://tradingeconomics.com/india/unemployment-rate (visited 1 January 2018).

85 Nishith Desai, Doing Business in India, available at http://www.nishithdesai.com/fileadmin/user_upload/pdfs/Research%20Papers/Doing_Business_in_India.pdf (visited January 1, 2019), at 45.

86 Anwarul Hoda & Durgesh Kumar Rai, Trade and Investment Barriers affecting International Production Networks in India, Working Paper 281 (2014), at 45.

87 Chinese Academy of International Trade and Economic Cooperation, Economic and Commercial Counsellor's Office of the Embassy of the People's Republic of China in Brazil & Ministry of Commerce of the People's Republic of China Department of Outward

3.3.4 China

The labour cost in China used to be low,[88] which was an important comparative advantage contributing to China's miraculous economic growth. However, Chinese labour cost has dramatically increased since the twenty first century.[89] According to a survey on enterprises in Nanjing, Chongqing and Luoyang, the annual growth of the labour cost reached 15.7% during 2005–2010, which significantly outpaced the growth of corporate profits.[90] Since the labour costs in the Association of Southeast Asian Nations ("ASEAN") are substantially lower than that in China, China is losing its labour-cost competitiveness.[91] The unemployment rate in China was around 3.8% in July 2018.[92] China implemented the one-child-per-family policy as from the 1980s, which resulted in the current ageing problem. China may even face a labour shortfall in 2021.[93] Although China started to implement the universal two-child policy in 2016, it is unlikely to reverse the population ageing.[94] China is also short of talented human resources. Some foreign enterprises complain that it is challenging to employ and retain Chinese talents at the management and highly skilled technical staff levels. Chinese education focuses more on theory than practical experience, and graduates have little experience working on projects or teams.[95] China needs to adjust its education system to cultivate more talented graduates with practical experience. As for foreign nationals working in China, China encourages the introduction of high-level talent, controls the number of medium-level employees, and restricts the introduction of low-skilled workers.[96]

Investment and Economic Cooperation, Guide on Foreign Investment and Cooperation: India (2018), at 65.

88 Dennis Tao Yang, Rising Wages: Has China Lost Its Global Labor Advantage?, EPWP#09-03 (2009), p. 1.

89 Yuming Cui & Changrong Lu, Are China's Unit Labor Costs Still Competitive? A Comparison with ASEAN Countries, 32(1) *Asian-Pacific Economic Literature* 59 (2018) 59.

90 Li Shi & Wan Haiyuan, China's Rising Labor Cost: Myths and Realities, 12(1) *China Economist* (2017) 59, 62.

91 *See* Yuming Cui & Changrong Lu, Are China's Unit Labor Costs Still Competitive? A Comparison with ASEAN Countries, 32(1) *Asian-Pacific Economic Literature* 59 (2018) 60.

92 Trading Economics, China Unemployment Rate, available at https://tradingeconomics.com/china/unemployment-rate (visited January 1, 2019).

93 Xinhua news, China Facing Labor Shortage due to One-Child Policy, available at http://www.china.org.cn/china/2015-10/21/content_36849280.htm (visited January 1, 2019).

94 Sabu S. Padmadas, Two-Child Policy in China: Rhetoric versus Reality' 40(2) *Annals of Human Biology* (2017) 97, 98.

95 PWC, Doing Business and Investing in China (2011), at 81.

96 *See* the State Council of the People's Republic of China, The Initiation of Pilot Scheme on Working Permit for Foreign Nationals, available at http://www.gov.cn/xinwen/2016-09/10/content_5107035.htm (visited January 1, 2019).

3.3.5 South Africa

The unemployment rate in South Africa is extremely high, and was around 27.5% in July 2018.[97] It is difficult for young South Africans aged 15–24 to find employment.[98] The South African education system is inadequate, which results in a shortage of skilled labours. Therefore, young South Africans do not possess the skills needed by the economy. Different from its peer countries, South Africa does not have as many as small firms that could absorb low skilled workers.[99] In addition, the historical apartheid prohibited the majority black population from entrepreneurship, and its legacy still exists, which has disadvantaged black people in their attempts to master business skills.[100] The South African labour market faces severe rigidities that prevent it from adjusting to exogenous shocks to the economy.[101] The high and persistent levels of unemployment in South Africa suggests that the price of labour should fall in order to clear the labour market. However, the South African labour costs have increased due to the increasing living expenditures. Compounding this, productivity increases have not corresponded to the increases in labour costs, which reduces the competitiveness of South Africa. The post-apartheid tightening of labor regulation has improved the protection for labour, but active collective bargaining and strong union pressure have reduced employment opportunities and contributed to the high unemployment rate.[102] As for foreign nationals, exceptionally skilled and qualified foreigners are encouraged to work in South Africa, which does not impose limits on employment.[103]

3.4 *Conclusions*

BRICS countries, as emerging economies, encounter various and serious problems in handling investment barriers. As regards market access, South Africa is more inclined to investment liberalization with little restrictions on foreign

---

97 Trading Economics, South Africa Unemployment Rate, available at https://tradingeconomics.com/south-africa/unemployment-rate (visited January 1, 2019).

98 Jorg Langbein & Michael Weber, Does Employing Workers or Accepting Work Pay? Analyzing Labor Costs in South Africa, World Bank Group Note 2018, at 2.

99 *See* Jeremy R. Magruder, High Unemployment Yet Few Small Firms: The Role of Centralized Bargaining in South Africa, 4(3) *American Conomic Journal: Applied Economics* 138 (2012) 139.

100 *See* Jeremy R. Magruder, High Unemployment Yet Few Small Firms: The Role of Centralized Bargaining in South Africa, 4(3) *American Economic Journal: Applied Economics* 138 (2012) 140.

101 Johannes Fedderke, The Cost of Rigidity: The Case of the South African Labor Market' ERSA Working Paper 290 (2012), at 1.

102 Jorg Langbein & Michael Weber, Does Employing Workers or Accepting Work Pay? Analyzing Labor Costs in South Africa, World Bank Group Note 2018, at 2.

103 Deloitte, Taxation and Investment in South Africa 2017, at 31.

investment admission, while other BRICS countries are more concerned with protection on domestic development of strategic sectors. Regarding investment facilitation, although Russia, among five BRICS countries, was ranked highest on ease of doing business in 2018 by the World Bank, its legal system is of severe problems, such as frequent amendment of law and lack of independent judicial system. Brazil and China have focused on promotion of investment facilitation by adopting measures at international and national levels. India is also making progress in improving its state of investment facilitation with elevated ranking in ease of doing business, however, its judicial system is still understaffed and lacks independence. In contrast, South Africa's decline in ranking in ease of doing business indicates that it must make more efforts to promote investment facilitation. As for the issue of labour, all the BRICS countries are insufficient to provide high-skilled labour, which is a barrier to inward high-tech foreign investment. In addition, the costs of labour in the BRICS, except Russia and India, are not competitive. The BRICS strict regulations on labour, aiming to protect domestic labour market, are far above an economic issue, in that those regulations are also associated with social issues like those of education, income distribution and social equality. A case in point is that South Africa attempts to employ current labour regulation to correct historical discrimination suffered by the disadvantaged population in early times.

In a word, it is urgent for all the BRICS countries to reduce severe investment barriers. However, the problems encountered by each BRICS country are embedded in divergent legal, social and historical systems. Those divergences frustrate the BRICS cooperation in reducing investment barriers, not to mention the difficulty for each BRICS country to make substantial commitments to address the barriers.

4 BRICS Countries' Investment Treaty Policies and Practice from the Perspective of Investment Barriers

With the rise of India and China, the world is changing from a unipolar order, which was driven by the U.S. in the 20th Century, to multipolar order.[104] Hence, neoliberalism that was promoted by the U.S. with "Washington Consensus" on privatization of public enterprises, liberalization of investment flows, and global governance of trade and investment, has been challenged.[105] The

104 M. Sornarajah, *Resistance and Change in the International Law on Foreign Investment* (Cambridge: Cambridge University Press, 2015), 55.

105 *Id*, at 11.

myths asserting that investment treaties lead to greater investment flows, and consequentially to economic development, and investor-state arbitration is a neutral method of dispute settlement, have been debunked.[106] The BRICS are now aware of framing their investment treaty policies according to their own realities and concerns, rather than following the steps of developed countries. Therefore, the investment barriers in the BRICS, as non-negligible economic factors, influence the BRICS investment treaty policies and practice.

4.1 *The Implications of Investment Barriers in the BRICS Countries on Their Investment Treaty Policies and Practice*

A state's treaty policy and practice are not isolated from its domestic system, which is embedded in its legal, economic, social and historical realities. Various and serious investment barriers existing in the BRICS indicate that it is difficult for the BRICS to adopt similar or coordinated investment treaty policies and practice. With more awareness of focusing on domestic development needs, the period of 2015–2016 seems a turning point for BRICS countries' deviation from their previous foreign investment policies. In 2015, Brail adopted a new Model BIT with an emphasis on investment cooperation and facilitation, the Indian government approved its final Model BIT ("Indian Model BIT (2015)"), and South Africa decided to terminate some BITs and developed a domestic framework, which is reflected in Protection of Investment Act, for foreign investment promotion and protection.[107] In 2016, Russia passed the Regulation on Entering into International Treaties on the Encouragement and Mutual Protection of Investments ("Guidelines (2016)") which established a new set of guidelines for future BITs. China has moved towards a liberal approach to BITs since 2003, but not yet developed a BIT model, and its BIT practice seems at a crossroads.[108]

As to investors and investment qualified under protection, the Brazilian Model CFIA (2015) employs a "control test", which requires that foreign investors should exert control or significant influence over the management of the invested enterprises.[109] Russia and India exclude citizens of a host state from seeking protection under Russia's Guidelines (2016) and Indian Model

106 Emma Aisbett, Bernali Choudhury, Oliver de Schutter, Frank Garcia, James Harrison, Song Hong, Lise Johnson, Mouhamadou Kane, Santiago Pena, Matthew Porterfield, Susan Sell, Stephen E. Shay & Louis T. Wells, *Rethinking International Investment Governance: Principles for the 21st Century* (2018), 7.

107 *See* M. Sornarajah, The Unworkability of "Balanced Treaties" and the Importance of Diversity of Approach Among the BRICS, 112 *AJILUnbound* 223–27 (2018).

108 *See* Chapter of China of this book.

109 Indian Model BIT (2015), art. 3.

BIT (2015), and require investors to conduct 'substantial business operation'.[110] China and South Africa adopted a broad definition of investment, which not only includes both enterprise and asset-based investment but also contains all essential rights and interests necessary for engaging in economic activities in China and South Africa.[111]

With regard to the standard of treatment, the Brazilian CFIA BIT (2015) includes traditional provisions such as national treatment and most-favoured nation ("MFN") treatment,[112] but does not have a fair and equitable treatment ("FET") clause. Russia's Guidelines 2016 is also silent on FET clause and specifies that the MFN cannot be used for treaty shopping.[113] The India 2015 Model BIT provides unique standards in the form of protection from (i) [d]enial of justice in any judicial or administrative proceedings; or (ii) fundamental breach of due process; or (iii) targeted discrimination on manifestly unjustified grounds, such as gender, race or religious belief; or (iv) manifestly abusive treatment, such as coercion, duress and harassment.[114] These standards, particularly denial of justice, are open to interpretation and hence entail unpredictability in their application in practice.[115] The Indian Model BIT (2015) also includes a national treatment clause but excludes MFN treatment. However, it is noteworthy that the Indian Model BIT (2015) does not apply to the measures by local governments,[116] which severely reduces foreign investment protection at the local level. Moreover, Article 2.4(ii) stipulates that the subject matter of taxation shall be non-justiciable and not open to review by any arbitral tribunal. This may be manipulated by the Host State to exclude any dispute from the jurisdiction of a tribunal by asserting that the measure in question relates to taxation.[117] China's new generation of BITs may cover a broad range of treatments, considering that the China-Tanzania BIT (2013) contains national

110 *See* Chapter of Russia of this book and art. 1:1.4 of Indian Model BIT(2015).

111 Stephan W. Schill, Tearing Down the Great Wall: the New Generation Investment Treaties of the People's Republic of China, 15 *Cardozo Journal of International and Comparative Law* 73 (2007) 85; South African Protection of Investment Act (2015), art. 2.

112 *See* Brazilian Model CFIA (2015), arts. 5, 6.

113 *See* Marianna Rybynok, The 2016 Russian Guidelines on Future BITs: Have Your Cake and Eat It, *Financier Worldwide Magazine* (2017), available at https://www.financierworldwide.com/the-2016-russian-guidelines-on-future-bits-have-your-cake-and-eat-it#.XYS9bdO4y5Y (visited August 1, 2019).

114 *See* Indian Model BIT (2015), art. 3:3.1.

115 Manu Thadikkaran, Model Text for the Indian Bilateral Investment Treaty: An Analysis, 8 *NUJS Law Review* 31 (2015) 36.

116 *See* Indian Model BIT (2015), art. 2.4(1).

117 *See* Manu Thadikkaran, supra note 115, at 35.

treatment, MFN and FET clauses,[118] and the Canada-China BIT (2012) includes the minimum standard of treatment, MFN and national treatment.[119] The South African Protection of Investment Act (2015) includes national treatment and fair administrative treatment, but excludes the MFN clause.[120]

As regards expropriation, the Brazilian Model CFIA (2015) only provides for direct expropriation,[121] and so do the following BITs, such as the Brazil-United Arab Emirates BIT (2019) and Brazil-Guyana BIT (2018), of which Article 7 is conspicuously entitled, "Direct Expropriation". Different from Brazil, Russia, China and India all recognize both categories of direct and indirect expropriation in investment treaty practice. The South African Protection of Investment Act (2015) is silent on expropriation, while South African parliament has just approved a proposal to amend its constitution to permit expropriation without compensation.[122]

As far as investor-state dispute settlement (ISDS) is concerned, the Brazilian Model CFIA (2015) does not allow investors to initiate arbitration against host states, but it does include a state-to-state dispute prevention clause and allows state-to-state arbitration.[123] Russia and China permit investor-state arbitration without exhaustion of local remedies in their investment policies and practice.[124] The Indian Model BIT (2015) also permits investor-state arbitration, but it requires exhaustion of local remedies with obligations to follow complicated procedures.[125] The South African Protection of Investment Act (2015) permits investors to resort to mediation or a competent court, independent tribunal or statutory body within South African to settle the disputes, but prohibits investor-state arbitration, while allowing home states to initiate international arbitration against South Africa subject to the exhaustion of domestic remedies.[126]

It is clear that BRICS countries have adopted divergent approaches to foreign investment issues, especially in relation to the substantive obligations that host states must perform. Nuanced and conspicuous differences simultaneously exist in BRICS countries' approaches, and these differences reflect various investment barriers that remain in the BRICS.

118 *See* China-Tanzania BIT (2013), arts. 3, 5, 5.
119 *See* Canada-China BIT (2012), arts. 4, 5, 6.
120 *See* South African Protection of Investment Act (2015), sections. 6, 8.
121 Brazilian Model CFIA(2015), art. 5.5.
122 *See* Chapter of South Africa of this book.
123 Brazilian Model CFIA(2015), arts. 23, 24.
124 *See* Chapters of Russia and China of this book.
125 Indian Model BIT(2015), Chapter IV.
126 South African Protection of Investment Act (2015), section. 13.

4.2 *Towards Investment Facilitation: a New Trend of BRICS Countries' Investment Treaty Policies and Practice*

Investment facilitation is a concept that includes the measures facilitating foreign investment, such as streamlining administrative procedures, promoting the dialogues between private investors and public authorities, and enhancing information exchange networks in the area of investment.[127] Since investment facilitation is more related with procedural issues, it is not difficult for a state to implement the measures of investment facilitation. Investment facilitation has become an emerging issue in recent years and attracts the BRICS attention.

4.2.1 Individual Efforts

As examined above, each BRICS country does make efforts to reduce investment barriers and thus enhance investment facilitation. Of course, different BRICS countries differ in this regard. Brazil and China appear more active in reducing investment barriers.

It is worth noting that the Brazilian Model CFIA (2015) emphasizes investment facilitation. The model includes 26 provisions in total, and in addition to transparency requirement on parties' legislations it also includes provisions on institutional governance and dispute prevention. A Joint Committee must be established for the administration of the BIT and the private sector may be invited to participate in the *ad hoc* working groups of the Joint Committee. Moreover, National Focal Points or "Ombudsman" will be designated to enhance the communication between investors and government authorities. Therefore, the new model is designed to enhance the cooperation between private investors and public authorities in order to take better care of investors' concerns. On the basis of the new BIT model, Brazil has signed ten BITs since 2015. Of these, the one concluded with Angola has come into force and the other nine BITs are not yet in force.[128]

Brazil has promoted its conception of investment facilitation not only at the bilateral level, but also advocates investment facilitation in the WTO.[129] Nevertheless, considering the long-time deadlock of WTO negotiations and recent WTO crisis, it seems impossible to reach such an agreement at the WTO. Even among the BRICS countries, although China and Russia supported

127 Kinda Mohamadieh, Reflections on the Discussion of Investment Facilitation, 8 *Investment Policy Brief* 1 (2017) 2.

128 Brazilian BIT information is available at the website of Investment Policy Hub of the UNCTAD, available at https://investmentpolicy.unctad.org/international-investment-agreements/countries/27/brazil (visited August 1, 2019).

129 Brazil requested to circulate its proposal on Investment Facilitation Agreement to WTO members on 31 January 2018.

negotiating an investment facilitation agreement at the WTO,[130] India and South Africa firmly opposed the discussion on investment facilitation at the G20 meeting and stated that investment facilitation could never be part of the WTO framework on grounds that it would undermine their "policy space".[131] Therefore, whether a regional or multilateral agreement on investment facilitation is able to be reached is highly dependent on whether it is possible to eradicate some countries' concerns regarding the infringement of their regulatory sovereignty.

China also emphasized the importance of investment facilitation and pushed forwards the discussion of investment issues during its presidency of G20 in 2016, which resulted in the G20's agreement on non-binding G20 Guiding Principles for Global Investment Policymaking (G20 Guiding Principles).[132] The G20 Guiding Principles aim to foster an open, transparent and conducive global policy environment for investment, promote coherence in national and international investment policymaking, and endorse inclusive economic growth and sustainable development.[133]

In addition, China submitted Possible Elements of Investment Facilitation to the WTO in April 2017, which provides non-exhaustive options for enhancing the transparency of the investment policy framework, improving the efficiency of administrative procedures relating to investment, and responding to developing and least-developed members' needs.[134] Moreover, China initiated the "Friends of Investment Facilitation for Development (FIFD)" group within the WTO and sponsored the Joint Ministerial Statement on Investment Facilitation for Development (Statement), which was signed by over 70 members in 2017. The Statement calls for structured discussions "with the aim of

---

130 The Ministers representing Brazil, Russia, China and other 41 WTO members released Joint Ministerial Statement on Investment Facilitation for Development in 2017, while the Ministers from India and South Africa did not joint it. See WT/MIN(17)/59.

131 *See* "India Objects to Discussing Investment Facilitation Issues at WTO" and "India Denies Blocking Agenda at the World Trade Organization Meet", available at https://www.livemint.com/Politics/B8klHCkPg4l9HwTUon5boL/India-objects-to-discussing-investment-facilitation-issues-a.html and https://economictimes.indiatimes.com/news/economy/policy/india-denies-blocking-agenda-at-world-trade-organisation-meet/articleshow/58674521.cms?from=mdr (visited August 1, 2019).

132 *See* Karl P. Sauvant, China Moves the G20 Toward an International Investment Framework and Investment Facilitation, in Julien Chaisse, ed., *China's Three-Prong Investment Strategy: Bilateral, Regional, and Global Tracks* (Oxford: Oxford University Press, 2018).

133 *See* Annex III: G20 Guiding Principles for Global Investment Policymaking, available at https://www.oecd.org/daf/inv/investment-policy/G20-Guiding-Principles-for-Global-Investment-Policymaking.pdf (visited August 1, 2019).

134 *See* WTO, Possible Elements of Investment Facilitation, JOB/GC/123, 26 April 2017.

developing a multilateral framework on investment facilitation. These discussions shall seek to identify and develop the elements of a framework for facilitating foreign direct investments that would: improve the transparency and predictability of investment measures; streamline and speed up administrative procedures and requirements; and enhance international cooperation, information sharing, the exchange of best practices, and relations with relevant stakeholders, including dispute prevention."[135]

4.2.2 Joint Efforts

The BRICS have approved numerous documents that address a wide range of issues including economic cooperation. Those documents that have bearing on investment facilitation can be divided into six categories: (1) the documents broadly addressing BRICS economic and trade cooperation,[136] (2) the documents focusing on BRICS investment facilitation,[137] (3) the documents addressing banking and finance,[138] (4) the documents coping with tax matters,[139] (5) the documents aimed to improve labor capacity and treatment,[140] (6) the documents on BRICS cooperation and coordination in standards.[141]

In particular, in 2014 the BRICS initiated the Trade and Investment Facilitation Action Plan.[142] The BRICS countries recognize that "joint efforts

135 *See* Joint Ministerial Statement on Investment Facilitation for Development, WT/MIN (17)/59, 13 December 2017.

136 These documents include annual BRICS Summit declarations, *BRICS Action Agenda on Economic and Trade Cooperation* (2017), *BRICS Trade and Investment Cooperation Framework* (2013), and *Action Plan for Deepening Industrial Cooperation among BRICS Countries* (2017), and *BRICS IPR Cooperation Guidelines* (2017). It is noted that *Action Plan for Deepening Industrial Cooperation among BRICS Countries* (2017) also addresses BRICS cooperation in the development of new industrial infrastructure and in the areas of standardization.

137 These documents include *Outlines for BRICS Investment Facilitation* (2017) and *BRICS Trade and Investment Facilitation Plan* (2014).

138 These documents include *Interbank Local Currency Credit Line Agreement under BRICS Interbank Cooperation Mechanism* (2017) and *Memorandum of Understanding between BRICS Export Credit Agencies and the New Development Bank on General Cooperation* (2017).

139 The representative document is *BRICS Memorandum of Cooperation in Respect of Tax Matters* (2017).

140 These documents include *BRICS Labour and Employment Ministers' Declaration* (2017) and *the BRICS Action Plan for Poverty Alleviation and Reduction through Skills* (2017).

141 The representative document is *Joint Declaration of BRICS Business Council on Regulatory Cooperation on Standards* (2017).

142 "Trade and Investment Facilitation Action Plan", available at https://www.tralac.org/news/article/5916-brics-trade-and-investment-facilitation-plan.html (visited September 1, 2019).

on trade and investment facilitation will benefit our business communities, strengthen and enhance trade and investment linkages among BRICS members, help boost the economic development and create jobs".[143] The Action Plan provides five principles enhancing the cooperation in investment facilitation, which include (a) increasing transparency and awareness; (b) promoting simplification and efficiency; (c)ensuring consistency and predictability; (d) enhancing communication and consultation; and (e) encouraging cooperation and harmonization.[144] The Action Plan further includes a menu of suggested actions. In terms of simplification and efficiency, for instance, the BRICS countries are encouraged to simplify custom documents, enhance the efficiency of examination and approval procedures for foreign investment, and to simplify commercial registration procedures. As far as cooperation and harmonization are concerned, the BRICS countries are encouraged to enhance cooperation and coordination in the areas of standardization, technical regulations and conformity assessment procedures, encourage the use of international standards as a basis for national standards and encourage cooperation in the promotion of technical and institutional capacity building.[145] Legally, however, to what extent these documents will make a difference in reducing investment barriers remains unclear because many of these documents are simply a "declaration" or "statement" without legal binding force. For instance, the BRICS Trade and Investment Facilitation Action Plan explicitly states that the BRICS countries are encouraged to implement, "on a voluntary basis", all or some of the suggested actions in the menu.[146] The BRICS Outlines is the same case. The document is aimed to enhance greater transparency of investment laws, regulations and policy measures, improve the efficiency of investment screening and approval, and promote cooperation between the private sector and other stakeholders. Should concrete measures be adopted pursuant to the BRICS Outlines, it is expected that investment barriers in the BRICS would be significantly reduced. Unfortunately, the BRICS Outlines, similar to the BRICS Trade and Investment Facilitation Action Plan, explicitly states that "[t]he above outlines will be considered on a voluntary basis".

143 *Id.*
144 *Id.*
145 *Id.*
146 *Id.*

5 Concluding Remarks

Most of BRICS countries are major investment destinations. Be that as it may, there are huge potential for them to attract more foreign investment by reducing investment barriers which are widespread in these countries. Investment barriers may also discourage the capital flow among the BRICS countries. From the legal perspective, the widespread investment barriers can to some degree explain BRICS countries reluctant to conclude liberal investment treaties, or to withdraw liberal investment treaties that they have concluded, which discourage the capital inflow. Currently, however, it seems that the BRICS start a correct direction of placing the priority on the improvement of investment facilitation both at the domestic level by reducing investment barriers and at the international level by advocating the investment facilitation in the reforming investment treaty regime.

Conclusion

Congyan Cai

There is a network of over 3,000 investment treaties governing foreign investment, most of which are BITs. For most of the time since its inception in the 1950s the aims and purposes, structure and content of the investment treaty regime, which were characterized by the bias for the rights and interests of foreign investors and against the public authority of host states, were decided by developed states while what developing states could do was either reject them or take them. That paradigm of the investment treaty regime was deeply rooted in international political, economic and ideological structures: in the 1960s and 1970s, newly independent developing states struggled for the New International Economic Order (NIEO) and so they often declined to negotiate investment treaties with developed states; in the 1980s and 1990s, many developing states began to embrace the neoliberalism advocated by developed states and thus concluded liberal investment treaties providing high standards of investment treatment and protection. The investment treaty regime was considered by many developing states to be an important instrument to attract foreign investment and, more generally, to embrace globalization. At roughly the same period, foreign investors began to frequently use investment treaties to challenge the public authority of host states, which was concurrent with the trend of growing power of non-state actors in international relations. International structures, however, have significantly changed since the late 1990s. The one-way capital flow from developed states to developing states that existed for decades has begun to change as some developing states, especially BRICS countries, have emerged as new major investment sources. More importantly, as treaty-based investment claims increase tremendously, host states, especially the developing states who are the major targets of investment claims, have recognized that the traditionally liberal paradigm of investment treaties should be reformed towards a more balanced one. Consequently, this balance has emerged as a preferred objective among states,[1] and the UNCTAD calls for balancing the rights and obligations of states and investors as a core principle

1 This Conclusion is written based on Congyan Cai, Balanced Investment Treaties and the BRICS, 112 *AJIL Unbound* 217 (2018).
See, e.g., UNCTAD, Investment Policy Framework for Sustainable Development at 8, UN Doc. UNCTAD/DIAE/PCB/2015/5 (2015).

 DOI:10.1163/9789004376991_010

of investment policymaking.[2] Indeed, measures aimed at making investment treaties balanced may be diverse. However, a balanced approach should neither overshoot on reform nor "depriv[e] the [international investment agreement regime] of its purpose of promoting and protecting investment."[3] For example, balance in ISDS means that investor-state claims mechanisms should be improved to prevent abuse, rather than totally abandoned, given that domestic remedies are often inadequate, that a state is often reluctant to bring international claims on behalf of its nationals against another state, and that foreign investors can decide on their own whether to rely on domestic or international remedies.

Against these backgrounds, both developed states and developing states have more interests in framing a more balanced investment treaty regime. It should be stressed that major developed states like the U.S. and EU, in updating their investment treaty programs, have taken a number of important measures or initiatives to give more respect of public authority of host states.[4]

In the twenty-first century, it is believed that developing states, especially like BRICS, are no longer "rule-takers" like they had done in the nineteenth century and twentieth century. However, a provocative question is: are they reformers or disruptors of investment treaty regime?

A definite conclusion is too early to draw at this stage when the process of reforming investment treaty regime around the world is ongoing. From a normative perspective, it is not unsound to suggest that the BRICS countries might be both reformers and disrupters.

On the one hand, the BRICS countries may be reformers, enhancing a more balanced and thus sustainable investment treaty regime. Although, as suggested above, developed states and developing states have interests in framing a more balanced investment treaty regime than before, in some sense the BRICS countries are better positioned than developed states to actually carry out the reform. This is because, like many other developing states where the robust investment climate – political, economic and legal etc. – is yet to be established, the BRICS countries are already very sensitive to economic sovereignty and how investment treaties function to help national development and, like developed states who are more concerned with the rights and interests of investors than the economic sovereignty, the BRICS countries who are

2 *Id.* at 6.

3 UNCTAD, Phase 2 of IIA Reform: Modernizing the Existing Stock of Old-Generation Treaties, IIA Issues Note, No. 2, June 2017, at. 2.

4 *See, e.g.*, U.S. Model BIT (2012), arts. 12, 13, 16, Annex A and Annex B; Canada-EU Comprehensive Economic and Trade Agreement (2014), Chapter 10.

emerging home states have growing interests in investment treatment and protection. Looking at that system as a whole, the BRICS in fact share many views, especially with respect to the spirit, principles, and substantive components of investment treaties. This much is apparent from the BRICS Perspective on International Investment Agreements.[5] Issued collectively by the BRICS in 2014, the statement asserted that investment treaties should strike a balance between the protection of investors and sovereign regulatory power and serve the sustainable development of host states. It also attached importance to robust domestic law and called for further improvement of and "build[ing] common approaches" to investment treaties.[6] It is thus suggested that BRICS countries could remedy two defects inherent in the investment treaties that developed states have advocated for decades.

The first is that the treaties have largely failed to serve developing state interests in attracting new investment. The common position among developed states has been that by strictly honoring their obligations, enforced through international ISDS, host states can help promote capital inflows and national development. But this position has proven flawed: contracting parties rarely cooperate or monitor implementation after concluding traditional investment treaties, which are best understood as a business deal between the host state and foreign investors. The causal relationship between signing investment treaties and increased investment has not been established. And the treaties do little to build developing countries' capacity to comply and attract investment. These circumstances, coupled with a surge in investment claims since the late 1990s, have led many developing countries to withdraw their support for the treaties.

The BRICS offer a more promising approach by suggesting that, in addition to imposing obligations on host states and according rights to investors, investment treaties should enable contracting parties to interact in a more constructive manner. This approach, for instance, was introduced in the Brazilian Model CFIA (2015). Under the CFIA, institutions and mechanisms, such as joint committees and ombudsmen, will emerge and execute meaningful mandates to monitor implementation of the agreements and promote cooperation between contracting parties to facilitate investment.[7] Continuous interaction between contracting parties can enhance capacity building and reduce

5 Press Release, South Africa Depeartment of Trade & Industry, BRICS Perspective on International Investment Agreements (July 15, 2014).

6 *Id.*

7 Brazilian Model CFIA (2015), arts. 17,18 and 22.

information asymmetry, which will not only help channel investment flows but also reduce the risk that host states will violate their obligations.

The second defect in traditional investment treaties is their inflexibility. Special and differentiated treatment, which is well established in the international trade system, finds no counterpart here, as investment rules are assumed to apply equally to the contracting parties. Negotiations typically proceed from a model text provided by developed countries without substantial departures or derogations. For instance, the United States has hardly made any compromises in its BIT negotiations over the years.[8] From preamble to operative provisions, the treaties leave no room for the special circumstances of host states in prescribing a BIT obligation (in particular, a "minimum" standard of treatment). As a result, investment tribunals have often found themselves at a loss as to whether the level of development of host states should be taken into account.[9]

BRICS countries are more likely than developed countries to support such an approach. Their receptivity can be inferred from the fact that the BRICS always support special and differentiated treatment in the international trade system and in their investment policies. In accordance with the South African Protection of Investment Act of 2015, foreign investment shall be provided with "physical security in accordance with minimum standards of customary international law" but "subject to available resources and capability."[10] That is, although South Africa accepts the minimum standard of customary law, the particularity of South Africa should also be considered. In similar fashion, China agreed in negotiating an investment treaty with the Association of South East Asian Nations (ASEAN) to consider the "different stages and pace of development among the Parties and the need for special and differential treatment and flexibility" for the newer ASEAN member states.[11]

On the other hand, however, the BRICS countries are likely to disrupt the international legal order on investment, bringing another imbalanced approach to investment treaties.

---

8 Kenneth J. Vandevelde, *U.S. International Investment Agreements* (Oxford: Oxford University Press, 2009) 32, 41.

9 *See* Nick Gallus, The Influence of the Host State's Level of Development on International Investment Treaty Standards of Protection, 6 *Journal of World Investment & Trade* 711 (2005) 735–726.

10 Protection of Investment Act of 2015, section 9.

11 Agreement on Investment of the Framework Agreement on Comprehensive Economic Cooperation Between the Association of Southeast Asian Nations and the People's Republic of China (2009), Preamble.

First consider India. In gradually opening its economy, India has largely embraced a liberal investment treaty policy.[12] But it was shocked by the *White Industries* case, the first award to find India liable to an investor,[13] and other investment claims followed.[14] In light of this experience, India approved a new Model BIT in 2015, updating its prior model from 2003. The Model BIT (2015) substantially curtails the protections accorded to foreign investment under the 2003 version.[15] For instance, the new model, unlike most investment treaties, does not provide for most-favored-nation treatment or fair and equitable treatment. As for investor-state dispute settlement, this model permits an investor to resort to international arbitration only after exhausting all domestic judicial and administrative remedies "for at least a period of five years from the date on which the investor first acquired knowledge of the measure in question."[16] This requirement represents a considerable departure from prevailing investment treaties and creates a new imbalance in favor of the host state.

Other steps by the Indian government have exacerbated this imbalance. In particular, India abandoned international investor-state claims altogether in a BIT signed with Brazil in 2017. And in 2016, India began to terminate a number of its investment treaties. As a result, twenty-two of eighty-three Indian BITs are no longer in force, including its treaty with China.[17]

South Africa has gone even further than India. The *Foresti* case,[18] like *White Industries* for India, prompted South Africa to review a national BIT policy that had been quite liberal since the 1990s. This review, completed in 2009, suggested that South Africa retain but substantially improve its investment treaties.[19] Nevertheless, the government decided in 2012 to start terminating these treaties.[20] To date, ten of a total of twenty-two South African BITs are no longer operative.[21] In their stead, the South African Parliament approved the

12 *Compare* Indian Model Text (2003) *with* the US Model BIT (2004).

13 *White Industries Austl. Ltd. v. Republic of India*, Final Award, UNCITRAL (Nov. 30, 2011).

14 "Investment Policy Hub: India-Cases as Respondent State", available at https://investmentpolicy.unctad.org/investment-dispute-settlement/country/96/india (visited July 13, 2019).

15 *See* Chapter 4. *See also* Grant Hanessian & Kabir Duggal, The Final 2015 Indian Model BIT: Is This the Change the World Wishes to See?, 32 *ICSID Review* 216 (2017).

16 Indian Model BIT (2015), art. 15.2.

17 *See* "Investment Policy Hub: India", available at https://investmentpolicy.unctad.org/international-investment-agreements/countries/96/india?type=tips (visited July 13, 2019).

18 *Foresti v. South Africa*, ICSID Case No. ARB(AF)/07/1 (Aug. 4, 2010).

19 South Africa Department of Trade and Industry, Bilateral Investment Treaty Policy Framework Review (hereinafter "South Africa BIT Review"), June 2009, Part II.

20 Peter Leon et al., *South Africa: South Africa Declines to Renew Bilateral Investment Treaties with European Union Member States*, Mondaq.Com (Oct. 5, 2012).

21 *See* "Investment Policy Hub: Brazil", available at https://investmentpolicy.unctad.org/international-investment-agreements/countries/27/brazil (visited July 13, 2019).

Protection of Investment Act of 2015, which provides that foreign investment will be governed exclusively by South African law after a transitional period.[22] Schlemmer has suggested that although domestic law should have played a more important role in the protection of foreign investment in the past, protections pursuant to domestic law alone will be inadequate going forward.[23] Like India, South Africa has created a new imbalance in favor of the state and against foreign investment.

The latest BIT policies of these two countries are also imbalanced in the weight they accord to the protection of their own outbound investment. In contrast with many other states in the developing world, India and South Africa, together with their BRICS peers, have emerged as major investment sources in addition to destinations. This development creates a need to balance state interests in not only maintaining public authority but also protecting overseas investors. In some ways, India and South Africa appear to recognize as much. For instance, in light of "sizable intra-Africa investments" by its nationals, South Africa has acknowledged the need to identify the best means of safeguarding those investments.[24] Moreover, Indian and South African experience in investment disputes would seem to underscore this need: To date, three of the four cases involving South Africa were brought by its own investors.[25] India has been a respondent state twenty-four times,[26] but Indian investors have also been claimants in seven cases[27] and the number is sure to increase as Indian businesses expand their overseas operations. Nevertheless, the latest BIT policies of India and South Africa do not adequately account for each state's growing need to protect investors.

In view of the imbalances, it is doubtful that some of the stronger reform measures that India and South Africa have instituted will operate well in practice. With respect to India, for example, several key players, especially the

---

22 Protection of Investment Act of 2015, sections 13, 15.

23 Engela C. Schlemmer, Dispute Settlement in Investment-Related Matters: South Africa and the BRICS, 112 *AJIL Unbound* 212 (2018).

24 South Africa BIT Review, supra note 19, at 7.

25 *See* "Investment Policy Hub: South Africa-Cases as Respondent State", available at; https://investmentpolicy.unctad.org/investment-dispute-settlement/country/195/south-africa/respondent (visited July 13, 2019) *See* "Investment Policy Hub: South Africa-Cases as Home State", available at https://investmentpolicy.unctad.org/investment-dispute-settlement/country/195/south-africa/investor (visited July 13, 2019).

26 *See* "Investment Policy Hub: India-Cases as Respondent State", available at https://investmentpolicy.unctad.org/investment-dispute-settlement/country/96/india (visited July 13, 2019).

27 *See* "Investment Policy Hub: India-Cases as Home State", available at https://investmentpolicy.unctad.org/investment-dispute-settlement/country/96/india (visited July 11, 2019).

United States, the European Union, and China, may decline to make substantial compromises in negotiating investment treaties. In 2007 and 2008, India began negotiating BITs with the European Union and the United States, respectively, but they have been deadlocked after ten years of marathon bargaining because India is reluctant to accept the high standards expected by Western powers.[28] It is safe to predict that neither the United States nor the European Union will negotiate with India on the basis of its 2015 Model BIT. Nor is China likely to negotiate a new BIT with India based on that model. India also seeks to have authoritative interpretations of its BIT provisions with some countries, but whether and to what extent its desired reforms will be accepted by other states remains to be seen.

To be sure, it is not inconceivable that India and/or South Africa will someday recognize that termination of investment treaties is inappropriate. In fact, South Africa acknowledged in its 2009 BIT review that "[d]emands for the conclusion of additional BITs are unlikely to recede."[29] As for India, the government appears open to some proposals (for instance, for an appellate body or similar mechanism)[30] that have been approved or are under consideration by others such as the European Union. But these are not the dominant views at present.

It is widely recognized that the emerging powers should have a greater say in international affairs, but some commentators are concerned about whether they can behave responsibly.[31] Effecting investment treaties with greater balance can help BRICS countries to gain broader recognition as responsible powers, shouldering and sharing the work of maintaining international peace and increasing international prosperity. The absence of a robust network of investment treaties among the BRICS currently prevents them from fully exploring their potential to reform investment treaties as a group. But certain commonalities in their approach, albeit broad and perhaps somewhat rhetorical, could arguably help them to improve their image and contribute to the balance of investment treaties over time.

---

28 Madhyam Kavaljit Singh, *The India–US Bilateral Investment Treaty Will Not Be an Easy Ride*, E. Asia F., Feb. 10, 2015; European Commission, *Overview of FTA and Other Trade Negotiations* (May 2018).

29 South Africa BIT Review, at 56.

30 *See, e.g.*, Indian Model BIT (2015), arts. 24, 29. *See also* Report of the High Level Committee to Review the Institutionalisation of Arbitration Mechanism in India, July 30, 2017, at 107, 113.

31 *See, e.g.*, Jorge G. Castañeda, Not Ready for Prime Time: Why Including Emerging Powers at the Helm Would Hurt Global Governance, 89 *Foreign Affairs* 109 (2010)109; Stewart *Patrick*, Irresponsible Stakeholders? The Difficulty of Integrating Rising Powers, 89 *Foreign Affairs* 44 (2010) 57.

Index

www.ingramcontent.com/pod-product-compliance
Lightning Source LLC
LaVergne TN
LVHW020635300926
849161LV00004B/712
* 9 7 8 9 0 0 4 3 7 6 9 8 4 *